Bikutsi

Transcultural Music Studies
Series Editor: Britta Sweers, University of Bern
Founding Series Co-editor: Simone Krüger Bridge, Liverpool John Moores University

Transcultural Music Studies publishes monographs and edited collections on contemporaneous explanations surrounding the nature of music and human beings in a (post-)global world. Books in this series encompass a comprehensively wide selection of subject matters alongside a shared interest in fieldwork – physical, virtual, historical – and its complex challenges and fascinations in a postcolonial age. Topics include music's use in social, collective and psychological life; musical individuals; music in globalization and migration; music education; music, ethnicity and gender; and environmental issues.

Published

Cultural Mapping and Musical Diversity
Edited by Britta Sweers and Sarah Ross

Provincial Headz
British Hip Hop and Critical Regionalism
Adam de Paor-Evans

The Lifetime Soundtrack
Music and Autobiographical Memory
Lauren Istvandity

Turkish Folk Music between Ghent and Turkey
Context, Performance, Function
Liselotte Sels

Bikutsi

A Beti Dance Music on the Rise, 1970–1990

Anja Brunner

equinox

SHEFFIELD UK   BRISTOL CT

Published by Equinox Publishing Ltd.

UK: Office 415, The Workstation, 15 Paternoster Row, Sheffield,
         South Yorkshire, S1 2BX
USA: ISD, 70 Enterprise Drive, Bristol, CT 06010

www.equinoxpub.com

First published 2021

British Library Cataloguing-in-Publication Data
A catalogue record for this book is available from the British Library.

ISBN-13   978 1 78179 785 3 (hardback)
           978 1 78179 786 0 (paperback)
           978 1 78179 787 7 (ePDF)
           978 1 80050 114 0 (ePub)

Library of Congress Cataloging-in-Publication Data
Names: Brunner, Anja, author.
Title: Bikutsi : a Beti dance music on the rise, 1970-1990 / Anja Brunner.
Other titles: Transcultural music studies.
Description: Bristol, CT : Equinox Publishing Ltd, 2021. | Series:
   Transcultural music studies | Includes bibliographical references and
   index. | Summary: "This book offers the first ethnographically informed,
   in-depth historical study of the Cameroonian popular music genre
   bikutsi. The thriving dance music in Cameroon's day-to-day life has its
   foundation in the specific historical processes of the 1970s and 1980s,
   which led to the recognition of bikutsi as a distinct genre of
   Cameroonian dance music. Examining these processes in detail, this book
   analyses the various factors involved in the rise of a popular music
   genre within a national music scene"-- Provided by publisher.
Identifiers: LCCN 2021005493 (print) | LCCN 2021005494 (ebook) | ISBN
   9781781797853 (hardback) | ISBN 9781781797860 (paperback) | ISBN
   9781781797877 (pdf) | ISBN 9781800501140 (epub)
Subjects: LCSH: Bikutsi--History and criticism. | Beti (African
   people)--Music--History and criticism. | Popular
   music--Cameroon--History and criticism.
Classification: LCC ML3503.C35 B78 2021 (print) | LCC ML3503.C35 (ebook)
   | DDC 781.63096711--dc23
LC record available at https://lccn.loc.gov/2021005493
LC ebook record available at https://lccn.loc.gov/2021005494

Typeset by S.J.I. Services, New Delhi, India

Contents

List of Figures

Notes to the Reader

The processes described in this book took place in the part of Cameroon where French is the dominant lingua franca. Consequently, French was the main language of my ethnographic research as well as most Cameroonian sources used in this book. To facilitate an understanding for readers not familiar with the French language, all French citations – from interviews or written sources – have been translated into English. The original French citations can be found in the respective endnotes. Any mistakes or misinterpretations in the translations are my own.

The local languages relevant to the analyses in this book are those of the Beti-Faŋ groups living in the southern part of Cameroon. These languages are tonal languages; different pitches as well as different durations of vowels are major signifiers in these languages. In Guthrie's classification of Bantu languages, the Beti-Faŋ languages appear as A.70 Yaounde-Fang Group. This group is further differentiated into five linguistic subgroups: A.71 Eton, A.72 Ewondo-Cluster with Mvëlë, Bakja (Badja), Yangafĕk, A.73 Bĕbĕle and Gbïgbïl, A.74 Bulu and Bĕne, and A.75 Fang (Guthrie 1970: 11). Of specific relevance for this book are the languages included in the Ewondo-Cluster (for more on ethnic and linguistic matters of the Beti see Chapter 3). The most standardized orthography of Ewondo follows the *Alphabet général des langues camerounaises* (Tadadjeu and Sadembouo 1979), which is based on the International Phonetic Alphabet (IPA). This orthography has been applied in this book. Tones are marked by ´ for high tone and ` for low tone; the accents ˇ and ˆ refer to a sliding tone from high to low or reverse. I wholeheartedly thank Prof. Dr Louis Martin Onguene Essono for his information on and help with the Ewondo orthography. All errors in orthographic matters are my own.

Acknowledgements/Remerciements

A project like this book takes years of research, writing, rewriting, and editing, and cannot be realized without the support of others. I had the great fortune and honour to work with many wonderful people during the years it took to publish this book. I want to acknowledge their contributions here.

First of all, I want to thank all the people who contributed to my research during my stays in Cameroon by providing information, helping with daily life, and/or becoming friends.

A huge thanks goes to the following musicians I had the honour to talk to and who kindly shared their experiences and knowledge with me during informal talks and interviews (in alphabetical order): Jean-Marie Ahanda (Les Têtes Brulées), Jean-Marie Ahanda (visitor to the Escalier Bar), René "Cosmos" Ahanda, Abanda Man Ekan, Oscar Zue Ella, "Ange" Ebogo Emerent, Ted Mekoulou, Ateba Albert Mvondo alias Atebass, Balla Pierre alias Zikoko, Mbambo Simon alias Johnny Cosmos, Nkodo Sitony, the late Claude Tchemeni, and the late Onana Zacharie alias Onana Chantal.

I also want to thank Mrs Eloundou née Tsimi Marie Romaine, Ms Leka Emmilienne, Mrs Noa née Edjili Ntsama Dorothée, and the women of Monatélé, who gave me a vivid impression of bikutsi as mainly female musical tradition.

The members of Balafon Star in Yaoundé helped me not only with information on many questions around Beti xylophones but also facilitated my participation in many events. I am very grateful especially to Jules Akoudou, Albert "Second" Ottou, and Salomon Akono for their patience with my questions and for their friendship. Jules Akoudou was an excellent research assistant and helped me with the transcriptions and translations of Ewondo lyrics and musical questions. *Abui ngang!*

My sincere gratitude goes out to Joachim Oelsner for his friendship and for sharing his formidable knowledge and expertise on Cameroonian music with me. I appreciated very much his motivation and devotion to documenting the rich musical traditions of Cameroon. With his expertise, every conversation with Joachim sparked new ideas and has opened new perspectives. Joachim, I hope this book meets, at least partially, your high expectations. Thanks for everything!

I would further like to thank Prof. Dr Louis Martin Onguene Essono for answering my questions on the languages of the Beti and the correct orthography of Ewondo. Thanks also goes to his then student Olivier Moussa Loumpata for his assistance with the transcriptions of the lyrics.

In addition, I am grateful to the following people: Dr François Bingono Bingono, who helped with various information and facilitated contact with musicians; he also supported the project as a whole. Jean-Maurice Noah shared with me his expertise on Cameroonian music and answered all my questions with patience. Prof. Albert Temgoua facilitated my arrival in Yaoundé and my first research steps. Christian Tsala Tsala made my travel to Monatélé possible and Abbé Antoine Awona was highly committed to teaching me some basic vocabulary in Ewondo.

The staff of the Bibliothèque Centrale de l'Université de Yaoundé I and the staff of Les Archives Nationales du Cameroun supported my research by providing easy access to the sources. Thank you very much.

A special thanks goes to those who became friends during my stays in Cameroon: Sali helped with all the small, daily problems that occur when living in a foreign country. He became a precious companion during my stays in Yaoundé and found solutions for all my troubles. Marthe always had a perfectly prepared meal for me and helped with many little things. Thanks to her I got to know the group Balafon Star. Sali and Marthe, thank you so much! A big thanks also to all the other inhabitants of the Cradat and Ecole de Poste quarters who helped me through daily life in Yaoundé.

And not least I want to say thank you to my dear sister Lydie-Chantal in Douala and her precious family. They welcomed me with so much cordiality to their home every time I arrived in Cameroon. Thank you very much for your support and the countless hours of joy in your house!

Many people in academia helped this book to become reality as well. At the University of Vienna (Austria) and the University of Bern (Switzerland), where I was employed as a researcher and teacher during the time of writing this book, I had the pleasure to work in an open-minded, supporting environment with wonderful people. I am grateful to all my colleagues for their support and friendship. Two individuals especially were generous with their time, knowledge, support, and friendship in reading parts of this manuscript and in talking over details again and again with me: Michael Parzer and Cornelia Gruber. My heartfelt gratitude to you! Special thanks are further due to Regine Allgayer-Kaufmann, August Schmidhofer, Gerhard Kubik, Britta Sweers, Sascha Wegner, and Henry Hope.

My field trips to Cameroon were funded by the Dean of the Faculty of Philological and Cultural Studies at the University of Vienna (Austria); my sincere thanks for this support.

I also thank Simone Krüger Bridge and Britta Sweers, the editors of the series *Transcultural Music Studies*, who supported the genesis of this book in all its facets. Further thanks goes to all the staff at Equinox Publishing for their great work and patience.

My sincere thanks to the two anonymous readers for their detailed comments and very useful criticism and to Andreas Hemming for his accurate and attentive editing work.

Of course, beyond academia, there are also people to be named and thanked: A big hug and a huge thank you is due to my beloved sons, Jakob and Simon. They had to forgo a good deal of time with their mum, especially during several intensive writing and editing periods. Thanks for making my life so miraculously wonderful. And last, but not least, my partner for life Gernot, thank you for everything.

***

Pendant mon séjour au Cameroun, beaucoup de personnes ont contribué à l'avancement de mes recherches et ont facilité ma vie quotidienne à Yaoundé.

Je tiens à remercier en premier lieu ceux qui ont eu la gentillesse de partager leurs expériences avec moi et de m'accorder une interview : Jean-Marie Ahanda (Les Têtes Brulées), Jean-Marie Ahanda (visiteur d'Escalier Bar), René "Cosmos" Ahanda, Oscar Zue Ella, "Ange" Ebogo Emerent, Ted Mekoulou, Ateba Albert Mvondo alias Atebass, Balla Pierre alias Zikoko, Mbambo Simon alias Johnny Cosmos, Nkodo Sitony, feu Claude Tchemeni, feu Onana Zacharie alias Onana Chantal et Abanda Man Ekan. Je vous suis très reconnaissante de m'avoir aidé avec des informations très valables qui ont rendu possible cette recherche. Je tiens aussi à remercier Mme Eloundou née Tsimi Marie Romaine, Leka Emmilienne and Mme Noa née Edjili Ntsama Dorothée ainsi que les femmes de Monatélé, qui m'ont donné une vive impression du bikutsi comme genre musicale reservé aux femmes.

Les membres de l'orchestre Balafon Star de Yaoundé m'ont aidé non seulement avec des informations sur la musique, mais ils ont aussi facilité ma participation à beaucoup des événements. Je suis très reconnaissante particulièrement à Jules Akoudou, Albert "Second" Ottou et Salomon Akono d'avoir répondu à mes questions avec patience et de m'avoir offert leur amitié. Jules Akoudou a été aussi un très bon assistent de recherche et m'a beaucoup aidé en ce qui concerne les transcriptions et traductions des paroles en Ewondo et des questions musicales. *Abui ngang!*

Je tiens à remercier tout particulièrement Joachim Oelsner pour son amitié et pour partager sa formidable expertise et connaissance sur la musique camerounaise avec moi. J'ai beaucoup apprécié sa motivation et son dévouement à la documentation des richesses de la musique au Cameroun. Chaque conversation avec Joachim a, grâce à son expertise, fait naître des nouvelles idées et m'a ouvert des nouvelles perspectives. Joachim, j'espère que ce livre correspond, au moins un peu, à tes attentes. Merci beaucoup pour tous!

Je tiens également à remercier Prof. Dr. Louis Martin Onguene Essono pour m'avoir aidé avec mes questions sur la langue Ewondo et son orthographie correcte. Un merci aussi à son étudiant Olivier Moussa Loumpata pour son aide avec les transcriptions.

En outre, je suis très reconnaissante aux personnes suivants : Dr. François Bingono Bingono m'a aidé avec des informations et des contacts musicaux, il a également encouragé le projet dans son intégralité. Jean-Maurice Noah a partagé avec moi son expertise sur la musique camerounaise et il a répondu avec patience à toutes mes questions. Prof. Albert Temgoua a facilité mon accueil à Yaoundé et les premiers pas de mes recherches. Christian Tsala Tsala a rendu possible les voyages à Monatélé. Abbé Antoine Awona m'a appris avec beaucoup d'engagement un vocabulaire de base en Ewondo.

Le personnel de la Bibliothèque Centrale de l'Université de Yaoundé I et le personnel des Archives Nationales du Cameroun m'ont soutenue dans mes recherches, soyez convaincus de ma profonde reconnaissance.

Je tiens particulièrement à adresser un grand merci à mes ami(e)s suivant(e)s: Sali m'a aidé à surmonter les petits problèmes quotidiens. Il est devenu un compagnon précieux pendant mes séjours à Yaoundé et a trouvé une solution à tous mes problèmes. Marthe avait toujours un repas très bien cuisiné pour moi et m'a aidé avec beaucoup des petites choses. C'est à cause d'elle que j'ai fait la connaissance de l'ensemble Balafon Star. Sali et Marthe, je vous remercie beaucoup ! Merci aussi à tous les autres habitants des quartiers Cradat et Ecole de Poste qui ont facilité ma vie quotidienne à Yaoundé.

Et non des moindres, je veux dire MERCI à ma chère sœur Lydie-Chantal à Douala. Elle et sa famille m'ont accueilli pendant chaque séjour au Cameroun avec beaucoup de cordialité et amitié. Un très grand merci pour votre soutien et les innombrables heures de joie dans votre maison!

À toutes les autres personnes qui m'ont aidé d'une manière ou d'une autre j'adresse un grand merci!

Chapter 1

Introduction: Putting Bikutsi in Context

The city of Yaoundé, the capital of Cameroon, is full of manifold sound-scapes filled with bikutsi music. The latest bikutsi hits blare out from the speakers of small street cafés; bikutsi is played live in clubs around town, where popular singers literally pass the microphone from one to another; xylophone ensembles perform bikutsi in neighbourhood bars. Bikutsi is the essential musical background for private and public festivities. The city hosts an annual bikutsi festival that lasts three days. When entering a music shop in Yaoundé, the bikutsi section is overwhelming and the most popular bikutsi singers are played in the background. Yaoundé and other towns in Cameroon, especially in the south, seem to vibrate with the fast, pounding rhythms that are characteristic for bikutsi.

How bikutsi music sounds and where it is performed can, however, vary greatly. At the time of writing this book, the musical universe of bikutsi included a capella songs sung by women, dance music played live by guitar-based modern dance bands and electronically produced and recorded in small backyard studios in Yaoundé, and dance music played by local xylophone ensembles. Even church hymns can be – provided the musical characteristics allow it – bikutsi. All these different musical phenomena are distinct to one another but still connected, especially through their common origin in the musical traditions of the ethnic groups of the Beti. The term bikutsi in this musical world is a generic denomination pointing to a conglomerate of musical phenomena which are all recognized as being bikutsi, regardless of their performance contexts or the instruments used.

This has not always been the case. Until the early 1980s, hardly anyone talked about bikutsi in Cameroon. At that time, bikutsi either referred to a particular genre of danced rhythmic patterns, usually in connection to xylo-phone performances, or to the repertoire of women's a cappella song-and-dance pieces performed mainly in female-only contexts. Academic studies on the music of the Beti ethnic groups did not even mention bikutsi before the 1980s. In newspaper articles, bikutsi, as a women's musical practice or specific rhythmic pattern, was mentioned only every now and then. Bikutsi simply was not a topic to talk about; it had not yet developed into the universal musical category within the Beti and Cameroonian musical landscape that it is today. The dance music scene of Yaoundé and other Cameroonian towns in the 1960s and 1970s was dominated by Latin American-derived dance music, especially merengue and soukous, and the popular music makossa, developed out of the musical traditions of the people living in the coastal regions around Douala. The rise of bikutsi only started in the early 1980s, when dance music performed by modern music groups, based mainly on electric guitars and percussion and drawing heavily on Beti musical traditions, was framed as "bikutsi", thereby establishing a new popular music genre within the Cameroonian music market. In the process of framing and cementing bikutsi as an identifiable popular music genre, not only did modern dance music in Cameroon change permanently, so did the semantic meanings of bikutsi and its relevance throughout Cameroon. Beti life especially was significantly altered. Music groups and singers as well as labels started to concentrate on bikutsi alone, and more and more people listened and danced to bikutsi. Bikutsi became a relevant and significant player in Cameroonian musical life and on the music market. This is also clearly reflected in academic works: since the 1980s, bikutsi has become a topic of scholarly analysis as a musical phenomenon, especially by Cameroonian scholars. This book explores this transformation in Cameroon's modern music in the 1970s and 1980s. It sets out to explain the rise of a dance music tradition of the Beti ethnic groups that led to the establishment of a distinct popular music genre in postcolonial Cameroon. While the musical phenomena from which the popular music genre bikutsi emerged are featured in brief, that is, xylophone dance music and women's song-and-dance pieces, the main focus of the book is on guitar-based bikutsi traditions and the question of how, why, and by whom, under which circumstances and changes bikutsi rose to become an identifiable, distinct popular music genre.

Local and Cosmopolitan: Bikutsi as African Popular Music

This study of bikutsi becoming a popular music genre necessarily draws on and inscribes itself into the dynamic and growing tradition of ethnomusicological African popular music studies. Popular music in Africa came into (ethno)musicological focus in the 1980s, and research increased since the 1990s (see, e.g., Kubik 1969, 1971–72; Nettl 1978; Coplan 1982; Stapleton and May 1987; Manuel 1988; Erlmann 1991, 1996; Ewens 1991; Graham 1989, 1992; Bender 2000) with an increasing interest among music listeners in the Western hemisphere as well as altered ideologies in the discipline that now accepted popular music as an important research topic. For Bruno Nettl, "research on popular music (admittedly in the broad sense of the word) has arguably become the mainstream" in the decade since 2000 (Nettl 2005: 188). Writing briefly on popular music in his work on issues in ethnomusicology, in defining what popular music is, Nettl simply refers to "mass-mediated music" known and loved by many and immediately adds that "it's not one music but many (with significant commonalities), everything from rock music and blues to rap, from Indian *bhangra* to Moroccan *rai*" (Nettl 2005: 188). In this sense of "popular musics" around the world, Nettl continues that "there is a tendency for each culture, or subculture, to develop a distinct popular music" (Nettl 2005: 187). This is exactly what happened with Beti music traditions in bikutsi. In line with Nettl's definition of popular musics, Kofi Agawu states that popular music "is first and foremost a repertoire" and proposes to speak of "*varieties* of African popular music" (Agawu 2003: 122). In this sense bikutsi is one of many distinct, locally embedded, and ethnically grounded popular musics around the world: it uses instruments characteristic for the making of popular music, it is to a certain extent mass-mediated, and it is dependent on marketing structures, media presence, and specific social contexts developed through the late twentieth century.

Entering the field of the study of African popular musics, one immediately encounters different categorizations of music along dichotomies of modern/traditional, Western/African, or global/local. Although concepts of hybridity and cosmopolitanism have increasingly taken hold in ethnomusicology, it seems that we are nevertheless still struggling to overcome the dichotomies that imply a hidden notion of "authentic" and "pure" African musical practices, presumably not influenced by music from a diffuse "outside", and the notion of a strictly "Western" music, that is, pop and rock music – including the implicit danger of essentialism (cf. Turino 2003: 58). Ethnomusicological studies especially on various popular musics have increasingly challenged these dichotomies, as these are often ethnically and locally embedded musical traditions using various traits of global popular music. Recent ethnographic work on music in African countries shows that there is a strong move towards less essentialist notions of musical practices (e.g., Feld 2012; Steingo 2016; Emielu 2018). In ethnomusicology we are well aware that musical phenomena around the world have always incorporated character-istics from "outside" their immediate area of origin and impact, in Africa especially via migration and church music, and during the twentieth century also through traits of popular music produced primarily in North America and Europe. At the same time, much music around the world is usually still associated with specific geographic areas or groups of people. Beti music and bikutsi are no exception. Even in its guitar-based and electronically pro-duced variants, bikutsi remains embedded in and connected to the regions in southern Cameroon inhabited by Beti ethnic groups. Accordingly, during my fieldwork with musicians, fans, and audiences in Cameroon I did not encounter conceptions of a "local" and "global" culture or a "modern" versus a "traditional" music in their understanding of bikutsi. Bikutsi, as most other popular music in Africa, eludes a clear categorization of "modern" versus "traditional" or "local" versus "global".

In an attempt to overcome these dichotomies, Motti Regev suggests the concept of "aesthetic cosmopolitanism" (Regev 2013; see also Regev 2007a, 2007b). "Aesthetic cosmopolitanism" refers to the conditions under which typical features of pop-rock music and distinct methods of music-making in the pop-rock traditions have been available around the world ever since its emergence. Using the history of popular music in Israel and Argentina as examples, Regev argues that "pop-rock was from an early stage a world phenomenon" (Regev 2007b: 322). Electric and electronic instruments, technological sound equipment, amplification, and other devices for sound manipulation have been present, available, and in use not only in the domi-nant centres of Anglo-American popular music, but also on their peripheries. In consequence, musicians around the world created popular music genres "of their own", usually sung in domestic languages, including local musical characteristics. In Africa during the twentieth century, many such varieties of popular music emerged, like mbalax in Senegal, zouglou in the Ivory Coast, or chimurenga in Zimbabwe. In Cameroon, one can cite the popular music genre makossa, and, of course, bikutsi. Due to their intrinsic local embedded-ness, these musical genres increasingly became powerful markers of local identity and have been perceived as legitimate musical expressions to per-form what Regev calls "ethno-national cultural uniqueness".

Drawing on the concept of "cultural fields" developed by the sociologist Pierre Bourdieu (see Bourdieu 1993, 2001) and extensions thereof, Regev situates any form of "ethno-national pop-rock" within a globe-spanning field of pop-rock wherein local musicians and other actors find their creative inspiration. As such, bikutsi and its predecessors are part of a dynamic global field of popular music. These musics and their respective musicians hardly ever assume dominant positions in this global field. They do, however, take part in the dynamics, structure, and hierarchies of this field (Regev 2007b, 2007a). Simultaneously, ethno-national pop-rock agents – including musicians, journalists, and other players in the context of musical production – are situated within a specific field of ethno-national culture, where they take part in negotiating legitimate cultural expressions and compete for profitable field positions and available capital (in the sense of Bourdieu, e.g., financial means, recognition, media presence) on a regional or national level (Regev 2007b: 323). As these two fields converge and intersect, according to Regev, "aesthetic cosmopolitanism" comes into being and enables the representation of ethno-national uniqueness based on contemporary art forms of pop-rock. In contrast to notions of aesthetic cosmopolitanism ascribed to the level of individuals (see, e.g., Turino 2000), Regev argues that it manifests on a "structural collective level, as a cultural condition that is inextricable from current ethno-national uniqueness" (Regev 2007b: 318–19). In Regev's theoretical model, this collective aesthetic cosmopolitanism was the outcome of the "historical event of pop-rock" during the second half of the twentieth century. This process culminated in the legitimization of pop-rock within the presentation of ethno-national culture, thereby extending or replacing former presentations via traditional music and folklore (Regev 2007b: 325–36).

With its potential to include any "outside", "global", or "Western" influences and features and the active role of local actors to choose among these influences consciously, this theoretical concept fits the development of bikutsi and can help to explain its framing as a popular music genre within the Cameroonian musical landscape. Bikutsi as an identifiable popular music genre developed at the intersection of the diverse global field of pop-rock music as it was locally embedded and the Cameroonian national and Beti ethnic field of musical production. Rather than explaining the emergence of bikutsi and the development of this specific Beti music as hybrid, as a mix of something "outside" Beti or Cameroonian reality and something "inside", this book analyses the development of guitar-based popular music bikutsi as intrinsically connected to local realities of ethnicity, nationality, politics, and musical availabilities, which include local musical traditions as well as forms of pop-rock music.

Cameroon, the Beti, and Bikutsi Stomping

The processes described and analysed in this book took place in a specific geographical, historical, and political setting, namely postcolonial southern Cameroon from immediately after independence in 1960 up to the 1980s. The Republic of Cameroon is situated geographically in the transition zone between West and Central Africa. It had in 2021 an estimated population of 28 million with the biggest cities being the coastal town Douala with around 3.7 million people and the political capital Yaoundé in the interior with around 4 million people.[1] Due to its internal diversity in terms of ethno-linguistic, cultural, religious, and ecological characteristics, Cameroon is often called "Africa in miniature". The country is home to over 200 different ethnic groups, each with particular languages, social structures, and cultural customs. Religious beliefs include Islam, Christianity, and animism. During the colonial era, the area of contemporary Cameroon was subject to much struggle and changing domination by different colonial powers, including Germany, France, and Great Britain. While German rule ended in 1916 during World War I, French rule lasted until 1960 and British rule until 1961. French and English remained official languages after independence; for most of the country, French is the dominant language.

Figure 1.1: Map of Cameroon (the circled area marks roughly the area inhabited by Beti).

The main geographical area of interest for the history of bikutsi is the region in the southern part of the country including the capital Yaoundé, with mainly Christian beliefs and French as the dominant language (see Figure 1.1). This part is mainly inhabited by Beti-Faŋ groups, who also inhabit territory beyond the borders of Cameroon, reaching into the neighbouring countries of Gabon, Equatorial Guinea, and Congo. The musical practices around bikutsi are bound to the musical traditions of these ethnic groups. To do justice to the manifold internal diversity of the Beti-Faŋ, it is more appropriate to speak of Beti-Faŋ "groups" or an ethnic cluster than of a single group. In early colonial times, the respective groups were subsumed under the term "Pahouin" (*fr.*) or "Pangwe" (*ger.*) (see Tessmann 1913). A collective identity of Beti-Faŋ was little developed before independence (Mehler 1993: 79); it was only with the establishment of colonial power structures and later the relevance of ethnic presentation within the postcolonial state that the feeling of belonging to a common ethnic conglomerate became pronounced among Beti-Faŋ.[2] The Beti-Faŋ ethnic groups share various cultural traits, including most musical traditions and instruments, and speak mutually intelligible tonal languages belonging to the Bantu languages. Studying the internal subdivisions and categorizations of Beti-Faŋ groups is a complex matter because the respective terms as well as the divisions themselves have undergone significant alterations and have been used in different ways throughout history. Already a brief glance at the ethnological accounts written during the course of the twentieth century reveals that there has always been considerable debate and some confusion over denominations, (self-)ascriptions, and differentiation among these linguistically and culturally close ethnic groups in southern Cameroon.[3] A very common categorization used for decades in academic writing was to differentiate between Beti, Bulu, and Faŋ groups (cf., e.g., Ngumu 1976b). Due to my own experience during field research I see the main differentiation rather between Beti groups and Faŋ groups wherein the Bulu figure as a Beti group.

In this study I use the term Beti in its narrow sense, referring specifically to the ethnic groups of the Beti living in the northern part of the Beti-Faŋ region, mainly in the administrative region Centre.[4] The region is covered by tropical rainforest and has a humid tropical rainforest climate, with two rainy and two dry seasons. These environmental conditions serve the Beti as an identity marker vis-à-vis other groups in Cameroon, calling themselves "the people of the forest". The term Beti can be translated as "the lords"; in French, it is usually translated as "les seigneurs" and in German as "die Herren". The word "beti" is the plural form of "nti", for which Théodore

Tsala gives two meanings in his Ewondo–French dictionary: the first is "sei-gneur", "maître", or "monsieur"; the second is "libre", in opposition to the word for slave (Tsala n.d.: 484). The second connotation of being free – free of preponderance and having power over others, of being superior in the social hierarchy – is not covered by most simple literal translations. For Philippe Laburthe-Tolra, the best translation is "non-barbare" or "civilisé" (Laburthe-Tolra 1977: 93).[5] The Beti have inhabited their current homelands since the seventeenth century when they migrated from across the river Sanaga (Laburthe-Tolra 1981a; Quinn 2006: 14). An essential myth shared by the Beti groups holds that the Beti crossed the river on the back of a large serpent, and this myth contributes to their notion of belonging to the same entity. Laburthe-Tolra explains that the term Beti was at the time of his research in the 1970s reserved for groups with the common origin of "au-delà du Fleuve", that is, "beyond the river" (Laburthe-Tolra 1977: 100).

Even in this narrow sense, however, the Beti are a group with important internal differentiations that can be traced to the successive arrival of Beti groups in the area. Their social and political organization was traditionally one of autonomous smaller groups; Beti individuals belong primarily to their specific residential units called *mvog*, founded by a male head of household. The term *mvog* is to a large extent synonymous with lineage; a new *mvog* was usually named after the founding person. While the identity as Beti serves mainly as a differentiation vis-à-vis neighbouring people, internally the smaller unit of *mvog* was the main identity marker (see Laburthe-Tolra 1977: 302–303, 424; Quinn 2006: 18). Additionally, the Beti differentiate main lin-eage lines that go back to the first lineages of sons and grandsons of one founding ancestor of the Beti. These lineages are called *ayong*, which was in academic studies translated as "race" as well as "nationality", "clan", or "tribe" (see Tchoungui 2000; Laburthe-Tolra 1977; Tsala n.d.). It is difficult to determine these lineages definitely in number, although some main ones are generally unchallengeable and considered to be the main Beti subgroups (cf. Laburthe-Tolra 1977: 97). These are Ewondo, Eton, Mvele, and Bene. Others, like the Manguisa, the Ntumu, or the Etoudi, appear in classifications either as main lineages themselves or as belonging to one.

It is important to note that the term Beti does not apply to the language spoken. "Beti" only designates the people, the community, but not their lan-guage. Thus, when referring to the language spoken by Beti, the specific dia-lectal variant connected to the main lineage should be employed. While there is a greater gap between the Faŋ and the Beti, there are minor but detectable variations between the mutually intelligible dialectal variants. However, in the course of the twentieth century and due to colonial practices, the variant spoken by the Beti groups living in and around Yaoundé, the Ewondo, has been established as the standard language used mostly by the church and being the first to be written down by the missionaries in colonial times. Therefore, when speaking of the language of all Beti people, the most often employed term is Ewondo (see Onguene Essono 2012). Yaoundé and its surroundings, the region primarily covered in this book, has been the region inhabited throughout the twentieth century by the Beti subgroup Ewondo.

The term "bikutsi" is used in all dialectal variants spoken by the Beti groups. Literally, bikutsi is a composite of three items: the plural particle "bi", the verb "kut" (or "kud"), and the noun "sí". The noun "sí" means "ground" or "floor", also "earth"; the verb "kut" means "to stomp" or "to hit", and "bi" is a particle signifying plural or repetition. Consequently, bikutsi literally means "to stomp on the floor (repeatedly)" or "to hit the ground again and again". In this basic meaning, bikutsi is evidently associated with motion, and particularly, with an action of dance. The term bikutsi is only used in musical contexts and describes a dance movement wherein the feet "stamp the ground". This most basic definition has remained relevant ever since: in Cameroon, people regularly refer to the stamping of the feet as a characteristic feature of any bikutsi music. When asked what the different rhythmic versions in bikutsi have in common, the musician Ebogo Emerent for example explained that "all that they have in common is the foot" (Ebogo Emerent, interview, August 23, 2010). And according to Abbé Antoine Awona, music is not bikutsi "if there are no feet" (Antoine Awona, personal conversation, December 3, 2007). As comprised in its literary meaning, bikutsi music is connected to the specific dance moves of stomping regularly on the ground. This counts for any bikutsi – no matter whether xylophone dance music, women's song-and-dance pieces, or the latest electronically produced bikutsi hit; the stamping on the ground as its main "origin" remains implicitly present, if not performed or mentioned explicitly. Even if not explicitly stated, the practice of stamping on the ground can and should resonate within the term bikutsi when used throughout this book.

Bikutsi, National Identity, and the Postcolonial Condition

The development of bikutsi in postcolonial Cameroon cannot be explained without considering the political realities in the postcolonial nation-state. This is not only because the establishment of bikutsi as a popular music genre owes much to the support of political authorities (see Chapter 7), but also because the day-to-day life of all Cameroonians is subject to specific practices of domination and interaction inherent to the postcolonial state. Popular music and (state) politics in Africa in the twentieth century have to a large extent been intertwined and form a complex relationship that has met with increasing interest among scholars since the turn of the twenty-first century.[6] Popular music in Africa has always been a means to comment on political realities, social problems, and economic developments, and has as such been subject to much censorship (Drewett and Cloonan 2006). On the other hand, politicians need musicians for adequate musical representation and support. Nyamnjoh and Fokwang observed that "political power in Cameroon and, indeed, the rest of Africa has tended to appropriate musicians and their creative efforts to seek or maintain themselves in power" (Nyamnjoh and Fokwang 2005: 253). Furthermore, musicians often rely on the financial and material support of the state and have therefore also tended to be loyal to political regimes.

Achille Mbeme, himself of Cameroonian origin and using Cameroon regularly as an example, shows in his work on the postcolonial African state that most African states have developed specific, historically conditioned, postcolonial political systems based on particular practices of domination and interaction (Mbembe 2001). Everyday life is marked by this postcolonial reality. Musical practices and musicians in Cameroon have, also due to their potential role in state presentation, played a relevant role within this form of politics. Mbembe argues that authoritarian African postcolonial regimes are based on a "trinity of violence, allocations, and transfers" (Mbembe 2001: 48; cf. 42–48). To maintain their marginally legitimized power, the potentates rely firstly on violent suppression and hierarchical relations taken over from the colonial era, such as the imprisonment of political critics and strong hierarchies in political organizations. Secondly, the postcolonial state is based on transfers, that is, on social or financial services for other members of the community that hark back to structures of social obligation prevalent in African communities, be it within a household or family or at the workplace. Transfers are a part of a "multi-faceted, never-ending debt to the community" (Mbembe 2001: 47). For example, a musician living in Yaoundé will only be able to go back to visit his family in the village, if he brings a certain amount of money to distribute. Allocations, the third dimension of the postcolonial state, are payments from the state to the people, for example via privatization or as wages. Such allocations guarantee the loyalty of the citizens and are at the same time a means of suppression and create dependencies. Rather than a renumeration for work, wages are seen as being a favour and privilege of the state given to the individual. The popular Cameroonian singer Anne-Marie Nzié has relied heavily on such allocations, as I have described in detail elsewhere (Brunner 2013). These three pillars of repression and coercion, social obligations, and the financial rewarding of loyalty by the state are intrinsic aspects of life in postcolonial Cameroon and as such are the context within which the processes around bikutsi music described in this book take place.

Cameroon has had two authoritarian potentates since its independence. Ahmadou Ahidjo, a Muslim from the north of the country, was President from 1960 to 1982. He was followed by Paul Biya, an ethnic Beti-Faŋ from the south, who despite some half-hearted moves towards more democracy, such as introducing a multi-party system in 1990, remains in power and has been re-elected by large margins repeatedly in 1997, 2004, 2011, and 2018. The structures of a postcolonial state as described by Mbembe have been more than apparent in both regimes. While severe repression including (according to rumours) torture and spying went hand-in-hand with allocations under Ahidjo, Biya had to struggle with a loss of state influence due to a lack of financial resources during an economic crisis in the 1980s.[7] With decreasing capital, the material foundation to fulfil the functions ascribed to the state after independence decreased; the state could not guarantee the well-being of all its citizens and lost much of its credibility (cf. Mbembe 2001: 66–101).

Musicians' lives and strategies in postcolonial Africa have to be interpreted as intertwined with and embedded in specific struggles over resources and strategies of the postcolonial state. Musicians are subject to repression and/or support within the postcolonial system: they depend on transfers within their communities and they rely on allocations from the state, be it in the form of engagements for concerts, regular wages through a position in a state-sponsored music group, or individual contributions. Seen from the perspective of the postcolonial state, the role of popular musicians since independence in Cameroon has been basically bound to one specific task: to contribute to the state's cultural representation in line with the need to build a national consciousness as a Cameroonian nation. After independence, Africa's political leaders have consistently aimed at the construction of durable states, assigning a central role in this process to the creation of a national consciousness or a sense of national belonging among often ethnically and culturally disparate citizens. Cameroon was no exception. The construction of the postcolonial state enforced through and supported by tight state control was accompanied by and acted out via an overbearing rhetoric of nation building (cf. DeLancey

1989; Nyamnjoh and Fokwang 2005). The consciousness of belonging to a shared nation is one of an "imagined community" (Anderson 1983), realized not via personal contact, but for example, through the media, cultural practices, language, and economic borders. Musical performances as a means to communicate and represent common features and symbols consequently played an important role in the imagination and creation of a Cameroonian national identity.

As with any form of identity, national identity is fragile and arbitrary in its nature, being a social construction that needs to be repeatedly and continuously acted out to persist or change (e.g., Butler 1990). In her study on cultural politics in Tanzania, Kelly M. Askew argues for analysing national identities as fluid concepts: "No less than individual or group identities do national identities wax and wane and undergo significant change" (Askew 2002: 12). Due to the inherent instability of national identity, it must be performed continuously, be it by rhetorical utterances by politicians or through musical practices labelled "national" or "Cameroonian". That said, no state control is as close or fixed in its specific implementation of a national image or specific cultural practices as ideally desired or intended. Citing Antonio Gramsci, Askew argues that "[a]spiring hegemonies, be they imposed from the top or the bottom, are always subject to perforation. Latent possibilities and alternative visions can never be fully nor permanently eradicated, however imposing a state bureaucracy may appear" (Askew 2002: 11). Although the cultural visions, activities, and plans of the ruling political elite provide the general framework for musicians in Cameroon, their implementation nevertheless takes place on a different, lower level. Musicians, audience, and other (musical) players forming the nation and being the citizens of the state perform – and in doing so negotiate – the musical representation of the nation. Musical practices in Cameroon are no exception to the general postcolonial rule, as I show elsewhere in detail (Brunner 2017; see also Brunner 2013). Especially in the immediate decades after independence, musicians engaged in transfer relations and benefited from state allocations, but they were also repressed – or avoided a priori activities that might lead to conflicts with the state (Brunner 2017). Political players, on the other hand, kept a close eye on the developments and people in the field of music, in order to ensure adequate musical representation. Musicians were forced to find a position in these political realities and the dominant notions of musical national representation. This embedding of music in the postcolonial Cameroonian state shaped the rise of bikutsi as a popular music genre in a direct and immediate manner and is the political frame in which the changes in music and musical landscape must be seen.

Bikutsi's Emergence as a Popular Music Genre

In the course of the developments described in this book, what is considered to be the musical practice called bikutsi expands significantly over time. In the following I will argue that this is due to bikutsi being framed as a popular music genre. While the repertoire and practice of song-and-dance pieces sung by women, introduced in more detail in Chapter 3, certainly counted as a specific Beti music genre in the 1970s, it is only through the change and expansion starting in the 1970s and taken up efficiently in the 1980s, that bikutsi became an identifiable popular music genre, introducing on the way a new meaning for the term bikutsi in general. Questions around (popular music) genre development and the connected social and musical constraints or opportunities have been explored especially in sociology and in popular music studies (Lena and Peterson 2006, 2008; Holt 2007; Winter 2013; cf. Fabbri 1981; Negus 1999). Genres are not only relevant in contexts where music is first and foremost a commodity (and it is one in most cases); they are an ordering force in everyday (musical) life and a reality in our everyday experience. To mark and define a music genre is a means of bringing some order into the endless variants of musical practices in this world and to provide some orientation (Gebesmair 2008). Especially in the field of popular music, but also in other musical worlds, we encounter music as being ordered, categorized, and classified along more or less fluid and flexible genre conventions and conceptions. In Cameroon, bikutsi arose as an ordering category and title for a music rising to popularity, and thereby changed the existing borders and distinctions relevant in the field of dance music as well as in the field of Beti music.

Music genres have a clear processual character. They cannot be conceptualized as something stable; genre boundaries as well as their specific definitions are fluid and negotiable. Fabian Holt defines a genre as "a category that refers to a particular kind of music in a distinctive web of production, circulation, and signification. It is a structuring force that organizes cultural practice and creates contexts and horizons for understanding music" (Holt 2008: 42; see also Holt 2007). In a similar way, Jennifer C. Lena and Richard A. Peterson see music genres "as systems of orientations, expectations, and conventions that bind together industry, performers, critics, and fans in making what they identify as a distinctive sort of music" (Lena and Peterson 2008: 698). For a genre to emerge and persist, continuous "genre-defining work" (Lena and Peterson 2006: 4) by individuals is needed, as genres are permanently negotiated in their (musical) characteristics and boundaries, and constituted by discourses and struggles over meaning (Frow 2006). In the constant struggle over musical meaning and belonging, a genre can serve as a landmark, as a point of reference, and as such it can be neglected, praised, extended in its definition, valued, described, contested, and negotiated.

There is, however, one major gap in the mentioned research on musical genres: the role of musical innovation and music characteristics within (popular) music genres has rarely been discussed (cf. Winter 2013). As Lena and Peterson observe, there exist two dominant approaches in the relevant disciplinary traditions: musicologists tend to identify genres alongside shared musical characteristics and define genres solely in musical terms; sociologists on the other hand put the social context in the foreground and leave musical matters aside (2008: 698). A fruitful approach to studying musical genre, however, combines and merges these two sides of the same coin. As Roy Shuker summarizes in the revised edition of his classic *Understanding Popular Music Culture*, music genres emerge out of and exist through several distinguishing features, the music itself being one of them (Shuker 2016: 113–14). For Shuker, "musical characteristics, which produce an identifiable sound, according to conventions of composition, instrumentation, and performance" are essential to the constitution of a musical genre (2016: 113–14). In addition, he mentions non-musical, stylistic attributes, institutional frames and practices, and the audience as relevant parameters in music genres (2016: 113–14; cf. Winter 2013). In studying music genres, then, analyses of musical characteristics, innovations, and changes have to be merged with research on their respective social and cultural embedding.

This is exactly what this book sets out to do. The rise of bikutsi to become an identifiable popular music genre cannot be explained solely on the basis of social and cultural factors, nor can it be explained only along musical lines. Rather, the developments in southern Cameroon in the 1970s and 1980s around Beti music and bikutsi is a constant intermingling of processes of musical experimentation and renewal, new social embedding, political change, technological innovation, and institutional and commercial framing. Only the complex intertwining and mutual interconnectivity of social, cultural, political, industrial, and musical parameters can explain why and how bikutsi became a structuring category on the musical landscape of Cameroon and within Beti music.

Fieldwork, Sources, and the Challenge of Reflexivity

The material for this book was collected during four periods of field research in Cameroon each lasting from a few weeks to a few months between 2007 and 2012. A lot of effort was put into collecting written sources, mainly newspaper articles from the French edition of the newspaper *Cameroon Tribune*.[8] I collected and evaluated about 1400 newspaper articles from the *Cameroon Tribune*, most of them on music, from the period from 1975 to 1990. The *Cameroon Tribune* was founded in 1974, when the state re-appropriated the French-owned *La Presse du Cameroun*.[9] Until the early 1990s, the *Cameroon Tribune* remained the only Cameroonian daily newspaper in the country. Legal reforms brought a liberalization of print media and consequently a boom in the publication of newspapers. Although it was the only available newspaper, the influence of the *Cameroon Tribune* in the 1970s and 1980s should not be overestimated. While it was the print publication with the largest distribution among Cameroonian citizens, especially in urban centres, and its content also spread by word of mouth, the newspaper only reached a small part of the population, especially when compared to the radio. Furthermore, the content of the newspaper articles was naturally biased, as the *Cameroon Tribune* was the main written voice of the authoritarian state. That said, in terms of the development of Cameroonian music in the 1970s and 1980s, this newspaper must be considered the central and most authoritative print resource available.

The other archival sources used for this work are commercial recordings, that is, vinyl records. A good number of commercial recordings of the 1970s and 1980s have been preserved in private collections and could at the time of research be easily acquired from specialized vendors at the Marché Central in Yaoundé. In addition to the thirty or so LPs and singles that I purchased myself, I also gained access to relevant music and information on the music through the archive Arc Musica, curated by the German Joachim Oelsner, a former "lector" of the German Academic Exchange Service (DAAD). The archive houses a large quantity of musical recordings and background information, painstakingly collected and archived by Joachim Oelsner and detailed in his in-depth work since the 1990s. Hundreds of tapes, a dozen or so LPs and singles, digitized versions of early reel-tape recordings, and a number of CDs provide as complete a picture as possible of music history in southern Cameroon, with a focus on Beti music traditions and bikutsi. Joachim Oelsner additionally collected a huge amount of information from newspapers and other written and visual sources, all sorted and structured on the basis of keywords, artists, and themes. The work of Joachim Oelsner and his considerable expertise on the history and events of music in Cameroon in the late twentieth century proved highly valuable for this research on bikutsi.

Out of the many music pieces listened to during research, I selected some for a detailed transcription and analysis. The selection was based on my own listening experiences as well as on extra-musical criteria, mainly the status of these songs (as identified in interviews or newspaper articles) as especially important for the processes around bikutsi or as being extremely popular at their time of release. Some of these transcriptions and analyses found their way into this book. Considering the debates on the choice of notational system for African music (for an overview see Grupe 2005; also Agawu 2003), I opted for different notational presentations depending on the phenomena described. I chose Western staff notation for longer parts with several instruments. In applying a notation that musicians and researchers around the world are mostly familiar with, I want to put bikutsi on an equal level with any other popular music in the world. However, my understanding of bikutsi as popular music is also informed by the notion of a specific African musical foundation, and my interpretation of bikutsi is also founded on the premises described in detail by Gerhard Kubik, for example in the concept of equal pulsation and the importance of circular elements (Kubik 2010: 1–84; 2004). Therefore, at some points I add to the Western staff notation rhythmical transcriptions following the system used by Kubik. While on the one hand this combination of notational systems is in accordance with my musical understanding of bikutsi as African music in a global field of popular music, on the other hand I am convinced that this combination also enables a better understanding of my analysis.

In addition to the historical data of newspaper articles and commercial recordings mentioned above, I collected ethnographic data during fieldwork. The material collected thus includes field notes, field diaries, CDs and tapes of contemporary bikutsi singers, notes on informal conversations, short ethnographic interviews with numerous people, and recordings of music events (mostly video recordings). Most of this material is archived at the Phonogrammarchiv, the Austrian Audiovisual Research Archive of the Austrian Academy of Science (see catalogue at http://www.phonogrammarchiv.at). These documentations of contemporary bikutsi served as background information and a contemporary foil on which I interpreted and evaluated the historical developments. At some points during this book where I deem it meaningful, I include ethnographic accounts and comparisons to the contemporary situation as I experienced it during fieldwork. In doing so I hope to live up to my ambition to present what I call an ethnographically informed history of the popular music genre bikutsi.

Last but not least, I undertook long interviews with selected musicians, a regular visitor of a nightclub in the 1980s, and a producer. All interviews were done in French, recorded with permission of the interviewees, and transcribed by myself for analysis. The interviews were semi-standardized, problem-centred interviews. The problem-centred interview combines the approach of narration-based interviews with the more standardized topical interviews. During a narration-based interview, the interviewer uses questions and remarks to evoke a narrative, not influencing the narration of the interviewee, in order to obtain unique and sometimes surprising stories. The topics and themes presented are not given by the interviewer. In the standardized topical interview, on the other hand, prepared questions are used to retrieve facts and opinions; the content of the interview is controlled by the interviewer. During a problem-centred interview, an open, narrated phase structured by the interviewee is followed by a phase structured by specific questions by the interviewer.[10] This interview form allows for new aspects to emerge and for the interviewees to present their individual life history and viewpoints on bikutsi history. At the same time, it provides space for specific clarifications concerning specific issues identified in other sources or through other interviews.

Ethnomusicologists are well aware that the position of the researcher is one of immediate importance in terms of the insights of ethnographic research – and this is also true for historical accounts. No historical account can be solely factual and objective; the position and background of the researcher and writer are of immediate importance. Sketched out in some keywords, my specific position during field research was that of a white, European (Austrian), female PhD candidate in her late twenties to her early thirties. I owe to this individual situation specific forms of communication and data accumulation, for example easily achieving an expert-student relationship with my interviewees, but also situations where it was not suitable for a woman, especially a white and European woman, to ask certain questions. Concerning my position in writing historical narratives on an African popular music, I am well aware of my temporal and cultural position and the representational power therein; I write in the second decade of the twenty-first century, in the centre of Europe, on the development of a Cameroonian popular music some fifty years ago. My outsider position to the research subject is a double one: in time and space. This fact called for continuous, careful considerations of interpretations and a high level of reflexivity, which I tried to accomplish by staying close to the available data in interpretation and writing. With this book, my aim is to provide a well-informed historical study, based on significant data, and written with as much reflection as possible concerning the data, the writing position, and scholarly pre-considerations. Thus, this work aims to be a contribution to an understanding of the processes towards bikutsi as an identifiable popular music genre and the lasting effects of this development.

Chapter 2

The Sound of Yaoundé in the 1970s

In an article in the *Cameroon Tribune* in 1979, the journalist and associate to the culture ministry Adala H. Gildo, himself a pianist, described the music in Yaoundé as particular to the Cameroonian musical landscape. He coined the term "musique made in Yaoundé" and thus highlighted the shared musical path that musicians and music groups in Yaoundé were following (Gildo 1979): while their musical repertoire in the 1970s was predominantly Afro-Caribbean-derived dance music inspired by Congolese popular music, in nightclubs and bars, the musicians of Yaoundé nevertheless increasingly and consciously drew on the Beti musical tradition in their performances. Gildo used the term "Soukouss-Bikudsi" to describe this musical trend and highlighted the groups Los Camaroes and Les Titans as "inspirers of the typical music 'made in Yaoundé' that draws its verve directly from the sources in the beti-fang folklore (and the like…)" (Gildo 1979).[1] This chapter introduces the field of modern dance music in the capital in terms of active musicians, political environment, production and dissemination, and musical repertoire. The music of the bands performing in Yaoundé in the 1970s provides the foundation for the framing of bikutsi as an identifiable popular music genre some years later.

Guitar Music in Yaoundé (and Cameroon) in the 1950s and 1960s

Bikutsi's development as an identifiable popular music genre is based on the introduction of the guitar as the central instrument in modern dance music. According to Andrew Kaye, the guitar has probably been present on the African continent since the late nineteenth century, but only became known and appreciated outside the colonial European communities in the 1920s and 1930s – at approximately the same time as the interest in this instrument grew in Europe (Kaye 1998: 352). Several musical styles using the guitar emerged during this era in African countries. Austin Emielu notes that what is called popular African music today is intrinsically connected to the introduction of the guitar; however, he also rightly insists that "the idea of a Western string instrument in the fashion and design of the acoustic guitar was not new to Africa" (Emielu 2018: 214). In Cameroon, guitars were known and played to some extent in the period before World War II (Ndachi Tagne 1990: 46–48). After WWII, the use of guitars spread in Cameroon as elsewhere in Africa and they became more and more established in musical entertainment. For example, Nzié Moïse Cromwell, known as Cromwell Nzié, was a popular guitarist in the 1950s after having served in the French army during WWII, releasing records with the Congolese label Opika (Ndachi Tagne 1990: 42). Cromwell Nzié was one of quite a few active and popular guitarists in the 1950s. Lobè Lobè Rameau was described in a newspaper article as a "pioneer of modern music" in Cameroon and known for the music he wrote for advertisements (E.N.B. 1977). Nelle Eyoum was credited with having coined the neologism "makossa" for what was later to become a particular type of Cameroonian guitar-based music (cf. Noah 2010). These guitarists composed and sang their own songs, usually in local languages, sometimes also in French. Most of these first-generation African guitarists were educated to some extent in a Western-style school system and associated in one way or another with the colonial economy or administration or various Christian missions. As Gerhard Kubik states, the guitar was "*the* instrument associated by young men with their struggle for a better position in the colonial hierarchy and eventual freedom for their countries" (Kubik 2009: 11). Predominantly, the guitar was played by young men in Cameroon – with one exception. Cromwell Nzié's sister Anne-Marie Nzié was one of the first, if not *the* first, woman to publicly play guitar in Cameroon. She became a successful and very popular solo singer and was given the name "The Golden Voice of Cameroon".[2] The role of the guitar in Cameroon's music received official recognition in a guitar contest organized by the Ministry of Information in 1963, which was won by Anne-Marie Nzié (Ndachi Tagne 1990: 100). The guitar was an instrument perfectly suited for entertainment music in African countries. As Kaye put it, the "indigenization" of the guitar was completed in the 1960s (Kaye 1998: 362).

In the 1960s, the electric guitar began to gain ground in African countries. Christopher Waterman found evidence that the first time an electric guitar was played in Lagos was probably in the late 1940s (Waterman 1990: 83); Chris Stapleton and Chris May mention that in what is today the Democratic

Republic of Congo the electric guitar was first played by Wendo Kolosoy in 1949 (Stapleton and May 1990: 144). In the dance music styles of Kinshasa/Leopoldville and Brazzaville, popularized as "Congolese Rumba", as well as other Afro-Caribbean dance music taken up by musicians in various African countries, the electric guitar became the most prominent instrument. In the 1960s, the instrument was known and played in Cameroon as well. Ndachi Tagne reports its use by Anne-Marie Nzié – together with her Hawaiian guitar – in this decade. The amplifier was carried on the back and was powered by batteries (Ndachi Tagne 1990: 135–36). Although acoustic guitars remained widely in use in the 1960s, electric guitars and associated music styles quickly spread in the country, especially in urban centres. Since the 1960s, guitar-based music groups are commonly called "modern", as they use instruments perceived as non-indigenous, foreign, and "modern" in contrast to other locally embedded instruments. These bands consisted of (electric) guitars, (electric) bass, percussion (usually congas and rattles) and singers and performed in different urban dance and entertainment venues. The musicians were most often male; Anne-Marie Nzié as a female instrumentalist and singer long remained an exception.

The music played by these groups was dance music popular at the time, often simply called "variété", and included Afro-Caribbean-derived music and *rumba congolaise*, but also slows, boleros, tangos, and waltzes. Further, French chansons and jazz made an impact. These musics were popular with the political and economic elite of Cameroonian society in their endeavour to live what they perceived to be a modern European lifestyle. Titi Joseph, a musician active in Yaoundé and Douala in the 1950s, played in music groups he called "reputed"; the occasions for playing before independence in 1960 were various galas, dinners, and festivities, for a mainly white public and the Cameroonian upper class. In these contexts, the musicians had to be able to read sheet music (Gildo 1978). Other, less reputed music groups worked in different performance contexts, but played a similar repertoire. Rather than galas and dinners, their main stages were urban bars and nightclubs and organized entertainment occasions such as village parties. Bands and musicians were regularly recorded by the local radio stations to be aired later and could sometimes release their music on commercial records with French labels. Especially active in the Beti region were the Congolese labels Opika and Ngoma (Ndachi Tagne 1990: 112).

In the 1960s, Afro-Caribbean dance music styles spread increasingly in Cameroon, especially through the dissemination of Congolese modern music. With music groups such as O.K. Jazz, led by Franco Luambo Makiadi, or

Ry-Co Jazz, the music genre rumba congolaise and its typical guitar-playing style became widely popular in Sub-Saharan Africa (White 2009; Stewart 2000). Additionally, styles like charanga, pachanga, rumba, son, merengue, and cha-cha became an essential part of the repertories of local dance bands. This musical orientation towards Afro-Caribbean styles was also referenced in the paratexts of music, such as the names of music groups. In Cameroon, Spanish names were common, like Los Camaroes or Los Calvinos. The nicknames of musicians were sometimes inspired by Congolese musicians, as was the case with guitarist Onana Zacharie who played with the group Les Vétérans in the 1980s and was commonly called "Onana Chantal" after a Congolese guitarist, because he played a solo made famous by that guitarist so well (Onana Zacharie, interview, September 12, 2008). The identification with Afro-Caribbean-derived music went beyond simple musical inspiration.

Merengue in Yaoundé: Cheramy de la Capitale

In the Beti region, one form of dance music was especially widespread in the 1960s and 1970s: merengue. Merengue is an Afro-Caribbean dance style commonly associated with the countries of Haiti and the Dominican Republic (see Austerlitz 1997; Averill 1997). The reasons why merengue (also written "meringue" in Cameroon) became so popular in southern Cameroon especially among Beti musicians remains unclear, but it has become an important dance music element in Beti music. The main protagonist of merengue music played by modern dance bands in the 1960s in Yaoundé was Apollinaire Owona, better known as Cheramy de la Capitale. Born in November 1926 near Yaoundé, the singer and saxophonist Cheramy began his life as a musician in 1956 when he formed a music group.[3] He was a taxi driver in Yaoundé prior to his musical career, but had already acquired the nickname Cheramy de la Capitale and was a regular visitor in bars and nightclubs, a cost-intensive activity mainly reserved for white people at that time. He learned to play saxophone with the then leader of the brass band Fanfare des Ewondos, one of the first brass groups in the region.[4] Cheramy then bought instruments from an expatriate to form his own music group and made music his profession.

Cheramy de la Capitale, often called "king of merengue", was one of the first Cameroonians in Yaoundé to engage a full modern dance band and perform with it in bars and pubs. The group played common Afro-Caribbean dance music, that is, merengue, tango, waltz, and samba with Ewondo lyrics. Playing saxophone and singing himself, the instrumentation of the group included electric guitars, string bass, and percussion. Cheramy was probably the first band leader in southern Cameroon to include electric guitars in his modern dance ensemble. Cheramy did some radio recordings, some of which can be found in the archive of Cameroon Radio Télévision, and released a few records (J.-M. Ahanda 1982d). Primarily, however, his music acquired popularity through live performances and via the radio. From the late 1950s to the late 1960s, Cheramy's band played in various dancing locations in Yaoundé: Canne à Sucre (Cheramy's home club), L'hôtel Aurore, L'hôtel Bellevue, Auberge Catalane, Cercle des jeunes, and Pezzana (A. Ahanda 1982). The journalist Antoine Ahanda later described Cheramy's status in Yaoundé in the 1960s: "In a Yaoundé that wanted to exude an aura of elegance while maintaining its provincial character with its houses made of woven mats, Cheramy was the star" (A. Ahanda 1982).[5] Cheramy and his music were associated with the middle and upper classes of the town. Accordingly, an evening with the band was described in the *Cameroon Tribune* by listing expensive drinks: "During the reception where the band played under a roof of palm trees, one drank champagne soda, the beers Stoubic, Kronenbourg, Beaufort Spécial, Slavia, Heineken, the red wines Kiravi and Bellevie" (A. Ahanda 1982).[6] Cheramy also played at official occasions, for example for the Cameroonian President.

Cheramy's professionalization and success as a musician was made possible because he had the financial resources acquired over long years working in other occupations. He was able to pay the members of the music group and buy the instruments. With his success, the income from his musical activities remained steady for about a decade. Beside his nightclub performances, appearances at prestigious wedding celebrations contributed significantly to his financial means. Today, many people in Yaoundé who were children in the 1960s or early 1970s have vivid memories of Cheramy's band accompanying wedding processions. After leaving church, a wedding procession followed. The wedding guests as well as other people marched and danced behind a truck on which the dance band played. Sometimes, Cheramy is even described as the inventor of these "wedding caravans". To celebrate a wedding with Cheramy's group was clearly a sign of wealth (A. Ahanda 1982).

In the early 1970s, however, Cheramy's popularity declined and the musician disappeared from Yaoundé's musical scene. This was due to the increasing range of music available in Yaoundé with ever more music groups and the trend to develop Beti music further, but also to declining financial means, which led people to hire less costly musical entertainment for their festivities, such as local xylophone ensembles. In 1982, Cheramy played a concert with two other musicians in the Centre Culturel Français in Yaoundé, but what was intended as a comeback did not carry fruit (J.-M. Ahanda 1982d). Cheramy lived his last years impoverished in a small house at the edge of Yaoundé. He died in May 2011. Of his music, a few recordings are preserved on magnetic tapes. Cheramy's music group served as a starting point and training for musicians that would later be successful in Yaoundé. The trumpeter and composer Tedjo Mekoulou, one of Yaoundé's most renowned jazz musicians in the 1970s, played with Cheramy whilst in college, and Mama Ohandja, popular throughout the 1970s, took his first steps with the group. For those who continued and extended the musical life of Yaoundé in the 1970s, Cheramy was a role model.

Cameroonian Afro-Caribbean Music in Yaoundé in the 1970s

With Cheramy de la Capitale's popularity decreasing, younger musicians took his place and kept the city's music scene alive. The best-known music groups of this era were Los Camaroes, Les Titans, Les Grands Esprits et Les Vétérans, as well as the singers Betti Joseph, Mama Ohandja, and Aloa Javis. They all contributed to the musical trends that led Adala Gildo to create the term "made in Yaoundé" or "Yaoundé sound" in 1979 for the dance music created in the Cameroonian capital. In line with the music of Cheramy, the "Yaoundé sound" of these urban guitar-based music groups throughout the 1970s remained Afro-Caribbean-derived dance music, that is, merengue, but even more so rumba congolaise, also called soukous. This dance music was widely disseminated via radio in Cameroon, and similar to developments in other African countries, Cameroonian music groups composed lyrics for songs in these dance styles in their own languages. On record singles, these songs were mainly labelled as "rumba", "soukous", or "merengue". The impact of these genres in Cameroonian/Beti music was enormous and lasting. Beti xylophone ensembles called *məndzáŋ* had integrated them into their Beti dance repertoire already in the 1960s (see Chapter 4), and even at the time of research, soukous and merengue figured prominently in performance repertoires – whether electronically produced, guitar-based, or played by urban məndzáŋ ensembles. They have been absorbed into Beti music and are now intrinsic to it; urban məndzáŋ ensembles perform soukous and merengue no different to how they play Beti dances.

The instrumentation of modern dance bands in Yaoundé in the 1970s match the genres played and usually included vocals (solo and chorus), electric guitars, electric bass guitar and percussion, mostly congas and/or rattles and bells. Electric amplification was already common. An article about the break-up of Los Camaroes in 1975 stated that there was an electronic organ in the instrumentation (Boyomo Assala 1975b). The instruments were commonly provided by the owners of the bar in which the group played or by someone else with the necessary financial means. The dependency on individuals with such financial means was significant: keyboards, organs, or a drum set were neither easily available nor affordable for club owners or musicians and they thus only played a minor role on a few recordings. Only in the mid-1970s did their use increase. Unlike the state-funded music groups that will be discussed later, wind instruments were also rare among groups performing in entertainment venues in the capital.

Musically, the rumba, soukous, and merengue pieces performed by Yaoundé-based music groups in the 1970s had an Afro-Caribbean foundation in their overall structure and characteristics. They are dance songs with a binary rhythmical foundation in typical 4/4 meter. They last from three to five minutes. The tempo varying from as slow as 100 bpm to around 140 bpm, most pieces are in the range of 120 to 130 bpm. All songs start with a short introductory section of a couple of measures, in most cases played solo by a guitar. Then the other instruments join in before the verse starts a few measures later. The verses can differ in length and structure, but are always followed by an instrumental part, commonly improvised by the lead guitar on top of the continued pattern played by the other instruments. This instrumental interlude might be reminiscent of the "jaleo" section in merengue or the "montuno" section in rumba, as described by Peter Manuel (Manuel 1988: 434). Another verse part follows, similar to the first. Then the songs end after a short instrumental part, either by fading out or more often with a closing chord on all instruments.

The basic structure of these Afro-Caribbean-inspired pieces is as follows:

instrumental intro
verse
instrumental interlude (guitar solo)
verse
instrumental ending (fade-out or closing chord)

The lyrics of this dance music were in Ewondo or, depending on the origin of the singers, other dialects used by the Beti people. This was one of the main reasons why the music journalist Adala Gildo classified the music as something distinct and called it "made in Yaoundé" (Gildo 1979). The main message of the dance music songs sung in Ewondo can be found in the verses. These are realized in different manners. In some songs, such as 'Amu Dze' sung by Messi Martin, the main melody is sung by one voice throughout. But more common is either a call-and-response structure with a two- or three-voice-choral answering the solo voice, or a two-voice realization of the melody. Two voices in the vocals are most often harmonized, mainly in thirds. The lyrics of the choral parts commonly remain the same throughout the song. The voices show no vibrato; melodic ornamentation is possible. The melodic progression commonly uses whole steps and thirds; large jumps in melody are rare. The tonal range often does not exceed a fifth, except for solo parts, where it can go up almost to an octave.

Whether call-and-response or not, the verses commonly consist of repeated short melodic phrases of one to four measures that are often taken up by the solo guitar as well. Generally, the pieces are built on such short ostinato patterns, with the rhythmic guitar and the bass repeating their phrases throughout the song. This is a feature that also exists in Congolese dance music (Kazadi 1973). The ostinato guitar patterns provide the basic foundation on top of which the lead guitar plays the vocal melody, melodic ornaments and interludes, and improvises in the instrumental sections. The guitar patterns often feature arpeggiated triads in the harmonic progression of the song or circle the fundamental notes of the chords. If using this framework, the harmonic progression can be interpreted as a tonic-dominant alteration, although the harmonic positions are often not clearly realized. Many of the songs available are in the key C major, some also in G major. Besides the accompanying guitar, it is mainly the bass supporting this harmonic progression by commonly providing the fundamentals of the respective chords. Furthermore, as opposed to later trends, the relatively simple bass lines also support the rhythmical structure with the main bass notes falling on-beat.

In many cases, the beat of the songs – in pulses divided into either two or four – is additionally realized by percussion instruments such as rattles or bells. They mark either the beat or double-beat structure, sometimes even the pulses. Additionally, congas are usually present in the rhythm section and provide the basic rhythmic pattern. For the rumba and soukous songs, the basic pattern is the son or rumba clave, which are central rhythmic patterns in Afro-Cuban dance music, presented in Figures 2.1 and 2.2. Although not realized on a distinctly heard percussion instrument like rhythm sticks, the son or rumba claves were the basic patterns of the pieces called rumba or soukous interchangeably. Thus, these pieces are clearly in the tradition of Congolese rumba dance music that itself can be traced back either to Cuban son or the local Congolese maringa dance (Mukuna 2001; Bender 2000). Mvondo Ateba Albert, commonly called Atebass, bass player in the popular band Les Têtes Brulées in the 1980s (see Chapter 7), demonstrated the souk-ous pattern as shown in Figure 2.3 by playing both the son and the rumba clave together on a drum set. The two patterns only differ in the third stroke of the pattern realized on the "4" in the son clave and on the "4+" in the rumba clave. Atebass played both on "4" and on "4+", with a slight accent on the latter.

Figure 2.1: Son clave.

Figure 2.2: Rumba clave.

In contrast to the soukous/rumba pieces, pieces titled merengue are not based on a clave, but provide a typical strong on-beat binary feeling of a 2/4 meter, sometimes also with a continuous fast rattle accompaniment on every pulse, reminiscent of the playing of the scraper *guiro* in Dominican merengue (Manuel 1995: 111). Atebass played the basic pattern as visualized in Figure 2.4.

		1		2		3		4		5		6		7		8	
pattern	(16)	x	.	.	x	.	.	x	x	.	.	x	.	x	.	.	.
beat		x	.	.	.	x	.	.	.	x	.	.	.	x	.	.	.

Figure 2.3: Soukous/rumba pattern (as played by Atebass on a drum set, recorded November 13, 2012).

		1		2		3		4		5		6		7		8	
pattern	(16)	x	.	x	.	.	x	.	.	x	.	x	.	.	x	.	.
beat		x	.	x	.	x	.	x	.	x	.	x	.	x	.	x	.

Figure 2.4: Merengue pattern (as played by Atebass, recorded November 13, 2012).

Listening to early 1970s recordings of "Yaoundé" music, the musical orientation towards Afro-Caribbean music is evident. However, there is also an
obvious tendency towards the conscious use of Beti music traditions. Even
if still labelled "rumba" or "soukous", some songs in the early 1970s already
sound similar to others that are named after Beti rhythms, such as 'Minkul
Mi Nem' by Elamau et son orchestre Les Grands Esprits or 'Kundug Bidza
Bidza' by Los Camaroes. Los Camaroes, with their guitarist Messi Martin,
was of particular importance in this development. Los Camaroes developed
out of the group Jazz Garo that played in northern Cameroon in the 1960s.
In terms of instruments, the group was typical for "modern" music groups at
the time with electric guitars, electric bass guitar, congas, and various percussion instruments. The singing was performed by various group members.
Mbambo Simon, one member of Los Camaroes, described the repertoire as
follows: "The musicians in the past familiarized themselves with the music
of other groups by listening. For example, we interpreted Congolese music,
the Cubans, the South Americans, the pachanga, these genres ... so, we were
a variété group" (Mbambo Simon, interview, August 29, 2008).[7] As well as
cover versions, the group also composed and played their own songs in their
mother tongues. Los Camaroes moved to play in Yaoundé in the early 1970s
and gained considerable popularity in the city, especially because they intensified the musical references to Beti music. This group is seen today as having had a central role in bikutsi history in Cameroon due to their music style
and the invention of the "balafon guitar" by Messi Martin, a form of guitar-
playing and preparation of the instrument that is reminiscent of məndzáŋ
playing, which will be discussed in detail in Chapter 5.

The occasional turns toward Beti folklore in modern dance music in
Yaoundé were noticed in reports on Yaoundé's music in the national newspaper. The music of Betti Joseph (also written Beti Joseph), born in the mid-
1950s, who performed in Yaoundé with his group Tympo Jazz in the 1970s,
was called "typique", indicating its inspiration in folklore (Boyomo Assala
1975d), and described as similar to the style of Los Camaroes (Boyomo Assala
1975a). In late 1974, the singer Mama Ohandja, nicknamed "Rossignol"
("Nightingale") because of his voice, and his group Confiance Jazz released
a 7-inch single that became widely popular in bars in Yaoundé (Boyomo
Assala 1975a, 1975c). It was a recording of the soukous piece 'Mbom Mezik'
with 'Man Ebon Wom' on the B-side. The latter was described in a review in
the *Cameroon Tribune* as "pop bikutsi (?)" – including the question mark in
brackets (NAP 1975). It can no longer be ascertained if the journalist added
the question mark because "bikutsi" was at that time still an unusual term

for describing this genre or because it was mixed with music the journalist perceived as being "pop".

Whatever the case, it shows that Beti traditions were clearly recognized in the music. How this was done musically will be the subject of analysis in Chapter 5, after the musical tradition of women's song-and-dance pieces and Beti xylophone music have been discussed in Chapters 3 and 4. It should be noted here that although the musical Beti connection became increasingly important, the musicians playing in the music groups were not necessarily of Beti origin. Often, only the lead singers had a Beti ethnic background. The musicians were recruited according to their musical skills; their ethnic background was of no relevance. While ethnicity and regional belonging was highlighted on a political level, as will be described below, the music scene in Yaoundé in the 1970s was not structured along ethnic lines. Also, the main goal was not necessarily to make "Beti" popular music by forcing this ethnic connection. The agenda was, rather, to develop "Cameroonian" music further, in line with the dominant political agenda, by using ethnic traditions in various ways – so why not also Beti music. In Yaoundé, however, the audience was probably especially open to Beti music as it was for many inhabitants their own, known, and habitual music. That said, Beti music as played by modern dance bands remained only one facet of a varied repertoire, with the main focus still being on the merengue and soukous repertoire.

Class Differences as Seen through Performance Locations

In the 1970s there existed a considerable range of different performance contexts for dance music in Yaoundé. Regular weekend musical entertainment in Yaoundé could be found in nightclubs such as the Black and White, the Philantrope or the Arizona – locations aimed at a wealthier audience, since there were entrance fees and the drinks were expensive. Francis Kingué's renowned music group, which played regularly at the Hotel Mont Fébé on a hill on the outskirts of Yaoundé, also addressed the wealthier part of the capital's population. The Centre Culturel Français or the musical programming at the Goethe Institute also clearly addressed an audience with sufficient financial means and a certain musical taste, offering jazz and classical music, often with foreign musicians in non-dancing, concert settings. Other performance spaces were invitation only and organized events especially were often restricted to members of the political and economic elite; here more renowned musicians, like Anne-Marie Nzié, provided the necessary musical entertainment. The bands mentioned above never performed at these locations.

Regular public concerts, by contrast, most often addressed a broader public, but the Yaoundé dance bands rarely performed in this context. Many musical events took place in the two cinemas Abbia and Capitole, which served as important performance locations not only for school bands, but for various popular artists, such as Ekambi Brillant, James Brown, Tokoto Ashanti, or Les Black Styl. In particular, artists performing the dance music genre *makossa*, widely popular in the 1970s, took to the stage here in regular Sunday afternoon concerts that addressed a younger public. Bigger events could be organized in stadiums, but these were rare in the 1970s.

While guitarists and acoustic music groups were often engaged to play for various festivities like weddings or baptisms, but also for events organized only for entertainment purposes in villages and towns in the 1950s, such events no longer played a major role for amplified music groups in the 1970s. For the groups mentioned, nightclubs and popular bars with stage and dance floor were the main performance spaces. The most accessible venues for weekend entertainment for urban residents in Yaoundé in general were bars around town, called "bars populaires". Some of them provided live music from a dance band, and these were the main performance locations for Yaoundé's merengue and soukous dance bands. One of the most popular dance bars at this time was the Mango Bar in the Elig-Effa quarter where Los Camaroes performed regularly. Another such bar, which gained even greater popularity in the 1980s, was the Escalier Bar in the Mvog Ada quarter, where Les Titans and Les Vétérans played. In the 1970s such venues were known locally as *bar-dancings*. Later, the more common term in Cameroon for locations providing live music became *cabaret*. Cabarets vary in size, target audience, and musical programme. The line between bar-dancings and cabaret is nevertheless blurred. A bar-dancing is a bar with a stage for performances. A cabaret can be a restaurant with live music but without a dance floor, a location with a stage for performances of any kind with a seated audience, or a nightclub-like venue with a big dance floor and a stage for the band. The latter, bigger dance-club venues were at the time of my field research in Yaoundé in the 2000s important locations of contemporary bikutsi pop in Yaoundé.

With the introduction of hi-fi systems in urban bars in the late 1970s, live music was put under serious pressure. In an article in 1978 entitled "In the kingdom of the muse, the stereo system reigns", the journalist Laurent-Charles Boyomo Assala expressed his anxiety: "As the rain chases away the nice weather, more and more the stereo system chases away our musicians from the nightclubs" (Boyomo Assala 1978).[8] With hi-fi systems making it possible to provide music with ease, performance opportunities for musicians disappeared. They were simply much more expensive than buying a hi-fi system and some records. Nevertheless, live music remained a vivid element in Yaoundé's musical entertainment scene.

While there was a clear and visible gap based on class and economic lines between possible performance locations, some musicians active in the modern music scene in the 1970s were able to switch between audiences and venues. Ted Mekoulou, jazz trumpeter and member of the police dance band, Echo Jazz de la Police, since the early 1970s, played at galas, formal dinners, and the jazz atelier organized by the Goethe Institute as well as in nightclubs – "to stay up to date with musical developments" (Ted Mekoulou, interview, August 22, 2010). In general, professional instrumentalists and music groups playing mainly in upper-class contexts had a broad repertoire so they could better switch between engagement requirements – from a jazz performance at the Centre Culturel Français, to a concert in the stadium, or a dinner party. The dance bands in Yaoundé that were central to developing Beti music on electric guitars, however, performed predominantly in bar-dancings and cabarets and were rarely hired to play political and representative events or perform in bigger concerts. Los Camaroes' appearance at the First Festival of Cameroonian Music in 1973 was a rare exception.

(Popular) Music and the Young Postcolonial Cameroonian State

As mentioned briefly in the introduction, Cameroon entered a process of nation-building and the establishment of a postcolonial state after independence in 1960. This also affected musicians. Cultural expressions of various kinds, including music, were to contribute to a common feeling of belonging to a new Cameroonian nation. As in other African countries and elsewhere, the search for and construction of "authentic" cultural practices and adequate cultural representations were central to the agenda. One of the main concerns for nation-building in Cameroon was the great diversity of ethnic groups, political traditions, and languages within the new country. The first President Ahmadou Ahidjo answered this challenge by implementing a rigid and centralized political system that concentrated all power in his hands. As historian Mark W. DeLancey wrote: "This identity problem, common to many African states, and the fear that the state might break apart before the process of nation building could occur, has often been the excuse or the cause of the construction of authoritarian political systems in Africa. Cameroon was to be no exception" (DeLancey 1989: 51; cf. Nyamnjoh 2005: 129). By employing strategies of centralization, coalition-building, and repression, Ahidjo built a state apparatus within which he controlled even the smallest aspect, down to the nomination of political officials at local village levels. He promoted "unity in diversity" and thus implemented a political system and rhetoric of ethnic equilibrium. The ideal of ethnic equilibrium was the main factor in virtually all political decisions. This strategy of establishing national stability and consciousness via ethnic and regional balancing, ironically, developed an increased consciousness for ethnicity and regional origins in the population. According to Yvette Monga, Ahidjo's "emphasis on regional and ethnic identities resulted in the creation of an acute, sustained awareness of ethnic belonging and regional affiliation" (Monga 2000: 726). While intended to serve a feeling of belonging to a "Cameroonian" entity, Ahidjo's politics led directly to an increased significance of ethnic and regional identity for Cameroonians that also strongly affected cultural matters.

"Cultural renewal" became an integral part of building the Cameroonian nation (Bahoken and Atangana 1976: 51; DeLancey and Mokeba Mbella 1990: 71), and musicians were lauded for playing "Cameroonian" music. The concept of "Cameroonian" music, however, was rather vague. As Kelly Askew has argued for Tanzania (Askew 2002), it was constantly subject to negotiation and very different musicians and musics could and were integrated into the concept. Musicians in the young Cameroonian state were expected to have adequate "Cameroonian" representation. Some musicians were singled out as examples, such as Anne-Marie Nzié, who developed a close relationship to the political elite during her career (Ndachi Tagne 1990; Brunner 2013), or the religious group of Pie-Claude Ngumu, who presented Cameroon at the FESTAC, the "Festival of African Arts and Culture" in 1966 in Dakar (Senegal) and in 1977 in Lagos (Nigeria). This was seen as adequately contributing to "cultural renewal".

While different ethnic musical stage performances, so-called folklore, were present in state representation, it also included popular music. In the 1970s especially, popular dance music became the focus of state cultural politics (Brunner 2017). In December 1973, the "Premier Festival de la Musique Camerounaise", the First Festival of Cameroonian Music, was held in the two biggest cities in the country, Yaoundé and Douala. It was a state-funded music festival organized by the Yaoundé-based businessman Rodolphe James

Moukoko and was aimed at presenting Cameroonian musicians. The invited guests included established musicians and some newcomers: Manu Dibango, Rachel Tchongui, Francis Bebey, Ekambi Brillant, André Marie Talla, Jean Bikoko, Eboa Lottin, Messi Martin, Nelle Eyoum, Anne-Marie Nzié, Medjo Me Ndzom Jacob, and Georges Anderson. Francis Bebey, already an internationally renowned Cameroonian music expert and musician, was invited, but had to cancel his performance due to a conflicting engagement as consultant for the UNESCO (Nbouwza 1974). According to Ndachi Tagne, the festival attracted around 50,000 spectators and was a rare occasion where so many musicians that most people only knew through the radio came together in one place (Ndachi Tagne 1990: 146–48).

By the end of the 1960s, the central place that the state granted musical performances in its official cultural representation could also be discerned in the military becoming involved with its own music groups. The army, the National Police, and the Republican Guards (the President's personal bodyguard, later called Presidential Guards) all had respective divisions for music. Although primarily marching bands with brass instruments for official events, all three armed branches also maintained modern dance music groups in the 1970s. The army band was called Les Bérets Verts, the Republican Guards had the Golden Sounds (renamed from Orchestre de la Garde Republicaine in 1975), and the National Police band was called Echo Jazz de la Capitale (also: Echo Jazz de la Police). As the orchestras and bands were maintained by the respective organizations, they were by far the best-equipped music groups at the time. For musicians, to join such a music group was a chance for relative financial security, which was rare, especially among musicians. However, the musicians would have had to join the respective force, which included obligations not connected to their music. This discouraged many; for others it was an acceptable sacrifice. The dance music groups played various political events, but also accompanied solo musicians at concerts or for commercial recordings. Furthermore, they performed at representative occasions of the state; the Golden Sounds of the Republican Guards were part of the Cameroonian delegation to the FESTAC 1977 in Nigeria. The musicians received musical training and they used sheet music, as Ted Mekoulou, leader of the National Police's Echo Jazz, recounted (Ted Mekoulou, interview, August 22, 2010). Thus, these music groups served as music schools and training institutions. Due to their status as well-financed state institutions, these bands had good instrumentation, regular musical practice, and well-trained musicians. In the 1970s, these three dance bands maintained by state forces came to be important actors in musical life in Cameroon as well as in representing the state internationally.

The military and police band's repertoires included common music trends in the 1970s – and not necessarily music with obvious "Cameroonian" connotations. Rather, their musical repertoire could – and was supposed to be – modern and cosmopolitan, up-to-date with the demands of the (dancing) audience. Their instrumentation was a big band formation typical at the time which included electric guitars, electric bass, piano, drums, and percussion as well as various wind instruments (see, e.g., the line-up of the Golden Sounds for their presentation at the FESTAC, as listed in the *Cameroon Tribune*, February 19, 1977: 8). Generally, wind instruments were already in use in the 1970s, but this was limited to those who could afford them, most often state-supported music groups. Guitar-based groups in Yaoundé in the early 1970s playing in bars and nightclubs did not use wind instruments – or at least they did not include them in their recordings. In terms of musical facilities and possibilities, the music groups of the state forces were on a different level from many civilian music groups at the time.

When discussing state activities towards music and musical representation in the 1970s, the Orchestre National cannot be left out. The desire to establish an Orchestre National was discussed in Cameroon throughout the 1970s in government and public forums. The prevalent vision for such an Orchestre National was based on the examples of other African states, especially Senegal and Guinea (for more on the state-sponsored orchestras in Guinea see Dave 2019: 19–50), where internationally-renowned national ensembles had already been established: "In the years 76/77, the government organized the recruiting of young people for theatre, music and dance; the dream was to found a big organization like the one of Daniel Sorano in Dakar or the National Orchestra of Guinea-Conakry" (Mboua 2004: 80).[9] A national dance ensemble had already existed since the late 1960s; dance groups had been sent by the government to participate in the FESTAC in Dakar in 1966 and other international events. According to the brief historical review published in 1989 in the *Cameroon Tribune* (Nnana 1989), the Ensemble National des Danses was officially recognized by governmental decree in 1968 and located within the Ministry of Education, Youth and Culture. At that time, it did not yet have a musical division. In the mid-1970s, the recruitment of musicians for a new division of the Ensemble National, the Orchestre National, started (Boyomo Assala 1976b). The requirement that musicians joining the Orchestre National must be able to read sheet music resulted in a public debate over the inclusion of indigenous instruments. In addition,

as Manu Dibango, who was in the selection committee, wrote in his autobiography, political demands were prioritized over musical criteria, the "only
concern was a certain balance between the different ethnic groups: each was
to be represented within this embryo of a band" (Dibango 1994: 81). Thus
ethnic and regional balance was highlighted and indigenous music experts
were excluded due to formal criteria. Despite the complications in recruiting,
the Orchestre National took up work in the late 1970s. One of its first public
appearances was in 1978 on the occasion of the twentieth anniversary of
President Ahidjo coming to power. The group consisted of 28 musicians with
a big band-like instrumentation; the band leader was Francis Kingué, who
had headed the dance band at the Hotel Mont Fébé for years. Most musicians
played "modern" instruments. Pictures in the *Cameroon Tribune* show electric guitars as well as a drum set and saxophones (Vamoulké 1978). That said,
some indigenous instruments were included as well, such as wooden bells
and drums of different regional origins: "The traditional instruments – as the
goal of the orchestra is amongst other things to integrate them – have made
timid appearances on stage" (Vamoulké 1978).[10]

Musically, the repertoire was somewhat different to common dance bands
at the time. With more pieces in the repertoire that had jazz or classical res-
onance, the music was meant more for listening and demonstrating Western-
oriented musical competence than for dancing. Some pieces were composed
by Cameroonian musicians, such as Eko Roosevelt or Adala Gildo (Soupa
1978). Highlighting the musical competence of Cameroonian composers and
their attempts to integrate traditional elements was central to the musical
concept. Nevertheless, the National Orchestra did not really become a show-
case for Cameroonian music, not in the 1970s and not since. Mboua wrote in
2004 that the three groups in the Ensemble produced little, and that the dance
group and the orchestra had lost most of their members while the theatre
ensemble performed only once a year for an official event (Mboua 2004: 82).

Musical Training: The Role of Secondary Schools

Sketching out the field of music in Yaoundé in the 1970s, it is important to
look at the possibilities of training for musicians, as musical knowledge and
skills are the most important capital for musicians. At this time, one of the
main training opportunities for future musicians were nightclubs and bars,
where young musicians tested their talent in the shadows of professional
musicians and were – if considered adept – taken under someone's wing.

Beside these informal training possibilities, a major role was played by urban secondary schools.

Many musicians active in Yaoundé since the 1970s who were involved in the creation of a Beti dance music played by modern music groups gained their musical knowledge during their school education in institutions that had a special focus on music. The most popular was the Collège Vogt in Yaoundé while other relevant schools included the Lycée Leclerc and the Collège de la Retraite. Several secondary schools put an emphasis on music education and supported their own school music groups. As Ted Mekoulou recounted, himself having been a student at the Collège Vogt in the 1960s, students were encouraged to learn an instrument in school and to join one of the school's music groups, be it a marching brass band ("fanfare", *fr.*) or a dance band. The different dance music groups of the secondary schools presented their skills regularly for the public during concerts and school group competitions. These events often took place on Sunday afternoons in cinemas, like Abbia and Capitole in Yaoundé; sometimes school bands performed in the Centre Culturel Français. The concerts were reported on in the national newspaper *Cameroon Tribune*.[11] Musical education for young Cameroonians was in line within the state's vision of cultural education and it was of importance to present the talented young musicians as promising future cultural actors for the country.

The repertoire of these school groups included cover versions of pieces from various music genres. According to the numerous and surprisingly long articles on school band concerts in the newspaper, these cover versions commonly included contemporary Anglo-American pop and rock music, such as pieces by James Brown, Jimi Hendrix, Santana, or the Beatles, but also cover versions of contemporary Cameroonian musicians. Among those mentioned, most were musicians mainly playing makossa and having considerable success on the Cameroonian music market at the time. These included Ekambi Brillant, André Marie-Tala and Toto Guillaume as well as jazz musician Manu Dibango. It is striking that Afro-Caribbean-derived music, like the rumba congolaise or merengue, were hardly mentioned as genres played by school bands. Cameroonian youth in the 1970s appears to have been drawn to pop and rock music as well as Cameroonian popular music, especially the nationally promoted genre makossa.[12] Merengue, soukous, and rumba were genres for older people, the generation that remembered the heyday of Congolese dance music in the 1960s. As Motti Regev suggested in his theory of aesthetic cosmopolitanism (Regev 2013; see also Chapter 1), from the early days of pop-rock music, teenage music groups in Cameroon were drawn to international pop-rock trends and local popular music stars.

Means of Dissemination: Radio Broadcasting and Recording Facilities

Radio broadcasting was in the 1970s the most important means for dissemination of music in Sub-Saharan Africa. Broadcast over portable transistor radios, the medium found its way into remote villages beginning in the mid-twentieth century, and due to its easy and cheap accessibility, it remained the most widespread source for information in Africa at the beginning of the twenty-first century. The Cameroonian government was well aware of the power of radio broadcasting and sought to use it to serve its ideals in its endeavour to promote the new nation-state. Radio broadcasting was, as Nyamnjoh put it, "singled out as the media that needed to be watched at close range" (Nyamnjoh 2005: 48). The control of communication media was for Ahidjo (and for his successor Biya) the most powerful tool for implementing the repressive postcolonial state system: "the postcolonial press from the 1960s to the 1980s was ... either the mouthpiece of the government or subjected to draconian laws and administrative censorship" (Nyamnjoh 2005: 42). Cameroon had until the 1990s only one state-owned national radio and did not allow other radio stations; consequently, radio programming was under tight political control.

The first radio transmitter in Cameroon was installed in Douala in 1941 and was used solely for information and propaganda during World War II. It was technically deficient and stopped broadcasting right after the war. Broadcasting resumed in 1946 and it was replaced by a more powerful transmitter in 1949, at which time programming expanded to 2.5 hours a day. In danger of being shut-down for financial reasons the radio officer in Douala managed to have commercials permitted in 1952, saving the broadcasting project. In 1954, Radio Douala was joined by another transmitter in Yaoundé, equipped by the French "Société de Radiodiffusion de la France d'Outre Mer" (SO.RA.F.O.M). Three years after independence, that is, in 1963, all the equipment and radio stations were transferred from the French to the Cameroonian state (Eonè 1986: 247). More radio stations were founded in the 1970s under Ahidjo in the major urban centres in the various regions of Cameroon. In the early 1980s, *Radio Cameroun* had ten regional radio stations, operating under the head of the "Poste Nationale" in Yaoundé (Eonè

1986). In 1987, radio and TV stations were fused under the leadership of Cameroon Radio et Television (CRTV).

The relevance of radio in Cameroon and its rapid growth after World War II can be easily shown in numbers: in a study on radio and its audiences published in 1986, Tjadè Eonè reported that the number of radio receivers in Cameroon was around ten thousand in 1960 and rose to 200,000 in 1967 and one million in 1979 (Eonè 1986: 118).[13] With an estimated 7.5 million inhabitants in the 1970s,[14] it is clear that radio broadcasting was *the* most important media in Cameroon, reaching the majority of inhabitants, especially in urban centres. This is underlined in the 1981 census (as cited in Eonè 1986: 35–37): 87 per cent of the people in Douala, the largest city in the country, indicated that they listened regularly to the radio and 99 per cent listened at least from time to time. Although these numbers only show tendencies, they show that in urban centres in Cameroon, virtually everyone had access to radio in the early 1980s. This is supported by the data on household appliances in Douala in 1981: while only 1.5 per cent of the population had a fixed telephone line and 35 per cent of the households a refrigerator, 65.5 per cent had a radio receiver and 54.3 per cent even had a radio tape recorder (Eonè 1986: 35). The importance of radio airplay in terms of political and cultural developments in the 1970s can consequently hardly be overestimated.

As mentioned, President Ahidjo saw the radio as an important means of establishing his vision of the Cameroonian state. In line with the concept of national unity through and with diversity, the provincial radio stations especially were expected to, as Nyamnjoh put it, "create programmes well adapted to local needs but in tune with the communal tasks of nationbuilding" (Nyamnjoh 2005: 130). The obvious state control of radio programming, however, resulted in Radio Cameroun losing much of its credibility with the population: "Cameroonians increasingly tuned to foreign radio stations like the BBC, Voice of America and Radio France Internationale, which despite the 'foreignness' of their perspectives were indeed the only 'uncensored' alternatives" (Nyamnjoh 2005: 166; cf. Eonè 1986: 44). Tuning into other radio stations, according to DeLancey, put the government on the defensive: news was reported that the government remained silent on certain incidents, forcing the latter to come out with its own, possibly correct version of events. In the end, Radio Cameroun lost much of its legitimacy and no one believed it anymore (DeLancey 1989: 65).

Nevertheless, despite the availability and better credibility of foreign radio programmes, according to Eonè, in the early 1980s the most listened to radio station in Cameroon was still Radio Cameroun: over 80 per cent of people questioned stated that they listened regularly to the national radio station, with no significant difference in terms of profession, age, or gender (Eonè 1986: 49–52). The stated reasons indicate that the political efforts to intensify national consciousness had to some extent been successful: identification with one's "own" radio station as the only "Cameroonian" radio station, access to national news, and Cameroonian music (Eonè 1986: 71–74). This identification was supported by the inclusion of official, private, and communal information, for example, death notices or planned festivities. At a time when telephones were few and far between, the radio was a very important tool for disseminating timely information quickly.

Looking at the range of programmes on the national radio (in October 1982), it varied from those concerned with news to documentaries, educational programming, commentary, and entertainment. The majority – 56 per cent – of these programmes were in French, followed by English at 28 per cent and programmes in various local languages at 16 per cent. Music was mainly broadcast in programmes for general entertainment, including radio games or humorous segments (called "Emissions de variété" by Eonè) and specific musical programmes. Programmes with music were by far in the majority: programmes categorized by Eonè as "Emissions de variété" made up 36.5 per cent of total programming, followed by "Avis et commentaires" (17.6 per cent) and "Info d'actualité" (14.4 per cent). Specific musical programming ranked fourth, making up 8 per cent of total programming (Eonè 1986: 144–50, 156).

Musical content was subject to strict control. According to Eonè, 70 per cent of all aired music had to be Cameroonian. Radio Cameroun played a significant role in promoting local music before it even reached the national music market and thereby had significant influence on that music market (Eonè 1986: 74, 139). As for the music played, Eonè only mentions "traditional" and "modern" music as genres and that most Cameroonian music that was played was makossa (Eonè 1986: 140, 74). Bikutsi as a popular music genre had yet to be established and makossa was in fact the only popular "Cameroonian" dance music genre widely released and listened to. Bahoken and Atangana stated in 1975 that "every Sunday, the entire country listens over the radio to a festival of national music in which are heard the various languages of the human communities who, inspired by the same patriotic fervour, share the wealth of their musical art" (Bahoken and Atangana 1976: 84). They highlighted the role of sound recordings as "play[ing] a unique part, because they facilitate mutual understanding of the musical expression of the different communities" (Bahoken and Atangana 1976: 89). Promoting various ethnic traditions, music and knowledge via radio went hand in hand with national politics. With the monopolist Radio Cameroun being such an important dissemination media, it becomes clear that it was of immediate importance for musicians to get their music played on the radio. Most music easily met the criteria of presenting ethnic traditions since it drew on regional musical traditions in some way. As long as no obvious anti-government or problematic political position could be discerned, the Cameroonian vision was to accept and integrate virtually all possible forms of artistic expression as part of Cameroonian diversity, including the music of groups active in Yaoundé in the 1970s.

For many music groups, radio played an additional role as a recording studio. Most musicians in the 1950s up to the 1970s and beyond recorded their music in small radio studios, most often for broadcasting use only, but at times also for the production of records. If they had the financial means, artists recorded abroad, especially in France, due to the better technical infrastructure. But these musicians were in the minority and most of the music of the 1970s was recorded in the rather modest studios of the radio stations. No sixteen-track recording studio existed in Cameroon in the 1970s. The tapes were then sent to France, sometimes remixed, and pressed onto records and were sent back to Cameroon to be sold. Recording opportunities improved when the newly constructed radio building in Yaoundé opened in 1982 with a newly equipped studio with a sixteen-track recording console. Subsequently, most music by musicians from Yaoundé was recorded in this studio.

Commercial music recordings – be they of local or foreign labels – were, as in other African countries, not widespread in Cameroon. Due to the high costs of record players and the records themselves, until the late 1970s listening privately to music at home remained a privilege of the wealthy. Nevertheless, musicians sought to release their music on LPs or singles for prestige purposes and for possible additional income. Initially, foreign labels were the only option until the 1960s and 1970s, when more and more Cameroonian labels emerged. The Congolese labels Opika and Ngoma released a good deal of Cameroonian music in the 1950s and 1960s (Ndachi Tagne 1990) and French labels such as Fiesta and Sonafric/SonoDisc were also important producers. In the 1960s, the first Cameroonian labels were founded, one of them being Africambiance. Africambiance was founded in 1964 and closed in the mid-1970s. It was run by Joseph Tamla, who worked in a high position at a state company. He was joined initially by the musicians Manu Dibango and Francis Bebey, who left the project shortly after its founding. For musical support, Tamla hired a Congolese group called Cercul du Jazz. The aim of the label was to produce and promote Cameroonian music, such as makossa, and the artists recording on Africambiance were, among others, Manu Dibango, Jean Bikoko, Nelle Eyoum, the xylophone group Richard Band de Zoétélé, and Anne-Marie Nzié (Ndachi Tagne 1990: 112, 121). Another important Cameroonian label was Disques Cousin, run by M. Njoga Mathias (Keye 1978), and Samson. The late 1970s and early 1980s brought increased growth in the sector; the first label dedicated specifically to bikutsi music was Ebobolo Fia (see Chapter 6). The Yaoundé-based dance bands presented above released their music with the labels Africambiance and even more so with Sonafric.

***

Developments in the 1970s in Yaoundé laid the foundation for what would later become the popular music genre bikutsi. Musicians in the capital's dance bands began to mix musical elements, experiment with new playing styles, try out new forms of musical expression, especially different elements taken from Beti musical tradition. These primarily dance music groups still tended to integrate these innovations into their merengue and soukous repertoires. These processes of musical innovation took place in a specific musical field set in postcolonial Cameroon, where music as a cultural expression was constructed as a part of nation-building. The political imperative to play one's "own" music, that is "Cameroonian" music, was omnipresent, and while not necessarily an immediate answer to such nationalist policies, the Yaoundé dance bands nevertheless acted within a general atmosphere of a search for one's "own" music and an increasing use of local music in one way or the other. In the 1970s these musical changes were recognized and described as something particular, but not marketed or highlighted in any special way. Merengue and soukous remained dominant, but Beti musical pieces joined the repertoire and developed increasingly as sources of inspiration. In Mark Slobin's model of local, regional and transnational visibility of music, local musics "are known by certain small-scale bounded audiences, and only by them" and regional musics – somewhat flexible in definition – reach a larger audience and can be bound to geographical regions or go beyond an immediate bounded area, for example, to diaspora communities, via recordings, broadcasting, and increasing mobility (Slobin 1993: 17, 18–19). The "musique made in Yaoundé" (Gildo 1979) was, at the end of the 1970s, on the way from being a local to being a regional music in Slobin's terms. In the case of Beti dance music played by modern dance bands in Yaoundé, it was known to urban residents visiting the performances, but increasingly expanded its audience throughout the 1970s via radio airplay, media presence, and commercial releases. Sometimes such a phase of creative musical change just fades out without any further development. In the case of bikutsi, however, the changes in the music during the 1970s were enduring and were the precondition for the establishment of bikutsi as a popular music genre in the 1980s.

Chapter 3

Women's Song-and-Dance Pieces: The "Original" Bikutsi

Before bikutsi also became a term for a popular music genre, it described both a Beti women's song-and-dance musical tradition and the step that is danced. Bikutsi literally means "to stomp on the floor" or "to hit the floor", and it is this movement that forms the foundation of the bikutsi dance as performed by women. These song-and-dance pieces occupy an important position in Beti women's lives. To understand the bikutsi universe thoroughly, understanding this practice as it will be introduced in all its facets in this chapter is a necessary element. It will be shown how these song-and-dance pieces, often called the "original" bikutsi, relate to today's popular music genre bikutsi.

General Remarks on Beti Music

As with any African musical tradition, conceptions around "music" in Beti culture differ from the Western notion of the term. As Kubik and others have shown for various African contexts (see, e.g., Kubik 2004), this fact becomes clear when looking at the linguistic terms employed in contexts described in Western terms as "musical". Like in other African languages, in the Beti languages there is no word to describe "music" in the same semantic way as in Western languages.[1] Terms signifying music in a general understanding are connected to playing musical instruments, dancing, and singing – and the vocabulary around "music" highlights the intrinsic connection between music, dance, and language (in our terms), as will be described briefly below.

Let us begin with the singing. In Ewondo, "to sing" is "yiá". It is mostly employed with a noun, a specification of what is sung: "yiá dziá", "to sing a song". Singing is not a practice reserved for specially trained individuals; on the contrary, everybody can sing and should sing. There is no specific train-ing concerning vocal formation. There are, however, aesthetic criteria around the voice, so that some people do have a voice that is not considered beauti-ful. This does not mean that the person is a bad singer: to sing badly, "abé" ("bad"), is to sing out of the rhythm, to have bad musical timing. Further, any aesthetic evaluation is connected to the quality of the content of the song, its message, and the way it comes across. Singing, therefore, is done by every-body, and the qualities of good singing are described in terms of rhythmical timing as well as the transmitted message.

Singing songs is in Beti culture an important activity and is often high-lighted as a core characteristic of Beti music. Beti music is to a large extent organized in "songs", maybe better described as meaningful musical pieces, which either have a clearly understandable or highly metaphorical and for outsiders often barely decodable message in its lyrics. Pierre Betene wrote in his article "Le Beti vu à travers ses Chants Traditionnels" that

> if we look at the life of the Beti, we are quickly impressed by the
> ease and spontaneity with which he sings. He sings at serious and
> sad events in his life as well as in moments of leisure and relax-
> ation. He sings while in a group and while alone, when he is small
> and when, his head white and [his body] bent under the weight of
> the years, in his hut watching his grandchildren and great grand-
> children. When happy, he sings, but also when in pain, in tears
> and in mourning, he still sings. (Betene 1973: 44)[2]

Betene recorded many examples of songs in Beti life: from lullabies to songs sung while working in the fields, from ritual songs and simply enter-taining songs to critical songs addressing individual behaviour or societal matters. Being a priest himself, he discussed at length songs in Beti reli-gious life. Singing can accompany much of daily life among the Beti people, including sad occasions, such as mourning events or burials. Even the spon-taneous expression of grief over someone's death is expressed in singing.[3]

That musical practice is generally connected to the communication of a message is also underlined by the use of the verb "kɔ́bɔ́", "to speak" or "to talk", for instrumental playing. The stick zither *mvɛd* can "speak", as do the slit drums *mìǹkúl* (singular: *ǹkúl*) or the xylophones *məndzáŋ*. The mìǹkúl play a special role in that they are not only used for accompanying dance but also as a communication medium. This "speaking" of instruments is possi-ble due to the meaning of pitch and duration of tones in this tonal language, which can be imitated on such instruments. That said, any instrument can "speak", including those, like guitars, introduced in Cameroon in the twentieth century.

Instruments, no matter what kind, are not "played" but "hit": the term used is "bòm", which means roughly "to hit" or "to beat on something". A similar term is "kùd" (or "kut", like in "bikutsi"), also signifying "to beat", but additionally used to describe the dance steps. A person playing an instrument is called "m̀bom", the "beater". A "m̀bom mvεd" is therefore the player of a mvεd, a "m̀bom məndzáŋ" the player of a məndzáŋ. But unlike many translations of these terms in the literature suggest, for example "man of the mvεd", "m̀bom" is not gendered and can be employed for men and women alike. Moreover, there are no obvious and pronounced social restrictions on who is allowed to play an instrument, to sing, or to dance. There are, however, as common around the world, certain rules concerning specific rituals or events, genres and instruments, as well as some unspoken norms with occasional exceptions. In general, dancing for entertainment reasons has traditionally been mainly a female matter, while playing instruments has tended to be male dominated.

Connected to singing and songs and accompanying played instruments is usually some kind of body movement or dancing. To talk about dancing, the Ewondo language provides numerous terms. The most general is the word "dzɔ́m", usually translated simply as "to dance" but also including the meaning of "to tremble". This word is close to "dzɔ́mɔ́", meaning "to celebrate", and situates dancing in the context of festivities and celebrations, as a practice connected to a specific emotional event. In the same line is the noun "abóg" for "festive event", "party", or "dance". Dancing can moreover be described by words of joy, like "fon" for "to cheer", or "tag" for "to be happy". All these terms do not imply the specific dancing quality. There are specific words to describe qualities of the dance, like "sɔ́lɔ́": "sɔ́lɔ́ abóg" is used to describe elegant, discreet, and allusive dancing. Another is the word "təg", meaning "to dance well". This is exemplified by a sentence in Tsala's dictionary, published in the 1950s: "Adzem vĕ ndzeman, ayem ki teg", which translated as "He only dances, but he cannot dance well" (Tsala n.d.: 602).[4]

Besides dancing in spontaneous and improvised ways as in bikutsi dancing, the Beti have specific dances connected to rituals and specific events. *Esáni* or *esána* is danced at funeral events, and *elak* (also written *elag*) is an entertainment dance for young men and women. Others include *mbali*, *koé*, or *ekaŋ*, all distinctly recognizable by cultural insiders based on their rhythmical structure and all connected to a specific dance. Any "rhythm" has an equivalent dance and vice versa; when musicians talk about a "rhythm", they refer simultaneously to a specific dance.

On the most general semantic level, many of these dances are understood and described as "bikutsi". This simplified use of the term bikutsi for all possible Beti dance variants is a result, according to many musicians of the elder generation, of the lack of detailed knowledge on the part of many people, including younger musicians, on the variety in Beti dances. This is also a result of the process described in this book, that is, the emergence and establishment of bikutsi as a popular music genre. A further plausible reason for this generalized use of the term is that the main feature of bikutsi – the dance movement of stomping on the floor – is also included in other dances. In its most narrow meaning as dance and rhythm, however, bikutsi does not involve other dances; it is a specific musical practice performed by women. It needs no specific festivities, being instead widely embedded in daily life.

Women's Bikutsi: Situations, Roles, Structure

Bikutsi can be danced and sung by women on virtually all occasions. Bikutsi songs are not necessarily part of a specific ritual or connected to a specific event; there only needs to be an occasion to dance and sing. This can – and often is – part of the daily routine, especially upon joyful occasions. Mbala Agnès Marie épouse Nkili described these occasions as simply being "good news", like the birth of a child or the arrival of a guest (Mbala 1985). Furthermore, bikutsi pieces are part of funeral and burial services for deceased women, the primary funeral dance esáni only being performed for honoured men (cf. Betene 1973: 61). Besides being performed during events and spontaneously in everyday life, women's bikutsi sessions can also be organized for simple entertainment purposes where women can gather to discuss important issues of any kind or exchange news and gossip. Singing and dancing bikutsi pieces are a matter of community, of several women getting together. Although the songs can also be sung alone and solo, for example while cooking or working in the field, or for calming children, when danced, more women will always be present and dance and sing together. This perspective on bikutsi as collective action was highlighted by Stella Engama in a short essay on bikutsi, wherein she assumed that the term "bikutsi" might also be derived from the term "bia-kudsi": "bia" meaning "we" and therefore meaning "we stomp the floor" (Engama 2001). In its most common form, then, bikutsi songs are sung and danced by a group of women, no matter if five or twenty; Mbala mentioned possible groups of up to a hundred women (Mbala 1985). In Yaoundé during the time of my research, women's bikutsi was mainly danced on Sundays at gatherings of women who belong to the same *tontine* (*fr.*). A tontine is at its core a small group of people who together manage their financial savings and loans informally and locally, often only embracing a village or a district of a town. The significance of a tontine often goes beyond organizing financial matters, also being a social organization with regular gatherings for exchanging news, developing friendships, and organizing mutual aid when in need – and singing and dancing together. Corresponding to the potentially everyday performance of bikutsi, there is no special costume to wear. Women commonly wear various forms of traditional dress called *kaba*, a very wide and loose gown going down to the ankles or at least below the knees, with long or short sleeves, made with generous amounts of fabric. If the voluminous dress gets in the way during a dance performance, the dancers will tie a band of cloth around their waists to keep the dress under control.

Performing bikutsi as a women's tradition is a complex matter involving singing, dancing, and dialogue. The women involved take different roles, which Mbala identifies as being the solo singer, accompanying singers, and dancers (Mbala 1985). Any women attending a bikutsi session can take any role, including the solo singer. These roles are not fixed to one specific person but change throughout the session. The differentiation between accompanying singers and dancers as made by Mbala is more an analytical one, as these roles are performed simultaneously; the women accompanying the solo singer might better be understood as being singer-dancers. The solo singer is also not only singing, but dancing as well. Singing, clapping hands, and dancing are in women's bikutsi sessions hardly separable.

Bikutsi song-and-dance pieces are performed in a circle formed by the women taking part. To accompany their singing and dancing, they always clap and stomp their feet rhythmically. Rattles, called *nyás*, held in the hands or tied to the ankles, are also often used (cf. Mba 1981: 161). Nyás exist in different versions, from "traditional" nyás made out of a calabash with seeds tied around it, to old tins filled with seeds. The main element of bikutsi song-and-dance pieces however is the singing: "it's not possible to perform bikutsi without the singing. The steps of the female dancers follow the rhythm" (Mbala 1985: 10–11).[5] The singing and accompanying clapping indicate the tempo, beat, and rhythmical structure for the song. The clapping is in most cases maintained throughout the piece.

Most bikutsi songs have a call-and-response structure; a verse sung by the solo singer is answered by the singer-dancers. The phrase sung by the choir remains generally the same throughout the song, while the solo singer's lyrics may vary in content. Mbala described three main elements of bikutsi songs: refrains (*mekasi* or *meyebe*), verses (*metanan*), and coda (*mesuu* or *medzōmi*).[6] Although not all elements are always present, some songs consisting only of verses without refrains, these are the basic elements found in bikutsi songs.

According to Mbala, the accompanying singer-dancers are called *be kasi be bia*. "Kasi" is a variant of the noun "kali", "to approve a said opinion". This term is derived from the verb "kalan" which means "to transmit a message"; "be" is a plural particle. "Bia", according to Mbala, is a term to indicate development and progression; Tsala, however, translates the word as "songs" ("chants", *fr.*) (Tsala n.d.: 92). This indicates the main role of the supporting bikutsi singer-dancers, namely to answer the message sung, to approve, and to transmit it. The word "kasi" is thus also at the core of the term "mekasi" for the repeated phrases sung by the choir in bikutsi pieces; the particle "me" signifies plurality or repetition.[7] These repeated parts can be short sentences and phrases, but can also be onomatopoetic, using sounds expressing regret or joy or imitating an animal. Their purpose is to comment, acclaim, and approve of the message sung by the respective solo singer.

The solo singer is called *ntanan bia*; she sings the *metanan*, the verses. According to Mbala, this word comes from the verb "tanan", meaning "to narrate" or "to develop". The prefix "me" again marks its plurality; the prefix "n" creates a noun, "bia" signifying the songs. Literary, "ntanan bia" then means "the narrator/the developer of the songs". This is essentially the task of the solo singer in bikutsi sessions: to develop a topic in the song, to transmit a message in her singing. The ntanan bia is the one who sings the verses, which are approved and commented upon by the singer-dancers in the refrains. The role of the ntanan bia is not always clear before the bikutsi performance; rather, the person who adopts the role of the solo and lead performer develops out of the situation. Initially part of the group of singer-dancers, one woman will spontaneously enter the circle, perhaps inspired by a certain word or idea of a previous singer or dancer. She takes on the role of the ntanan bia and starts her song. It can happen that more than one woman steps into the middle of the circle at the same time. The most persistent, according to Mbala, will force the others back to their role as accompanying singer-dancers.

Although the main task of a ntanan bia is to sing, a good voice is not the main criteria for a good solo performance. As Mbala noted, "even the raspiest of voices can execute bikutsi pieces marvellously" (Mbala 1985: 163).[8] Rather than a certain aesthetic in the sound of a voice, the acting out of the song's content by the performer is important. The singer tries to evoke the situation in the song with her voice as well as by gestures and facial expressions, for example when lowering the voice to imitate a lover whispering to another. The best ntanan bia then are actors in their singing, dancing, and transmission of content.

Refrains and verses can vary greatly in length. Accordingly, the songs themselves can be of almost any duration, depending on the ability of the singer-dancers and the content the song is supposed to transmit. Moreover, it is also possible that more than one ntanan bia perform the solo of one song. When the song performance comes to an end, it can be closed by a coda, called *mesuu* or *medzōmi* (Mbala 1985). "Mesuu" derives from the verb "sus" for "to descend"; "medzōmi" includes the noun "dzombo" for "a part at the end of an object", for example the branch ending the tree.[9] Not all songs have a coda, and Mbala described various possibilities for ending a song. The most common, however, is to repeat the refrain followed by an expression, phrase, or verse indicating the end in the words themselves. This is then again followed by the refrain.

One part of bikutsi performances apart from the song structure should be mentioned here: the *oyə́ŋá*. Oyə́ŋá, also *oyáŋá*, is a cry of joy, a scream of pleasure, of fun, of admiration and of approval, produced using the head-voice. This cry, only executed by women, not by men, is a spontaneous expression of deep joyful sentiment and can be heard, for example, when a woman learns about good news. During bikutsi sessions, an oyə́ŋá can comment on excellent dancing or on the heartfelt approval to the message of the song. It can also be simply an expression of joy. The signification depends on its intonation as well as its length. Oyə́ŋá can be heard in everyday life, but is also an intrinsic element in any energetic and joyful bikutsi performance (Ngumu 1976b: 61; Mba 1981: 162; Mbala 1985: 28).

Women's Bikutsi: Topics and Messages in the Lyrics

Although joy, fun, and energetic dancing are important ingredients in bikutsi performances, an important focus is placed on the content of the song. Every bikutsi song has a message. Consequently, applying Western categories, Mbala as well as Stanislas Awona describe bikutsi as a "literary genre" (Mbala 1985: 69; Awona n.d.: 87). Based on an analysis of recorded bikutsi songs archived in the Centre Fédéral Linguistique et Culturel, Awona grouped the vast repertoire of possible topics into seven types of bikutsi songs, noting at the same time that the list is not exhaustive:

- songs of advice for young women and brides
- songs on the anxiety felt at puberty
- humorous, lascivious songs addressed at lovers or unfaithful husbands
- idyllic and poetic songs describing the ideal man or husband
- laments and melancholy songs expressing irritation and disgust at one's treatment by husband or co-wives
- songs expressing nostalgic feelings and reminiscences for the home village left upon marriage as well as songs of appreciation towards the political regime
- funeral songs. (Awona n.d.: 87)

Mbala categorized bikutsi songs in her analysis in a similar manner. She differentiated between "lyrical songs" ("chants lyrics", *fr.*) and "impersonal songs" ("chants impersonnel", *fr.*) (Mbala 1985: 191). Lyrical songs are about individual experiences, often in a dramatic narrated form. She noted that about 90 per cent of bikutsi songs could be categorized as lyrical songs. Impersonal songs, by contrast, treat public moral issues and are used to express considerations and opinions – positive or critical – of social and political questions, on a local, regional, or national level.

Mbala sees the possible topics of bikutsi songs in similar terms as those cited by Awona. First, she presents songs describing individuals physically as well as morally and in their respective social situation and behaviour: the woman as lover, concubine, and wife (then including her relationship to her husband and her roles as mother and daughter-in-law) and the man as lover, husband, and father. The descriptive forms vary from critical to satirical, loving or approving. Second, Mbala describes songs about "la vie comme elle va" (*fr.*), "life as it goes" (Mbala 1985: 411). Therein she includes songs with general topics relevant in society, such as the negative influence of alcohol or witchcraft, or the decline of the family as a fundamental element of society. She also includes songs on death, on historical developments, or on famous people from the community in this category. Mbala makes clear that the range of topics in bikutsi songs start with issues important at a very young age until those concerning old age and death.[10] No topic is left out of the bikutsi repertoire – with the exception of heroic songs. Bikutsi songs comment on every aspect of – mainly female – life from lullabies and childhood games to advice concerning the household and education, love, marriage and

marital life, sexuality and erotic issues, but also politics, positive and negative male behaviour, moral concerns in society, personal complaints and feelings, and songs accompanying death. Bikutsi songs accompany (female) life
and were and are an important means of female expression in society as well
as an institution to communicate and express personal feelings and opinions.

Much research attention is usually paid to the aspect of criticizing and
mocking patriarchal society as well as critiquing male behaviour in male-
female relationships and sexual relations. Already in 1913, Günther Tessmann
wrote of women's songs in his ethnography (while admitting not having had
much access to female cultural practices): "I myself cannot quite get a grasp
of this complicated stuff and only understand so much that the whole cor-
nucopia of female mockery and female passion for gossiping is poured out
over the men" (Tessmann 1913: 94–95).[11] The examples for bikutsi songs
provided by Pierre Betene all address men, some in a satirical or negative
manner, others in praise (Betene 1973: 53–59). Bikutsi sessions as female-
only performances are a central space for female expression, the sole occasion in Beti society where women can speak their mind, especially in terms
of discussing men and male behaviour, for which no other forum is available
to them. As such, bikutsi songs have a specific role in Beti society.

The art of speaking including an appropriate and sophisticated form of
expression and use of language is an important aspect of bikutsi songs. The
lyrics are often highly metaphorical, using elaborate images to mask their
messages, and can therefore not always be easily decoded by people unfa-
miliar with the situation, the context, or the people performing. The language
used in female bikutsi songs has consequently been described as being similar to a secret code: "In fact, the language of the songs is to such an extent
enigmatic that one needs to be initiated beforehand to seize its essence"
(Awona n.d.: 87).[12] Bikutsi songs were mainly meant to address the immediate community in which they were performed. However, even if only performed in a female-only group, it was certain that any specifically addressed
individual would hear about it, even if not present. As Mbala noted, the messages of bikutsi songs were not only transmitted among the women present
but potentially beyond this immediate circle. Due to this possible influence of
the message sent out into the world via female bikutsi songs, they are often
described as the space in which women can make themselves heard – and
are heard. In traditional Beti society, a woman's role did not include communicating her opinions and thoughts freely, especially not directly to the
men of the community. Bikutsi performances were therefore an important
female institution for influencing community matters, taking part in political

discussions, and manipulating individual behaviour. Further, bikutsi performances among women were repeatedly described as the central space in the community reserved only for women. Therein they could express their sorrows, joy, and anxieties, as well as solve conflicts among themselves.

Women's Bikutsi: The Dancing

Bikutsi songs are accompanied by certain body movements or dancing when they are performed in a group and the situation allows for it, corresponding to the rhythmical foundation of the song. The most obvious and always present moves are the hand clapping and the regular stomping of the feet. When a ntanan bia starts a song, she indicates this by starting to clap her hands in time to the rhythm and tempo of the song she is going to sing and introduces the refrain. The other singer-dancers join in and repeat the refrain, above which the solo singer then starts her verses. The rhythm given by the solo singer can last for a song, but can on occasion change therein.

Bikutsi performances generally have two parts: the first stage with the focus on singing is followed by a second stage reserved mainly for dancing. Mbala called the first part "nsebelan abog", signifying approximately "the slow beginning of the dance or the celebration".[13] The second part is called "ntegan nkuk", derived from the words "teg" for "to loosen" and "nkuk" for "torso", meaning "the loosening of the torso", referring to a common dance move performed during this phase. A similar structure is described by Wenzeslaus Mba although using different names for the two parts: the first he called "mekali me dzia" or "meteg me dzia", referring in the use of the term "dzia" to the focus in this part on the singing. The second stage he called "meteg me abog", the term "abog" indicating the focus on the dancing (Mba 1981: 162). This variation in naming the parts possibly has its roots in regional differences or in changes over time. The always literal description of things happening during the performance, however, make both designations plausible. The main point is that there are two phases in a bikutsi performance: one concerned with the message or the song, being rather slow and laid back, and the following, concerned with dancing, with more bodily energy than before.

This structure corresponds to the singing, that is, the developing of the message of the song, the singing of the verses and refrains in a call-and-response manner, and then a shift to the coda with its energetic dancing – an expression of joy and of dancing skill. Often started by the solo singer herself after finishing her song, during the coda, other singer-dancers in the group can enter the circle for a solo dancing performance. At the time of Mbala's writing, the dance was based on certain basic elements that Mbala described as the bending up-and-down of the upper body and a corresponding up-and-down motion of the feet (Mbala 1985: 279–80). During the "message" part, Mbala mentioned four main body parts involved in the dance: the neck, the arms, the feet, and the hips (Mbala 1985: 273–74). She further exemplified different types of dancing: "the ordinary step" ("le pas ordinaire", *fr.*), that is, lifting the right foot while swinging the left arm, then lifting the left foot accompanied by the right arm (276). This basic movement is then extended to more complex dance moves depending on individual ability or the necessities of different rhythmical structures. Moreover, it can also occur in bikutsi sessions that the ntanan bia commands the singer-dancers: she tells them how to move, almost testing their dancing abilities. The dancing of the solo singer herself includes complementing her main task with facial expressions and gestures in accordance with the story she is telling (Mbala 1985: 271–83). My own observations of women's bikutsi performances verified the descriptions of the basic moves described by Mbala.

To be a good dancer requires physical suppleness and plenty of energy and endurance. Like singing bikutsi, dancing is learned by imitation and experimentation in childhood and youth, and not through specific training. A woman's dancing ability is tied to her general worth, especially concerning her health. As the name indicates, bikutsi dancing often involves much forceful stomping on the ground, with both feet and accompanied by arm and head movements. Mastering this form of dancing is seen as an indicator of a woman's health and fertility. If she is not able to really "stomp the floor" and jump with both feet as expected during a bikutsi piece, because, for example, she might later complain of stomach pain, she is not considered healthy and potentially unable to bear children successfully. In turn she would not be considered a suitable candidate as a possible future wife for a son or nephew. Bikutsi performances therefore not only provide joy, and opportunities for social comment, lament and critique; they are also occasions for evaluating others and distinguishing and presenting oneself.

Contemporary Female Bikutsi: Analytical Observations

During my own field research in Monatele, a small town in the Eton region, I documented several women's song-and-dance pieces. I talked to a bikutsi singer who then performed two songs spontaneously. Further, an evening bikutsi session was organized especially for me in which eight women living nearby took part. While both recordings were not made in what might be called "authentic" situations, they nevertheless provide an insight into contemporary female bikutsi performance and a means to review historical descriptions. Furthermore, as none of the cited authors presented any musical analysis of women's bikutsi songs, this material made it possible to carry out a basic analysis of the music. These observations, discussed below, are based on just a few songs, so I do not claim a general validity. Nevertheless, I feel the need to add to the descriptions above some observations concerning the music of bikutsi performances that will be of relevance for the discussion of guitar-based bikutsi later.

In terms of content, the documented songs included, as discussed above, moral advice as well as spontaneous reactions to the situation. This varied from laments of being left alone as an elder woman, demands to be respected as a person, laments about changes in society, an homage to the man of the house and the woman of the house, the benefits of being in a group, praise for myself as scholar and guest, and the suffering of the people and the need for change. Figure 3.1 shows the lyrics of a short bikutsi song performed by Mme Eloundou née Tsimi Marié Romaine, accompanied by Leka Emmilienne and Mme Noa Née Edjili Ntsama Dorothée. Therein the singer laments to her own family, especially the men, that nobody knocks at her door anymore, that she is all alone. The interpretation of this song given to me was that the woman had been left by her husband for another woman. She closed the song with general moral advice, also used in another song: "In life, if you take nothing seriously, you will not yield anything serious".[14] During the dance part the singer shouted encouragement to the dancers and sometimes added onomatopoetic rhythmical sounds.

> Descendants of my father,
>
> I am surprised, I wonder,
>
> I live in a deplorable situation,
>
> for some time nobody knocks at my door anymore.
>
> In life, if you take nothing seriously, you will not yield anything serious.
>
> This message is addressed to the men, the descendants of my father.

Figure 3.1: Lyrics of a short bikutsi song, performed in Monatele, December 2007. Translation by Anja Brunner, on the basis of the French translation of the original song in Eton region by Christian Tsala Tsala.

The overall structure of all songs documented was as described above. They always started with a singing part, mostly in call-and-response, followed by a more energetic dancing part. The songs were mostly accompanied by hand clapping; one song was an exception, being a lullaby. In the group performance, one woman used a whistle and a rattle instead of clapping her hands; she rattled in rhythm with clapping, and the whistle added an intermittent additional sound element.

The dancing during the dance session made it clear why the dance is called bikutsi: the women in the middle of the circle, sometimes two at the same time dancing together, jumped up a little to then stomp with both feet on the floor. Neither the jumping nor the height of the jump was the relevant part, but the end of the jump, the stomping. The jumps were not high, just a few centimetres off the ground. These stomps, which often produced an equivalent sound, always met with a hand-clapping beat, with stomping and clapping on the same pulse. The tempo of the performances was rather fast; it was commonly around 160 beats (hand claps) per minute, but could go up to 170 or down to 150 as well, also within one song. The relation of the foot steps to the accompanying hand clapping during the singing part varied and subsumed either two or three claps, that is, songs had a binary or ternary beat structure. Most of the songs I documented had a binary beat–foot structure. The dancers in the circle commonly lifted their feet while staying on the spot; sometimes the women turned back to front and moved in one direction in the circle. Then they tended to tap one foot on the floor before stepping down, instead of lifting it up. During the dancing part the movements changed and every clap was accompanied simultaneously by a stomp, most often with both feet, accompanied by movements of arms and upper body.

The melodies sung either by the solo voice or the chorus hardly ever exceeded an octave in tonal range; chorus parts were commonly in two or three voices, harmonized generally in thirds. However, the intonation of the tones was not always very clear, but slid to a certain pitch up or down a semi-tone. In terms of the rhythmical level of the songs, most songs provided a ternary subdivision of the beat. The accents of the melodies tended to fall in between the beats realized by hand clapping and steps on the ground (see example in Figure 3.2). The harmonic structure of the songs alternated between two basic tones, possibly interpreted as tonic-dominant alteration. These features reappear in other bikutsi music genres, most obviously in the guitar version (see Chapter 5).

Figure 3.2: Melody of a women's bikutsi song (part of the chorus). Transcribed by Anja Brunner. The reader should be aware that this transcription in Western notation only approximately reproduces the actually sung tone pitches. The main focus is on the overall melody and the rhythmic relation.

With these observations on contemporary women's bikutsi song-and-dance pieces, existing research is complemented with information on the genre's musical and rhythmical aspects. Not only in lyrical content, but also in dancing and rhythmical features, similarities and influences are present both in 1970s guitar music as well as in bikutsi pieces from the early twenty-first century, as will be discussed in the subsequent chapters, especially in Chapter 5.

Research on Women's Bikutsi and Changes in its Perception

When studying past research on Beti music, it is striking that early ethnographic work did not mention the female practice of bikutsi, despite its central role in (female) Beti life. Indeed, dances and songs performed by women alone were mentioned, but they were not called bikutsi. Erich M. von Hornbostel transcribed a "Weibergesang" ("women's song") that might have been a bikutsi piece (Hornbostel 1913: 345). The French-language monograph by Pierre Alexandre and Jacques Binet published in 1958 provided several descriptions of dances, but none akin to bikutsi (Alexandre and Binet 1958: 126–27). The French anthropologist Philippe Laburthe-Tolra, who studied extensively the life, history, and culture of the Beti only mentioned bikutsi in a footnote with reference to the work of P. Mviena published in 1970 (Laburthe-Tolra 1977; Mviena 1970). Thus it was left to Cameroonian scholars and researchers to first discuss bikutsi as an important female practice and give it its rightful position in the Beti musical traditions. Most important here is the extensive work of Mbala Agnès Marie épouse Nkili, cited at length above. She wrote a doctoral thesis in 1985 at the University of Paris-Nanterre on the bikutsi tradition of the women of the Mvele, a Beti subgroup living east of Yaoundé (Mbala 1985). Contrary to the habitual use of bikutsi as a generic term in the singular ("le bikutsi") as was common at the time of my research, Mbala wrote about "*les* bikutsi". This use of bikutsi as a plural noun can point to the repetitive stomping on the ground. Given her descriptions of numerous bikutsi events, it also reveals her concept – and probably the concept of women's bikutsi at the time – of bikutsi as being a description for a collection of songs and dances. Bikutsi as a female practice was also examined by Wenzeslaus Mba (Mba 1981) in his dissertation and in a work on Cameroonian dances published in the late 1960s by the Ministère de l'education, de la Jeunesse et de la Culture (Awona n.d.). Bikutsi as a female tradition was briefly mentioned in the works of P. Mviena, Pierre Betene, and Pie-Claude Ngumu (Mviena 1970; Betene 1973; Ngumu 1989). In the 1990s, Louis-Martin Onguene Essono published an article with a focus on the political meaning of bikutsi songs (Onguene Essono 1996).

The lack of descriptions of bikutsi in early work on Beti culture by European scholars can be explained in two ways. First, male European travellers either ignored or overlooked this female activity or did not find access to it. However, since other female musical practices were described in their works, this does not suffice as an explanation. It is more probable that a unified term to describe this phenomenon was lacking, or rather, bikutsi was not something worth documenting. Women's songs and dances were not necessarily called bikutsi, the term also being a simple description of doing something to music. Thus, the songs and dances termed as such did not stand out as something special in the cultural universe studied by early ethnographers and were therefore possibly not perceived as relevant. Only with developments after independence, the emergence of a Cameroonian (Beti) research tradition, and the changes in popular dance music did these songs come more into focus, initially for Cameroonian writers and researchers. This theory that bikutsi was not recognized as relevant because it was omnipresent is supported by a note in Mbala's work. She wrote that the Mvele only have dances that are accompanied by stomping on the ground (Mbala 1985: 10). Any dance, therefore, was potentially bikutsi – as already revealed by the plural usage of the term. However, there was still a difference compared to dances accompanied by instruments such as the mìǹkúl or məndzáŋ. There are hints that suggest that bikutsi mainly meant women's song-and-dance pieces accompanied only by hand clapping and rattles with a focus on the lyrical content of the songs as well as the dancing abilities of the women. Other dances or rhythms danced had specific names, like elak, esáni, or mbali, and were also danced by men. While these were commonly included when speaking of bikutsi in general at the time of my own research, this was not the case in the first half of the twentieth century.

Women's Bikutsi as the "Origin" of the Popular Music Genre

Women's bikutsi is located in a fundamentally different context than the popular music genre bikutsi. While the first is performed by female groups on various daily occasions, with rattles and hand clapping as accompaniment, and in more private spaces, the second is presented with various musical instruments, in public spaces designated for dancing and in a specific, typical concert setting. So, in what way is the female tradition of bikutsi of relevance for bikutsi as a popular music genre? In her analysis, Mbala briefly commented on the use of new instruments for bikutsi pieces, noting that "to the traditional hand clapping are nowadays added modern instruments like the saxophone and the guitar" (Mbala 1985: 496).[15] For Mbala, there is little difference beyond the use of the instruments, and in fact, musicians often just reinterpreted women's bikutsi songs on their modern instruments. That women's bikutsi songs had been taken up by bikutsi musicians was claimed repeatedly by my informants, commonly in connection with notions of "stealing" rural music, without compensation and without acknowledging copyright. Jean Maurice Noah estimated in 2004 that around 80 per cent of modern bikutsi songs were based on bikutsi songs performed and composed by women in rural villages (Noah 2004: 20). Even if this number is not accurate, the fact that numerous people in Cameroon pointed out female creativity as the main source for bikutsi songs is sufficient to underline the importance of this female tradition as inspiration for bikutsi as a popular music genre, past and present. Musically, parallels exist and will be pointed out in more detail in the analyses of the following chapters.

That said, a significant difference between these two versions of bikutsi must be mentioned: the novel use of instruments brought about a significant transformation in terms of gender. "Original" bikutsi was performed by women alone. With the inclusion of musical instruments, bikutsi performances became male-dominated – both the instrumentalists as well as the singers. The dancing, however, remained a primarily female practice, although men also danced in urban bar and nightclub contexts at the time of my research. With the emergence of bikutsi as a popular music genre, bikutsi was no longer a solely female practice; with the exception of some female singers, guitar-based bikutsi became a primarily male musical practice.

In summary, bikutsi as a popular music genre and bikutsi pieces danced and sung by Beti women belong to the same musical universe; they are similar in musical structure and characteristics. In a way, they are two sides of the same coin or two ends of the same spectrum. In the discussion that follows, it should be kept in mind that especially for women, bikutsi songs remain very important: they accompany every aspect of life and are a means for dealing with difficulties in the community and other matters, to ask for help, to express joy, and so on. While many musical and dance aspects of the genre have remained virtually unchanged over the last few decades, other aspects of bikutsi as a women's tradition have undergone innovation. For example, today it is sometimes performed by professional ensembles and recorded. And it is being increasingly perceived as a noteworthy Beti tradition. Nevertheless, bikutsi as a women's practice has remained a local, female part of daily life. As one woman once put it in a personal conversation: "bikutsi, that's our life, that's our way to live". Bikutsi – be it a women's tradition, a general mode of song and dance, or a popular music genre – is simply an intrinsic part of Beti life.

Chapter 4

Bikutsi on the Məndzáŋ: Dance Music on Xylophone Ensembles

One innovation was of special importance in the adoption of Beti songs and dances by modern dance bands: the imitation of the local xylophone music on electric guitars. The local Beti xylophones are called məndzáŋ in Ewondo or "balafons" in vernacular French. Their repertoire and their playing style were the main inspiration for musicians active in the 1960s and 1970s experimenting with the inclusion of Beti dance music into their modern dance repertoires. Since then, mutual exchanges of songs and features between modern dance bands and məndzáŋ ensembles have become common. In this chapter, I discuss məndzáŋ playing and repertoire in southern Cameroon with a specific focus on those general historical changes connected to the emergence of modern Beti dance music.

Məndzáŋ in Traditional Society: Ongɛd

The term "məndzáŋ" is plural; a "ndzáŋ" in Ewondo is a xylophone key, and the particle "me" indicates its plurality. Consequently, when talking about the məndzáŋ one is literally referring to the multitude of keys of one instrument. At the same time, the term can refer to an ensemble of instruments. To differentiate between the two, in the following, when talking about a group of xylophone instruments performing together, I will speak of a "məndzáŋ ensemble". In general, məndzáŋ ensembles are associated with festivities of any kind. Their music is not ritual, but dance music, music for entertainment and amusement, for celebrating, played for example at weddings or birth parties. However, it is worth briefly mentioning the other versions of məndzáŋ music: the *ongɛd* and, in the next section, the playing of məndzáŋ ensembles in church.

In the first decades of the twentieth century, məndzáŋ ensembles were mainly associated with the power of regional Beti chiefs. Every chief maintained a group of musicians, and commonly also dancers, at his command. On important official occasions, a məndzáŋ ensemble accompanied the chief to show his wealth, power, and prestige. Such occasions could be visits to neighbouring chiefs, traditional festivities as well as national celebrations, like French national holidays (Mba 1981: 197). Jules Akoudou from the məndzáŋ ensemble Balafon Star remembered that in his childhood in the late 1970s, the chief of his village had a məndzáŋ ensemble at his disposal (email communication, May 30, 2011).

Hornbostel (1913) described in his chapter on "Pangwe" music – a term for Beti-Faŋ music at colonial times – two types of xylophone instruments. The first, which he called the "simple" type, was made from trunks of the banana tree on which the keys were fixed. The second, according to Hornbostel, "more refined" (German: "vollkommener") type, had a wooden frame, calabash resonators, and a curved bar to keep the instrument from the player's body.[1] This second type of xylophone was commonly called ongɛd and was associated with traditional society. Ongɛd xylophones were used for representation purposes by chiefs and accompanying traditional ceremonies. Although I personally did not come across such a xylophone type during my research in Yaoundé, the ongɛd was still present in rural areas in Cameroon. These ongɛd xylophones were described to me as portable, with a curved bar, like those described by Hornbostel. They were played while standing or walking, with the instrument hanging from the player's neck and held away from the body by the bar. The "modern" version of the məndzáŋ, in contrast, is not portable, but built into a wooden box.

Introducing Məndzáŋ to Christian Worship: "Les balafons de l'église"

At the time of my research, the "balafon" was an important part of Christian worship in Cameroon, a marked difference to colonial times, when the use of the məndzáŋ as well as other indigenous instruments in church was forbidden. Due to their profane character and in line with the goal of introducing African people to European standards of Christian belief, the missionaries in Cameroon banned any indigenous musical practices. Church music was accompanied in colonial times by an organ alone; and although missionaries translated the texts of many songs into local languages in order to improve the understanding of the Bible's messages, məndzáŋ and other Beti instruments remained absent from Christian worship until around independence in 1960.

It is often hard to tell in retrospect who started a development, and this is also the case for who first introduced məndzáŋ music to Christian worship. Pie-Claude Ngumu describes a məndzáŋ ensemble as part of a mass in the parish Saint Luc de Tala in the Eton region in 1961 (Ngumu 1976b: 10). According to Joachim Oelsner, founder of the music archive Arc Musica in Yaoundé, the introduction of indigenous Beti instruments to Christian worship started with the Benedictine father Luitfred Marfurt in the Grand Seminaire Otélé in Mont Febé, Yaoundé. He released a single titled 'Les psalmodies du Cameroon' in the 1960s with his music group (personal conversation with Joachim Oelsner, October 2012). Mba described the first use of indigenous Beti instruments in the Yaoundé Cathedral in 1962 on the occasion of the ordination mass of the first bishop of Cameroonian descent in the region: "Then, on the second of January 1962, it was a true canonization of traditional instruments that participated officially in a liturgical mass and made thus heard their voice for the first time in the Cathedral in Yaoundé" (Mba 1981: 187).[2] The reactions of those in attendance were positive; to hear indigenous instruments in church was widely appreciated. Indigenous instruments, including məndzáŋ, were thus introduced to Christian worship in the early 1960s at the latest.

One person proved to be especially prominent for his innovations to church music in the 1960s: the musician, composer, ethnologist, and priest Pie Claude Ngumu, who according to Joachim Oelsner was a student of Luitfred Marfurt. Ngumu's ensemble Maîtrise des chanteurs à la Croix d'Ébène de Yaoundé, founded in 1963 in the parish of Ndjon-Melen in Yaoundé, consisted of a mixed choir and the instruments məndzáŋ, mìǹkúl, the single-headed drum *m̀bɛ*, and the stick zither mvɛd. The group was made up, at its core, of 35 members (cf. Ngumu 1971) and was part of the Cameroonian delegation at the Pan-African Festival in Algiers in 1969. Ngumu himself was an active composer of religious music and included various Beti instruments in his work. His 'Messe Ewondo' won the "Grand Prix de Disque" at the Premier Festival des Arts Nègres in Dakar in 1966 (Ngumu 1971).

Other religious music groups also started to introduce məndzáŋ and other Beti instruments in their musical performance in the 1960s, among them the choir of St. Kisito de Mvog Mbi, then led by Wenzeslaus Mba, the choir Nkukuma David and the choir Sacré Coeur de Mokolo (cf. Mba

1981: 197). Religious choir music was also released on commercial records. In 1976 the choir St. Kisito released an LP, advertised in the national newspaper as "only the second album of Cameroonian religious music" after a recording of Ngumu's 'La messe à Yaoundé' (N.A. 1976). With the introduction of məndzáŋ and other indigenous instruments to religious contexts, dance slowly "crept in", as noted in a newspaper article in 1975: "The dance, gently of course, set an end to the traditional dichotomy between soul and body, indicating that in the new liturgy the human as a whole, spirit, soul and body, has to be devoted from now on to the search for the absolute" (Nyano 1975).[3] Certain gestures and movements were introduced slowly into church services since the late 1960s in connection with the musical changes (Mba 1981: 220–22).

With the fruitful and innovative introduction of məndzáŋ ensembles to the Christian context, məndzáŋ music became accepted and welcomed in a domain of life that was immensely important for Cameroonians in the southern regions of the country. Cameroon was missionized by Catholics as well as diverse Protestant churches with incredible success in the first decades of the twentieth century, and Christian belief became a vital and essential aspect in the life of most Cameroonians. Therefore, the introduction of məndzáŋ music to Christian worship also had an impact on the perception of the məndzáŋ in general: it enhanced its status as an acceptable and valuable instrument and at the same time indigenized an area that had formerly been thoroughly in the domain of missionary influence. This process was clearly in line with the "Africanization" taking place across the continent in church as well as in government activities. The developments contributed, beginning with independence, to processes of nation-building that propagated a "return" to supposed traditional values, styles, musics, and cultural traditions (cf., e.g., Bayart 1979, DeLancey 1989; cf. Chapter 2). For example, in his presentation of the Maîtrise des chanteurs à la Croix d'Ébène de Yaoundé, Ngumu cited a statement of the Minister of Education, Youth and Culture who commented positively on the work of the group: it "supports the creation of a true and authentic adaptation of religion to the African mentality and life" (Ngumu 1971: 14).[4] The notion of "authenticity", that is, what was truly "African" in the sense of turning away from any colonial influences to revive African traditions, was omnipresent in Africa in the 1960s and 1970s, a period in which most African states were in the throes of gaining and cementing their independence. In the twenty-first century, məndzáŋ remain an integral part of church music in the Beti regions in Cameroon.

Məndzáŋ Dance Music

In addition to their representational role in traditional society, məndzáŋ were used to play dance music at various social gatherings. Dancing for fun and entertainment was usually done to məndzáŋ music. In this function as dance music instruments, they became popular in urban drinking venues and bars in the 1960s, parallel to the introduction of indigenous instruments to Christian traditions in southern Cameroon. In contrast to ideals of indigenization and "Africanization" behind the inclusion of məndzáŋ in Christian contexts, məndzáŋ appear in urban bars as a result of ongoing processes of urbanization. With more and more people migrating from rural areas to the urban centres, especially Yaoundé, after World War II, the need and demand for familiar forms and genres of entertainment in the new environment grew, leading to the establishment of urban xylophone ensembles. Yaoundé being part of the region inhabited mainly by Beti-Faŋ, məndzáŋ ensembles playing Beti music were of course familiar in the region of Yaoundé. What changed was the setting in which they performed. Ted Mekoulou, jazz trumpeter and composer in Yaoundé since the 1970s and head of the music group Echo Jazz de la Police, recalled in an interview that məndzáŋ ensembles played in urban pubs called "bars populaires", where people living close by drank in their leisure time: "In certain bars, they accepted that they [the məndzáŋ ensemble] came, that they set up outside and played" (Ted Mekoulou, interview, August 22, 2010).[5] According to Mekoulou, the ensembles were paid not by the owner or manager of the bar, but by the audience: "If you wanted [to hear] a certain piece, you paid, that's how it was".[6] But he added that it was not possible for the musicians to earn a living in this way; therefore, the musicians must have had other occupations beside their musical activities.

Məndzáŋ groups playing entertainment dance music were popular throughout southern Cameroon; some were recorded on reel-to-reel tapes to be played at the local radio stations or released one or more records. Mostly, the məndzáŋ players also sang themselves. One məndzáŋ ensemble became especially popular in the region: the Richard Band de Zoétélé, led by Richard Nze. Like Ngumu's ensemble, the group was also part of the Cameroonian delegation at the Pan-African Festival in Algiers in 1969, and in 1974 they took part at an international festival in Canada, together with other Cameroonian artists. In a newspaper article from 1979 on the occasion of a concert by the group, a journalist stated that the group had been especially popular from 1970 to 1974: "It is with a lot of pleasure that the public listened to the repertoire of the Richard band, that consisted of old pieces, like Meringue Mariage, Menga yen aval adzo, that, as we remember, a lot of Cameroonians were crazy about between 1970 and 1974" (B.M. 1979).[7] The group recorded for the radio station and released a couple of records in the 1960s and early 1970s. Ethnomusicologist Gerhard Kubik came across the group during his research in Cameroon in the 1960s and mentioned it in his article on Cameroon in the *New Grove Dictionary of Music and Musicians* as a "famous group of 'modern' xylophone players" (Kubik 2001: 877). The attribute "modern" appears here to refer to the repertoire played. In line with the popularity of merengue and rumba dance music, urban məndzáŋ ensembles included popular pieces from these genres in their repertoire, one of the first to do so probably being the Richard Band de Zoétélé. The songs were either cover versions of existing songs or newly composed songs in local languages.

As Kubik reported, məndzáŋ ensembles playing dance music could be found not only in towns but in rural areas as well: "Xylophone ensembles modelled after Richard Nze's played all over southern Cameroon at village dance parties for youths at one time" (Kubik 2001: 877). So while Ngumu and others started to use məndzáŋ to accompany Christian hymns, dance music məndzáŋ ensembles adjusted to musical fashion and arranged popular dance pieces for their instruments. These məndzáŋ ensembles continued to play typical local dance music as well, like the dance elak: "Groups such as the Roddy Band de Mengbwa recorded in the Ebolowa area, typically performing merengue, rumba, rumba boucher, cha cha cha and an adaptation of a local dance in a fast 12-pulse rhythm called elak" (Kubik 2001: 877). Here can be seen the connection to Beti music on electric guitars: local dances played typically on the məndzáŋ were adapted to the guitar and later to the electric guitar to be performed by modern dance bands. Today, məndzáŋ music and dance music played by modern music groups have been thoroughly intertwined and connected.

Despite this exchange and mutual adaptation, however, it must be mentioned that the status of məndzáŋ ensembles remained different to that of guitar-based music groups, as musician, journalist, and painter Jean-Marie Ahanda recalled. The founder of the group Les Têtes Brulées in the 1980s (see Chapter 7) recounted in an interview that in Yaoundé in his youth, guitar-based music groups commonly accompanied wedding celebrations, a tradition connected to the popular musician of the 1960s, Cheramy de la Capitale (see Chapter 2). With increasing financial restraints, however, people began to hire məndzáŋ ensembles because they were cheaper: "What I experienced when growing up in Yaoundé [in the late 1960s, early 1970s], was that at weddings, the people put an amplifier or a modern dance band with guitars on a van, and they danced in the street, marching behind ... And bit by bit, one could see that those who did not have the means took the balafons, and often the balafons came from far away, from the villages" (Jean-Marie Ahanda, interview, December 11, 2007).[8] Compared to modern music groups that stood for modernity, urbanity, and a cosmopolitan lifestyle, məndzáŋ ensembles were associated with the urban poor and traditional ways of life.

Different Types of Məndzáŋ

These two different settings of hymns in church and merengue in urban bars and their respective repertoire brought about changes to the məndzáŋ tradition. The instruments were adapted to this new purpose: in their construction, in the roles they played within the ensemble, and finally, in their tonal range. These observations verify those of Artur Simon, who documented a məndzáŋ dance music ensemble in the 1980s and mentioned the differences in fabrication as well as the changed tuning and repertoire compared to older instruments (Simon 1987; 1992). Retracing these changes is possible because məndzáŋ ensembles and their instruments have been described repeatedly over the last century. The first such description of məndzáŋ music is from Erich Moritz von Hornbostel in his chapter on music in the ethnographic study of the "Pangwe" by the ethnologist and botanist Günter Tessmann (1913). The next available source on məndzáŋ is from the 1970s, when the ethnomusicologist and priest Pie Claude Ngumu, then a PhD student at the University of Vienna under the supervision of the ethnomusicologist Gerhard Kubik, undertook a close study of məndzáŋ making, tuning, and playing. As mentioned, Ngumu was also an active musician and composer, having founded a religious music group in Yaoundé consisting of a choir and various indigenous instruments (Ngumu 1976b). A few years later, another Cameroonian priest and musician, Wenzeslaus Mba, did research on Beti music for his PhD thesis at a German university (Universität des Saarlandes, Saarbrücken) and dealt with məndzáŋ music as well, therein critically reflecting on Ngumu's findings (Mba 1981). Further, we have partially unpublished accounts by Gerhard Kubik, who undertook research in Cameroon in the 1960s and also documented məndzáŋ ensembles (cf. recordings and field notes archived at the Phonogrammarchiv, the Austrian Audiovisual Research Archive of the Austrian Academy of Sciences in Vienna; Kubik 1985).

As already mentioned briefly above, traditional ongɛd xylophones were portable instruments with fixed keys and a curved bar, using calabashes as resonators that were played while standing or walking. It was this type of xylophone that Ngumu presented as being used by the "Maîtrise" (Ngumu 1971). On pictures of religious choirs and their instrumental accompaniment from the 1970s found in the national newspaper, however, the məndzáŋ had a wooden, often painted, corpus standing on the ground with the calabashes built in. The musicians are seated on a stool, the keys approximately at the height of their knees. At the time of my own research, instruments of this sort continued to be played, for example at the cathedral in the missionary quarter Mvolyé in Yaoundé.

Məndzáŋ dance music ensembles in the early 1970s, such as the Richard Band de Zoétélé, used instruments built as wooden boxes. A photograph in the *Cameroon Tribune* published in 1974 showed the Richard Band de Zoétélé playing this kind of instrument (Bolap 1974). In contrast to the instruments used in church, these məndzáŋ were higher and players could comfortably stand behind them. A picture of the André-Band-Esse, that "played at evening dances for the public on weekends in the region" in the Berlin Phonogrammarchiv from the 1980s, showed that this type of məndzáŋ constructed as a higher wooden box was also used by this group (Simon and Noah Messomo 2005: 70).

At the time of my research in the first decade of the twenty-first century, both variations of "boxed" xylophones were being used by məndzáŋ ensembles I worked with in Yaoundé. The group Balafon Star had higher instruments that the player could stand behind; the instruments used in the cabarets and bars were more often instruments to be played while seated.

It can be surmised that this change in the construction of the instrument was due to the stationary nature of the performance context in churches and for evening entertainment and festive events. Performers no longer needed to walk with the instrument. While it is unclear if this shift in how the instrument was played first took place in the context of church music or in the bars, or if it was a parallel or linked development, since Hornbostel did not describe boxed xylophones at the beginning of the century, it seems certain that the change in construction took place in later decades in response to these changes in the performance context.

Towards a Modern Dance Repertoire: Məndzáŋ Instruments and their Roles in the Ensemble

In their descriptions and analyses of məndzáŋ ensembles, both Pie-Claude Ngumu (1976b) and Wenzeslaus Mba (1981) described five xylophone instrument types that together formed a full ensemble. Théodore Tsala in his *Dictionnaire Ewondo-Français* also speaks of five types of məndzáŋ (Tsala n.d.: 350–51). All these authors were priests and musicians, so their main focus was on church music or traditional xylophone playing; dance music ensembles were not mentioned. Məndzáŋ dance music ensembles are slightly different, especially in their number, as they only use three to four instruments. Ngumu's and Mba's descriptions provide valuable insights on general aspects of the instruments that are also true for məndzáŋ ensembles in urban entertainment contexts. Although their descriptions vary in some small details, the commonalities are preponderant. The following description is based on their work (Ngumu 1976b; Mba 1981).[9]

The lead instrument in a məndzáŋ ensemble is the *oŋvəg*. The name was probably derived from the word "oŋvəg" used for people who make their voice heard. Using the then common hexatonic scale, the oŋvəg had nine keys providing a tonal range of just over an octave. The player of the oŋvəg was responsible for the progression of the piece, its beginning and its end. It was usually the most skilled məndzáŋ players that played this instrument. Similar playing competence was needed for the second instrument, the *olɔ̀lɔ̀ŋ*, supporting the melodic patterns played by the oŋvəg. The word "olɔ̀lɔ̀ŋ" actually means "whistling". The range of the olɔ̀lɔ̀ŋ was an octave higher than the oŋvəg, "like whistling compared to the normal human voice" (Mba 1981: 184).[10] The third instrument was the *akuda-oŋvəg*, responsible for the accompaniment. Its tonal range was similar to the oŋvəg with a few notes added in the lower register. The fourth instrument, the *nyă-məndzáŋ*, was considered the "mother xylophone". It consisted of the first three notes of the scale of the oŋvəg that were then repeated an octave lower; it thus only had six keys (divided by one muted key). Its role was more rhythmic than melodic, as the corresponding notes of the octaves played together with both hands provided a basic repeated pattern forming a foundation for the melody. The last instrument was the *èndùm*, which had two notes with several muted keys between them. The name was derived from the sound of the instrument, as Ngumu explained (Ngumu 1976b: 33). One note of the èndùm matched the lowest note of the nyă-məndzáŋ, the other note did not correspond to the scale. It had a very low sound that, as Mba put it, was "on the edge between noise and sound" (Mba 1981: 185).[11] The èndùm played a rhythmical role in the ensemble.

Məndzáŋ ensembles also included a percussion section, commonly consisting of one or more rattles (nyás) and the tall single-headed drum *m̀bɛ*. The m̀bɛ is made out of a hollow tree trunk of about 25 cm in diameter, covered on one end by a membrane that is fixed to the corpus by a cord and wooden wedges (see Figure 4.1). The drum is played standing on the floor, the player stands upright and plays with both hands. The m̀bɛ has a significant rhythmic role, marking the time and the beat of the pieces.

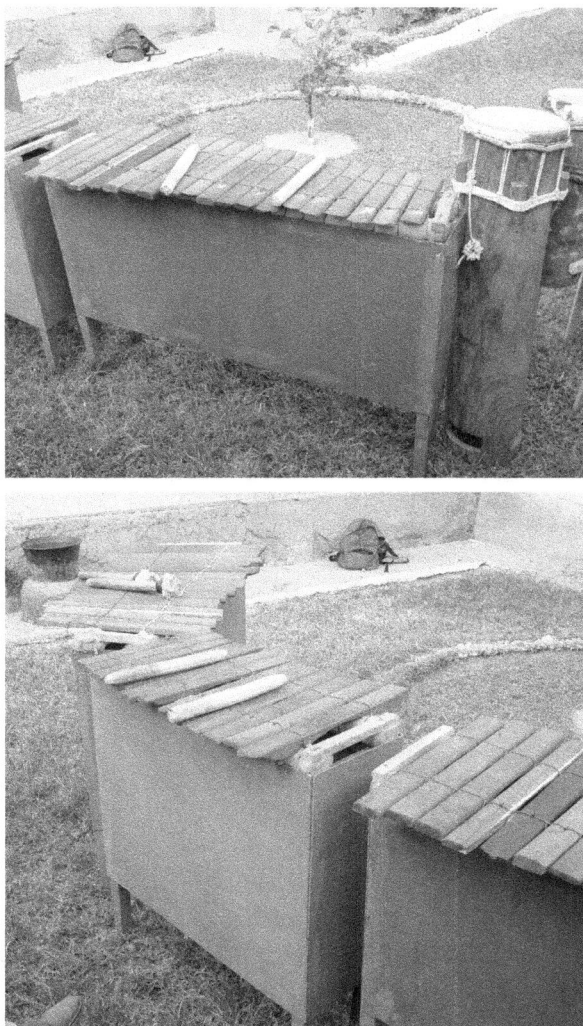

Figure 4.1: Məndzáŋ and the drum m̀bɛ used by the group Balafon Star at an event in January 2008. Photographs by Anja Brunner.

This ensemble size and the roles of the instruments are standard for traditional ensembles. In church contexts there are usually five or six instruments
in an ensemble. Comparing it to other repertoires, the xylophone player Jules
Akoudou described their playing as "carré" (*fr.*), that is, strict, with every
instrument having its part in a composition.

Ensembles performing urban dance music use fewer instruments. The
active məndzáŋ ensembles playing entertainment dance music that I documented in Yaoundé only consisted of three or four məndzáŋ, accompanied
by percussion instruments. A rattle and the m̀bɛ drum were always present
and sometimes Conga-like instruments were added. In one case in 2010, an
ensemble playing in a cabaret in Yaoundé had a drum set instead of a m̀bɛ.
Despite the reduced size of the ensemble, the names of the məndzáŋ instruments remain the same. The ensemble Balafon Star that I worked with primarily had three instruments in addition to the percussion section: an oŋvəg,
an olɔ̀lɔ̀ŋ, and an ɛ̀ndùm. With this setup they performed at weddings and first
communion parties. When performing in cabarets in Yaoundé, they had four
məndzáŋ, adding an akuda-oŋvəg. The nyǎ-məndzáŋ, according to Ngumu
responsible for the rhythmical foundation mainly played in octaves, was
apparently the instrument that could be omitted most easily in the ensemble,
although for Albert Noah Messomo it was indispensable (Noah Messomo
1980, cited in Simon and Noah Messomo 2005). For music performed by
məndzáŋ dance ensembles, however, it is apparently not indispensable.

The məndzáŋ player Jules Akoudou from Balafon Star explained that an
ensemble of three or four instruments was most common for məndzáŋ dance
ensembles (personal conversation, October 2012). When asked why they did
not also include a nyǎ-məndzáŋ, the answer was simply: "We do not see
the role of a fifth balafon, what would it play?" According to Akoudou, the
number of instruments was the main difference between the məndzáŋ music
played in churches and that played in bars and festive occasions. This is not
a new phenomenon: the same instrumentation with three instruments was
used by the dance ensemble André-Band-Esse in the 1980s (Simon and Noah
Messomo 2005: 27). And it was also used by the Richard Band de Zoétélé,
the picture in the *Cameroon Tribune* showing the group playing three xylophones, a m̀bɛ, and a pair of nyás (Bolap 1974).

When asked about the role of the məndzáŋ in a contemporary ensemble,
the musicians of Balafon Star used terminology adapted from popular music:
they said that the olɔ̀lɔ̀ŋ was the "solo". It introduced the piece, played an
important role during instrumental sections, and indicated changes in the
piece such as the transition from vocal to instrumental sections, a new song, or

the end of the song. The oŋvəg played a mainly accompanying role, guiding the singer. They called it "l'accompagnement". It was more present in parts with singing. The akuda-oŋvəg complemented the oŋvəg and the ɛndùm was simply called "bass məndzáŋ". Documented performances of contemporary məndzáŋ ensembles verify that the olɔlɔŋ was the lead instrument, beginning and ending the piece and leading the ensemble, a role assigned in the past to the oŋvəg. This shift in the number and roles of the instruments can be traced to the different needs inherent to the new repertoire: Afro-Caribbean influenced dance music such as merengue or soukous demands a different instrumentation than traditional xylophone music, and the məndzáŋ ensembles were adapted to these needs. When guitar-based ensembles play pieces from traditional məndzáŋ repertoires, they divide up the roles as well: the solo guitar plays the whistling olɔlɔŋ part while the rhythm guitar takes over the role of the oŋvəg. The bass guitar corresponds to the ɛndùm. The indispensable percussion instruments nyás and m̀bɛ are replaced by congas during merengue and rumba crazes and later by a standard drum set.

Changes in Tonal System and Tuning

This adaptation to a popular dance music repertoire like merengue and souk-ous brought about changes in the tonal system and tuning of the instruments. Ngumu describes an ongoing process of transition from a hexatonic to a heptatonic scale in the 1970s. According to the colonial anthropologist and zoologist Georg August Zenker, head of the colonial station in Yaoundé at the end of the nineteenth century, the scale of the xylophones was similar to the heptatonic European system, only "the seventh tone was missing" (cited in Simon and Noah Messomo 2005). Documenting the building of the instruments for a məndzáŋ ensemble, Ngumu describes the builder adding an additional key to the then common nine keys on the oŋvəg, thereby adding a new tone to the scale. He told Ngumu that he had seen this variation in another region: "The xylophone he had known and played in his childhood only had nine keys ..., for the construction of the first instrument. But in time he discovered, specifically during a stay in the Etenga region, that some məndzáŋ groups had introduced a new tone between key 1 and key 6" (Ngumu 1976b: 37).[12] This note was called "esandi", meaning something like "troublemaker" or "spoil sport". As Ngumu interpreted it, this was most likely in reference to its alien status in the usual tonal system (cf. Kubik 1985: 34). The height of the tone was, as Ngumu further noted, found by singing a specific məndzáŋ melody in which this additional tone appeared. Ngumu did not note the melody, but it may well have been a piece of Congolese music or merengue arranged for məndzáŋ.

Ngumu also studied closely the tuning of a məndzáŋ belonging to Gerhard Kubik, his doctoral supervisor at the University of Vienna, which the latter bought in southern Cameroon in 1964. Ngumu reported that no important interval – specifically the octave, the third and the fourth – corresponded to the Western diatonic scale: an octave was always higher than 1200 cents, the thirds were always in between minor and major third, and the fourths also did not match the European system of 500 cents but were always slightly higher (Ngumu 1976b: 46–47). However, the tuning of the instruments could be much closer to the Western diatonic scale. Kubik stated in his article on African tone systems that his own measurements showed scales of a near-equiheptatonic division of the octave, the standard interval in the mind of the musicians being around 160 to 180 cents (Kubik 1985: 35). He did suggest a reason for this difference, namely that "from the perceptual viewpoint of someone raised in a musical culture which uses a near-equiheptatonic system the Western diatonic scale do, re, mi, fa, sol, la, si ... may just fall within the margin of tolerance of this system", and thus be one possible variant of the heptatonic system used (Kubik 1985: 50–51). Citing, amongst others, Beti ethnic groups in southern Cameroon, Kubik remarked that in some African regions the Western diatonic scale had been adopted completely so that no difference to the traditional scale was conceived any more. In southern Cameroon, this adjustment began with the German colonial presence at the end of the nineteenth century. The leader of a xylophone group playing mainly Cuban and Congolese music in the 1960s had clearly internalized the ideal of the Western diatonic scale (Kubik 1985: 51–52).

There was no doubt during my field research that the heptatonic scale was predominant, if not omnipresent in the musical practice in Yaoundé, and probably beyond. With the adaption of foreign music genres, like merengue, and the diffusion of different pop-rock music traditions via various media as well as the increasing use of the respective instruments, the diatonic scale had entered Cameroonian and Beti musical practices. Contemporary məndzáŋ were tuned in or close to a diatonic major scale. According to the musicians of Balafon Star, məndzáŋ were tuned to diatonic scale by their makers if the buyer did not specify an alternative tuning. On one occasion I saw a məndzáŋ whose keys had labelled stickers showing their tone: Do, Re, Mi, etc. (see Figure 4.2). The transition from a close to equiheptatonic scale to a Western diatonic tuning as observed by Kubik in the 1980s has probably come to its conclusion for the time being, at least among urban məndzáŋ ensembles in Yaoundé.

Figure 4.2: Məndzáŋ with stickers on the keys showing the pitch in diatonic scale, using the Do-Re-Mi-system. Photograph by Anja Brunner.

In addition to the change in tuning and the adoption of a new repertoire, the tonal range has also been extended significantly compared to the traditional ongɛd. Ngumu and Mba describe the oɱvəg as having eleven notes, the akuda-oɱvəg ten, the nyǎ-məndzáŋ six, and the ɛ̀ndùm only two. By the 1980s though, the number of keys had generally increased. The oɱvəg of the André-Band-Essé, for example, had sixteen notes, the olòlòŋ twelve, and the ɛ̀ndùm ten (Simon and Noah Messomo 2005: 70). The five-piece ensemble of Nsimi Yetulu documented by the Berlin Phonogrammarchiv played portable instruments with a smaller tonal range more typical for the traditional ongɛd ensemble (Simon and Noah Messomo 2005). While portable instruments are necessarily limited in their tonal range, modern məndzáŋ instruments can easily be extended in their tonal range as they do not need to be carried.

The məndzáŋ I observed in Yaoundé during my fieldwork had an even broader tonal range than those of the André-Band-Essé in the 1980s: the oŋvəg had thirteen or fourteen keys, the olɔ̀lɔ̀ŋ around twenty, the akuda-oŋvəg around fourteen, and the èndùm fourteen to sixteen keys. According to Jules Akoudou, this extension of the tonal range occurred in response to the trend towards interpreting popular songs from other musical genres made popular via radio or records.

The wider tonal range was of great importance for the musical expression of the musicians, as I witnessed in a bar in a suburb of Yaoundé, when məndzáŋ players from Balafon Star were hired to perform on instruments that were not their own. The three məndzáŋ available were significantly smaller than the instruments they usually played: the oŋvəg had ten keys, the olɔ̀lɔ̀ŋ seventeen, and the èndùm nine. The size of the instruments in this case had to do with the financial limitations of the musicians. After the performance the musicians complained about the "bad instruments" with their limited tonal range and lamented that "it's not possible to express oneself properly" (personal conversation with members of Balafon Star, September 2008). A wider range of notes was necessary for aesthetically adequate musical expression; to cover a certain tonal range on the instruments had become part of the concept of an ideal məndzáŋ built for dance music.

Məndzáŋ Dance Music in Yaoundé from the 1980s to the 2000s

Having become an important part of the urban entertainment landscape in the 1970s, məndzáŋ dance music ensembles continued to be present in Yaoundé in the 1980s and 1990s. While bikutsi as a popular music genre rose to wider popularity in Yaoundé and beyond, with groups like Les Vétérans and Les Têtes Brulées and singers such as Ange Ebogo Emerent and Nkodo Sitony (see Chapter 7), məndzáŋ ensembles performed at weddings and other festivities as well as in urban bars. Məndzáŋ ensembles became an integral part of the representation of Cameroonian national culture, in line with the stress on "re-Africanization" or revival and the representation of one's "own" traditions. In the 1980s, one məndzáŋ ensemble was mentioned regularly in the state-owned newspaper: that of Albert Noah Messomo based in the Bastos quarter in Yaoundé. The group performed at locations associated with elite culture and the promotion of Cameroonian music, for example, in the Centre Culturel Français and in the Palais de Congrès in Yaoundé. Despite the attention gained by this one balafon ensemble, məndzáŋ music as a whole continued to have limited prestige, especially compared to popular dance music played by modern music groups. According to the musician Jean-Marie Ahanda, one məndzáŋ ensemble in the 1980s played in a bar close to the popular cabaret Escalier Bar with remarkable success. As opposed to the cabarets, there was no entrance fee to the bars where məndzáŋ were played, a fact that may have added to the perception of məndzáŋ music as being music for the poor: people who could not afford the entrance fee and prices in the cabarets listened to live məndzáŋ music.

In the 1980s and 1990s, məndzáŋ ensembles were not widely recorded or marketed on the ever-growing Cameroonian music market. Instead, there was even some concern that the məndzáŋ tradition was about to disappear. In a newspaper article, a reader stated that the ensembles were becoming rare, even in the villages (Emvana Emiro 1986), and Albert Noah Messomo argued along the same lines in his master's thesis, remarking that the lack of məndzáŋ players was due to living conditions and the rural exodus (Noah Messomo 1980: 98–99; see also Noah Messomo 1995). But məndzáŋ music did not disappear. While during the 1980s and 1990s most attention was focused on the newly established popular music genre bikutsi, after 2000, məndzáŋ ensembles in Yaoundé regained popularity – and two factors appear to have been central to this resurgence: xylophone ensembles were again released on recordings with significant commercial success and məndzáŋ ensembles entered a new performance arena – the urban cabaret.

Since around 2000, məndzáŋ players have gained more media attention, ensembles have been revived, recordings made, and məndzáŋ ensembles have been hired increasingly to play in prestigious cabarets. In general, the instrument is quite popular with Yaoundé's audience. One məndzáŋ player and his ensemble stood out especially in Yaoundé during my fieldwork: that of Akim Kondor, a məndzáŋ player from the district of Lekié in the region Centre who had resided for years in Yaoundé. And two songs became especially popular: 'Faux Complice', released in 2001, and 'Ma yi bon eboan aiwa', released in 2007. These songs in their released versions were recorded and mixed in a professional studio. Other məndzáŋ ensembles that had existed in the 1960s and 1970s were re-established in the 2000s. One such case was the Richard Band de Zoetélé, which was reformed by Bernard Ngbwa. The group released two CDs with re-recordings of pieces from the 1960s.[13] Similarly, the Rocher Jazz Band de Mezesse reformed with original and new members and re-released its songs on two CDs at the turn of the new century. Its leader Ndoua Akame alias "Decrampon" died in 2009. There did exist, nevertheless, a difference between the old məndzáŋ ensembles experiencing a revival and the younger musicians emerging new on the scene: the "revival" bands had a lot of merengue and soukous based pieces in their repertoire while younger musicians such as Akim Kondor were more influenced by bikutsi in establishing their repertoire.

The increased attention given to məndzáŋ apparent in the increased number of commercial recordings went hand in hand with an expansion of venues for məndzáŋ ensemble performances: in the 2000s, they entered the nightclubs and cabarets. As trumpeter Ted Mekoulou stated in an interview, "only now do people pay whole balafon ensembles to play in their nightclub" (Ted Mekoulou, interview, August 22, 2010).[14] During my stays, məndzáŋ ensembles performed regularly in cabarets in Yaoundé. In 2008, a popular location for məndzáŋ performances was a cabaret in the Nkomo quarter in Yaoundé called "Détente". In 2010, the musicians had switched to another cabaret in the Kondengui quarter called "La Couronne", which had opened that year near the popular cabaret "Carrossel" where live bikutsi music was played by a modern dance band. The ensemble playing the venue in both cases was that of Akim Kondor, supported by musicians from Balafon Star. By the time of my visit in November 2012, other məndzáŋ players had taken over after financial disputes. However, the music of both venues was still məndzáŋ music. Other urban bars also had məndzáŋ music, like the "New Martino Bar" in the Elig-Essono quarter, where in 2012 an ensemble played every Sunday afternoon into the night. This ensemble had four boxed xylophones, a m̀bɛ, a nyás, and locally constructed congas. It is evident that məndzáŋ music was showing no sign of disappearing; it had become a flexible musical tradition adapting regularly to new demands and trends in urban musical life.

From Merengue to Bikutsi: An Evening in a Məndzáŋ Cabaret

I will conclude this chapter on məndzáŋ music with a description of a typical evening in a cabaret with a məndzáŋ ensemble. These evenings in "balafon cabarets" are in setting, repertoire, and course of events similar to the cabarets in which modern music groups perform contemporary bikutsi and as such belong to the same domain of urban entertainment. The two locations with məndzáŋ performances I visited most often during my field research were in the Nkomo and Kondengui quarters and were similar to one another in many of their features. The buildings held a large, roofed rectangular room with walls on three sides; the fourth, long side open to an area of compacted earth. There, fast food, like grilled fish, could be bought. The rooms were equipped with plastic tables and chairs, some of which were outside as well; waitresses brought drinks to the seated guests, alcoholic drinks being the rule rather than the exception. People were dressed casually; guests dressed in traditional robes or festive clothes were rare. The public was mixed, half female, half male, and often people sat together in bigger groups.

Inside, along one of the shorter walls, was built an elevated stage where the məndzáŋ ensemble played. An open space between the stage and the tables served as a dance floor. The instruments were amplified, with elevated speakers to the left and right of the stage. The cabaret "La Couronne" in Kondengui also had a wall painting behind the stage showing a məndzáŋ player, a singer, and two dancers on a stage like that in the cabaret itself. In contrast to these məndzáŋ cabarets, those where bikutsi was performed by modern music groups were closed to the street. This was probably due to the necessary control needed to ensure the entrance fee was paid. Məndzáŋ cabarets did not ask for an entrance fee. Apart from this detail they seemed very much alike.

Məndzáŋ ensembles were, when hired for a cabaret on a regular basis, expected to play on weekends, meaning from Friday to Sunday. This regular engagement with a cabaret brought an important benefit for the musicians: a regular income. They were no longer solely dependent on occasional engagements for parties and celebrations, but could – more or less – count on a degree of financial security. But as I witnessed with Balafon Star, this could also bring restraints leading to scheduling problems: an engagement with the cabaret could then collide with other possible jobs, such as weddings, which also took place on weekends. In such cases, the ensemble then tried to play the weddings in the afternoon and continued to the cabaret in the evening.

The ensembles playing in the two locations were the same: the main act was the ensemble of Akim Kondor supported by musicians from Balafon Star. The same moderator led through the evening and the comedian and mvɛd player Balla Pierre, known as Zikoko, also played on all observed evenings. The course of events was therefore quite similar in both bars.

An evening in a cabaret entertained by a məndzáŋ ensemble started around eight or nine o'clock in the evening. In the first part of the evening, often called "prélude", the musicians from Balafon Star played. The pieces performed were usually cover versions of well-known songs of Cameroonian musicians, often older well-known soukous or merengue pieces, such as 'Amu Dze' and 'Elig Effa' by Messi Martin or 'Ma ba Nze' by Anne-Marie

Nzié. The musicians performed medleys that could last up to 40 minutes, playing basic accompanying patterns, but singing different melodies.

Figure 4.3: Full dance floor in the cabaret La Couronne, August 2010. Photograph by Anja Brunner.

A moderator guided the audience through the programme, announced new singers, special dancers or the məndzáŋ ensemble, and introduced people present in the audience. After the prélude, sometime between ten and eleven o'clock, the moderator introduced Zikoko, who then performed for around twenty to thirty minutes. His performance was a collage of mvɛd playing and singing, accompanied by percussion, storytelling with humorous and moral content, and solo dancing. Then the musicians returned to the stage, this time Akim Kondor's headlining ensemble, although the musicians from Balafon Star often helped out. The evening continued as before, with the məndzáŋ playing all night, although the repertoire changed to bikutsi. While the early evening was reserved for slower and softer music genres, as night approached it came time for the faster stamping of bikutsi dance music. Throughout the evening, different singers alternated on stage, primarily members of Balafon Star, but others invited by the ensemble to sing one or two songs as well. Audience members could also join the band on stage to sing a piece. Members of the ensemble provided the response in the call-and-response patterns. Sometimes, gifted dancers from the audience went on stage to present their dancing skills or newly invented dance styles. Music and dancing continued until early in the morning, the dancing getting wilder as the night wore on (and the audience became drunker), and always with bikutsi music (see Figure 4.3).

The instruments used in the cabarets were xylophones built into wooden corpuses with the musicians seated behind; the tuning was (close to) diatonic. There were four məndzáŋ: oŋvəg, olɔ̀lɔ̀ŋ, ɛ̀ndùm, and akuda-oŋvəg on all occasions, accompanied by various percussion instruments, that is, conga-like instruments, usually paired with a rattle and a m̀bɛ. Even when a drum set was included, as in the cabaret "La Couronne" on one evening I was present in 2012 (and probably more often), the congas were played too, sometimes with nyás, and the m̀bɛ was replaced by the big drum on the drum set. Additionally, a slit drum, a ǹkúl, was played in many songs in this performance. When I asked why a drum set had been included, the musicians appeared indifferent. The answer was simply that the "patron", the owner of the cabaret, had wanted a drum set and the ǹkúl. It appears that musical decisions were not always in the hands of the musicians themselves. For them, so it seemed, playing in a cabaret was sometimes less an artistic challenge than a job like any other that brought them an income.

The repertoire included merengue and soukous pieces as well as bikutsi songs. The repertoire varied from early guitar-based bikutsi à la Los Camaroes (see Chapters 2 and 5) to new pop songs such as commercial hits at the time from the singers Lady Ponce or Majoie Aie. People danced frequently, especially later at night. It was probably this dancing atmosphere as well as the free entry that attracted many people and led to ever more such cabarets opening in Yaoundé. The məndzáŋ cabarets came to seriously rival the established cabarets with their popular guitar-based bikutsi performances. It was rumoured in 2010 that owners and patrons of the "Carrossel", one of the most popular bikutsi cabarets in Yaoundé, described the məndzáŋ cabaret "La Couronne" nearby as a "problem" or a "rival", as it was free to enter and had "the same music", albeit performed on məndzáŋ. The situation was described in an online review of Akim Kondor, who at the time played at the balafon cabaret "La Couronne": "So you are on the street where Carrossel is and the cars fighting for parking spots spill out dozens of people at the entrance of another cabaret, La Couronne. The competition of this little neighbour, so they say here, is of the kind that the revellers come to whoop it up there before they move on to the renowned Carrossel".[15] The balafon cabarets thus provided a welcome and cheap opportunity for bikutsi dancing on weekends. In contrast to other bikutsi cabarets with live music by modern dance bands, the məndzáŋ cabarets were less about presenting stardom than about footloose dancing. Additionally, one could dwell on a nostalgic feeling of "traditional" music, a theme that popped up regularly in the accompanying talk of the moderator. While the lower social status of the məndzáŋ remained, in the course of the 2000s, məndzáŋ ensembles had found a niche in urban weekend entertainment and regained much of their former popularity.

* * *

Məndzáŋ music was subject to considerable change in the course of the twentieth century. Rather than sticking to a specific repertoire, məndzáŋ ensembles playing dance music were always up-to-date with the latest dance music trends and adapted these in order to meet the audience's expectations. At the same time, dance music typically played on the məndzáŋ, that is, traditional Beti dances, became a central inspiration for guitarists and other musicians playing and composing modern dance music. Imitating məndzáŋ pieces and sounds on the electric guitar, as will be discussed in the following chapter, was an important musical innovation in the music of Yaoundé's bands in the 1970s. Dance music performed with electric guitars, congas, and so on drew on dance pieces performed by məndzáŋ ensembles and vice versa. The repertoire of məndzáŋ ensembles and modern music groups have long overlapped, sometimes more, sometimes less, and they have had a similar entertainment function – to accompany dancing. Here appears what Motti Regev called "aesthetic cosmopolitanism" in relation to "ethno-national uniqueness": "As a form of ethno-national uniqueness, aesthetic cosmopolitanism comes into being with the institutionalization of contemporary forms of art such as film and pop-rock music as legitimate expressions of such uniqueness" (Regev 2007a: 127). Since the 1960s, music taken from the global pop-rock field has been intrinsic to məndzáŋ playing and to guitar dance music and it has become a central aspect of Beti-Cameroonian music.

Chapter 5

Musical Changes towards Beti Music by Modern Dance Bands in Yaoundé in the 1970s

While the core of the repertoires performed by music groups in Yaoundé in the 1970s continued to be merengue and soukous pieces, increasingly and consciously they adopted elements and songs from the Beti musical tradition into their musical practice. This generation of musicians, presented briefly in Chapter 2, was the pioneering generation in the development of bikutsi as a popular music genre. They introduced Beti musical features into their dance music, a change that had a lasting impact on musical practice in Yaoundé. Looking at selected songs from popular bands at the time, in this chapter I analyse the musical changes occurring in the music of Yaoundé in the late 1970s that made it a modern Beti music. While many features of the then prevalent merengue and rumba repertoire persist, two important changes are introduced: the "balafon guitar" and the wide use of traditional patterns as a rhythmical foundation. Using Motti Regev's theoretical model, the music is the outcome of the merging of two musical fields: local Beti traditions as ethno-national musical practice and the multifaceted field of pop-rock-music of which Cameroonian urban dance music is a part.

Music in Transition: From Rumba to Elak

In the transformation taking place in the repertoire of Yaoundé's modern music groups, some musical characteristics of Afro-Caribbean dance music persisted. The guitar-playing and the rhythmical structures, however, referred increasingly to Beti musical traditions. In the following I discuss these aspects using the song 'Bekono Nga Nkonda' by Messi Martin and Los Camaroes, released on a 7-inch single in 1969, as an example. Alongside the singer and guitarist Messi Martin being presented as the "father" of modern bikutsi, this piece is often cited in Cameroonian popular history as the "first" modern bikutsi song on electric guitars and therefore the starting point for the development leading to bikutsi as an identifiable popular music genre in Cameroon. As Adala Gildo claimed in an article in 1979, "the guitar-balafon style that can be discovered in the theme 'Bekono Nga Nkonda' created by the band Los Camaroes truly marks the launch of a new style in the 'typical' music or Cameroonian variété music" (Gildo 1979).[1] While such ascriptions remain a media construction and divulge more the need for a "starting point" for journalistic historical writing than the definitive "birth" of a new musical tradition or phenomenon, the song 'Bekono Nga Nkonda' was and is an extremely popular piece in Cameroon and a "bikutsi classic". It has certain characteristics that show the transition from rumba to Beti music in guitar-based modern dance music in Yaoundé. As such, it fits perfectly as an example piece to demonstrate the innovations in music towards modern Beti dance music.

The recording of 'Bekono Nga Nkonda' that was eventually ascribed a place in Cameroon music history as the "first bikutsi piece performed by a modern dance band" was not the first recorded version of the song, which was performed by Los Camaroes with their singer and guitarist Messi Martin. The best-known version was released by Sonafric in 1969 (SAF 1501) with the song 'Mengala Maurice' on the B-side, another Messi Martin classic. Previously the song had been released on the label Africambiance (AA 190). And even earlier, the group Los Camaroes had recorded a rumba version merely entitled "Bekono" (AA 188).[2] This rumba version of the song has a similar theme, that is, the pain of being far away from one's mother, but was played entirely in the rumba/soukous tradition. It is also melodically different from the later versions. That said, it was clearly the foundation for the song 'Bekono Nga Nkonda', which was composed as an "elak", a popular Beti dance. Thus, the song that became popular – at the time of release as well as in history – was therefore not a completely new composition but the transformation of an existing song. The song was recorded and re-released numerous times in the following decades, in newly arranged versions as well. The following analysis is based on the recording released by Sonafric in 1969, which was the one that likely became popular in the early 1970s.

Ewondo

chorus:
osug mə bəkóno ngə́ ǹkonda osug mə məmá

chorus
nâ á ngá líg mə etám etám te mɔ́n á mɔ́ ǎ mɔ́n ǹkonda

chorus
nâ á ngá líg mə dzɔgo á ǹdzɔ́ŋ tə mə və́ dzóm ǎ mɔ́n ǹkonda

chorus
aben ayab aben etun ǎ ndómənə dzáma ǎ mɔ́n ǹkonda

chorus
eh ǎ məmá ǹkonda ǹkama amú dzé
yə wə á líg mə etám etám tə é dzóm á mɔ́
eh a bəkóno ngá ǹkonda engóngɔ́l e wə
yə abím ǹdzug yə wə a nɔŋ ě bɔ́ŋ bə́

təgə yén tɔ ǹbɔ̌g ǹbɔg a nə wə a ndá sí eh
eh a pə́pa ǹkonda ǹkama o nə abé ǹnə́m
e wə a bə́lə mə nɔŋ ákǎ ǹkonda amú dzé

yə wə á líg bəkóno ngá ǹkonda étám dzié
o líg məsi mə́ ǹkonda ǹkama engóngɔ́l eh
o líg ákogo ébana ǹkonda étám dzié
eh a pə́pa ǹkonda ǹkama o nə abé ǹnə́m
eh a pə́pa ǹkonda ǹkama amú dzé
yə wə à líg ǹkama ǹkonda ǹkama étám dzié
eh bivindi bí daŋ engóngɔ́l
sə á kig é dzóm yə á mí á vuŋ ai dzɔ́ mú
aben ayab aben etun ǎ ndómənə dzama
yə wə á líg mə etám etám tə é dzóm á mɔ́
mǐ sug mə bəkóno ngá ǹkonda mǐ sug mə məmá eh
nâ á ngá líg mə etám etám tə ai dzam á mɔ́ ǎ mɔ́n ǹkonda

chorus
aben ayab aben etun ǎ mɔ́ngɔ́ nyí ǎ mɔ́n ǹkonda
chorus
yə wə a líg mə dzogo óyɔ́ tə mə və dzóm ǎ mɔ́n ǹkonda

English

chorus:
Send my regards to Mme Bekono Nga Nkonda [Mrs. Bekono married Nkonda], send my regards to my mother

My mother left me all alone, without a child

chorus
My mother abandoned me in broad daylight without giving anything to me, child of Nkonda

chorus
She is not tall, she is not short, my son, child of Nkonda
chorus

Eh, Mama Nkonda Akama, is this friendship?
You leave me alone with nothing
Bekono married Nkonda, what a pity
All the pain you took on you those poor children

None of them stays with you
Eh, Papa Nkonda Akama, what a bad heart
You come to take Aka Nkonda away from me, why?

You leave Bekono married Nkonda all alone
You leave Messi, the son of Nkonda, in misery
You leave Akogo Ebana Nkonda all alone
Eh, Papa Nkonda Nkama, what a bad heart
Eh, Papa Nkonda Nkama, pourquoi
You leave Akama Nkonda Nkama all alone
You leave the beautiful black in the misery
I am not into things like that
He is not tall, he is not short, my son
You leave me all alone without child
Send my regards to Bekono Nga Nkonda, send my regards to my mother
She left me alone, without child, the son of Nkonda

chorus
He is not tall, he is not short, my child, the child of Nkonda
chorus
You went while I was fast asleep, you gave me nothing

chorus	*chorus*
eh bəkóno ngá ǹkonda engóngɔ́l ă mɔ́n ǹkonda	Eh, Bekono Nga Nkonda, what a misery, son of Nkonda

[percussion solo]

eh aben ayab aben etun engóngɔ́l ai wə	Eh, he is not tall, he is not short, my son, what misery for you
ă məsi mə ǹkonda ǹkama engóngɔ́l ai wə	Messi Me Nkonda Nkama, what misery for you
ăbím ǹdzug yə wə á nɔŋ ai biə́m bí	With all the effort those things cost me
sə á kig éngúŋ yə á bá vùŋ ai dzɔ́ mú	I don't support your pride
yə və nə masɔ́ áwɔ́lɔ́ m̀banga a ndómənə dzama	My son, you tell me that you come from Douala
təgə a yén tɔ é dzóm yə á wə ázu mə é dzɔ́ á mɔ́	I don't see any presents and parcels
yə nə́ wə a sɔ́ ákónolinga é dzóm dzí	You come from Akonolinga, you, the thing here
təgə a yén tɔ mfə́g yə á wə a zu mə ai wə́ á mɔ́	You did not keep me anything in the bag
eh məsi mə́ ǹkonda ǹkama engóngɔ́l	Messi Me Nkonda Nkama, what a misery for you
yə wə à kɔ́bɔ mə ebɛ é faná ásŏŋ a ndómənə dzama	You speak to me with a piece of bamboo [toothpick] in your mouth, my son
eh aben ayab aben etun àmú dzé	Eh, he is not tall, he is not short, why?
mǐ sug mə bəkóno ngá ǹkonda mǐ sug mə məmá	Send my regards to Bekono Nga Nkonda, send my regards to my mother
nâ á ngá líg mə etám etám tè. mɔ́n á mɔ́ á mɔ́n ǹkonda	You leave me all alone without child, the son of Nkonda

chorus	*chorus*
aben ayab aben etun ă ndómənə dzama	He is not tall, he is not short, my son
chorus	*chorus*
nâ á ŋgá líg mə mə́ dzogo etám tə mə və́ dzóm ă mɔ́n ǹkonda	You left me in broad daylight, without leaving me anything
chorus	*chorus*
yə wə à líg mə etám etám tə ai dzóm á mvús ă mɔ́n ǹkonda	You leave me alone without anyone behind me
chorus	*chorus*
yə wə à líg mə mə́ dzógo óyɔ́ tə mə və́ dzóm ă mɔ́n ǹkonda	You are gone although I was fast asleep, you gave me nothing, the child Nkonda
chorus	*chorus*
aben ayab aben etun ă ndómənə dzama ă mɔ́n ǹkonda	He is not tall, he is not short, my son, child of Nkonda
chorus	*chorus*
eh bəkóno ngá ǹkonda amú dzé ă mɔ́n ǹkonda	Eh, Bekono Nga Nkonda, why, child of Nkonda
chorus	*chorus*

Figure 5.1: Lyrics of the song 'Bekono Nga Nkonda' by Los Camaroes in Ewondo and English. Transcribed from the recording and translated into French by Jules Akoudou, translated into English by Anja Brunner. I thank Olivier Moussa Loumpata and Prof. Dr Louis Martin Onguene Essono for their help with the Ewondo orthography.

In terms of its contents and lyrics, the song was in line with others of the time, dealing with daily family or relationship issues. In this case, the singer Messi Martin chose to address a rather personal topic. 'Bekono Nga Nkonda' literally means "Bekono married Nkonda". Bekono was the maiden name of a woman who married a man called Nkonda. As Nkonda was Messi Martin's father's name, the song can be interpreted as the story of his mother. In the lyrics, Messi Martin clearly cites his own childhood, which he spent mostly without his father (see Figure 5.1): the repeated line of the chorus is "Send my regards to Mrs. Bekono nga Nkonda, my mother". The core message of the songs seems fairly obvious and simple: one should not leave a mother with her children alone; she needs support and help; and whoever abandons a mother is morally disreputable. The song 'Bekono Nga Nkonda' lasts 4:30 minutes at a tempo of about 132 bpm. It is thus in both length and tempo comparable with Beti dances and merengue and rumba songs, the latter genres having tempos between 120 and 140 bpm, Beti dances on guitar from around 130 to 150 bpm. The instruments used in the song also align with the common instrumentation of modern music groups with guitars, a bass guitar, congas, and bells. The vocals are provided by a solo voice, sung by Messi Martin, and a chorus in two voices.

The main structure of the song corresponds to the then common composition of dance songs as described in Chapter 2. Starting with a guitar intro at the length of one such phrase, all the other instruments join in simultaneously with a vocal "hey" (see transcription in Figure 5.2). The intro on the accompanying guitar is already the phrase that is further repeated throughout the song without variation (see third line in the score in Figure 5.2). After two more bars during which all instruments introduce their basic patterns, a call-and-response part by choral and solo singers follows, followed further by a solo verse and again a call-and-response part. With a sound like "drrrr", that Beti singers often use to indicate a change or stop in the music to accompanying musicians (usually descending slightly in pitch), the solo singer introduces a break that lasts about 20 seconds, during which only the congas and the bells continue. An instrumental interlude and again a solo verse follow. The song ends after a repeated call-and-response part by a jointly sung exclamation in a proximate triad-chord.

The song is built on short patterns of 24 pulses that are repeated throughout the song with some variations. The beginning of the song is shown in a transcription in Figure 5.2. I decided on standard score notation in order to make the transcription readable to as many readers as possible. The 24/8 measure used shows the length of the phrases of the song and illustrates the underlying pulse pattern; one eight note refers to one pulse and the length of the pattern corresponds to one bar. The main beat divides the basic 24-pulse pattern into eight parts of three pulses each (see, for example, the accompanying guitar and bass in the transcription), sometimes realized in patterns of six pulses (see bells and congas). This ternary division of the beat is common in much Beti dance music. The beat provides the main orientation for the accompanying dance steps. Compared to bikutsi music at the time of my research, where it was common to mark the beat with the bass drum or an electronic equivalent, in 1970s guitar-based Beti music, the main dance beat is seldom clearly realized on a distinguishable instrument and is therefore hard to find for non-initiates. This is also the case in the song 'Bekono Nga Nkonda'. The main beat orientation and the basic rhythmic foundation of the "elak" dance in the song here is in the conga pattern and the rattle, as will be discussed in detail below. When notated in Western notation, the most useful time is not the 4/4 time used for Congolese or Latin American-derived dance music, but 12/8 or 24/8 time. As some basic patterns, here the bell, count fewer pulses, a notation in 6/8 would also be possible and is also used for Beti dance music (see, e.g., Touré 2005: 35–41).

In short, the structure of the song 'Bekono Nga Nkonda' is:

guitar introduction (bar 1), "hey!"
instrumental intro (bars 2–3)
call-and-response part (bars 4–10)
solo verse (bars 11–29)
call-and-response part (bars 30–36)
percussion solo (bars 37–43)
instrumental interlude (bars 44–48)
solo verse (bars 49–61)
call-and-response part (bars 62–74)

The structure of the song 'Bekono Nga Nkonda' is similar to contemporary merengue and soukous pieces. While transcribed as following one another, the parts in fact overlap in their opening and closing motifs. For example, the solo voice takes up the choral melody when passing over to the chorus part; the last bar of the solo part can then also be seen as already belonging to the call-and-response part. The melodic phrases, both by the choral and the solo voices, seem to be typical for the time. In the call-and-response section, the choral phrase starts and provides the basis, with the solo voice sounding more like it is interjecting in the choral parts rather than interacting with them. The solo melody is more flexible in its melodic organization and seems to improvise slightly in order to meet the necessities of the tonal language. That said, according to linguist Louis Martin Onguene Essono, the language tones can and frequently are altered to fit the melody (personal communication, November 2012). One feature of the singing style is especially striking: the sound of "éééé" at the end of some phrases, in this song primarily in the chorus. This can be observed in many Beti songs and is a characteristic of Beti singing used to underline and enforce the message as well as to indicate the end of the phrase. Neither the solo and the chorus melodies nor the guitar patterns exceed an octave in their tonal range. The vocal melodies consist mainly of half and whole steps; the choral parts are harmonized in thirds. The song is played on the recording in C major. As for its harmonic structure, the song seems to circulate around the tones C and G, also possibly interpreted as tonic-dominant progression; all vocal melodic phrases end on G; the guitar patterns circle around C. This harmonic structure points again to the persisting relevance of the merengue and soukous tradition in which this piece is embedded; other elements clearly indicate the musical changes in progress at the time. One of the main features of this process was the imitation of məndzáŋ playing by the guitar. Another was the conscious dancing of traditional dance steps to music played on modern instruments. Both aspects will be discussed in detail, whereby I continue to use the song 'Bekono Nga Nkonda' as an example.

Voice
Voice
Tempo: 133 bpm (beat: 3 pulses)
Electric Guitar
Electric Guitar
Electric Bass
Slap
Congas
Vo.
hey!
Vo.
hey!
El. Guit.
El. Guit.
El. B.
Sla.
Co.

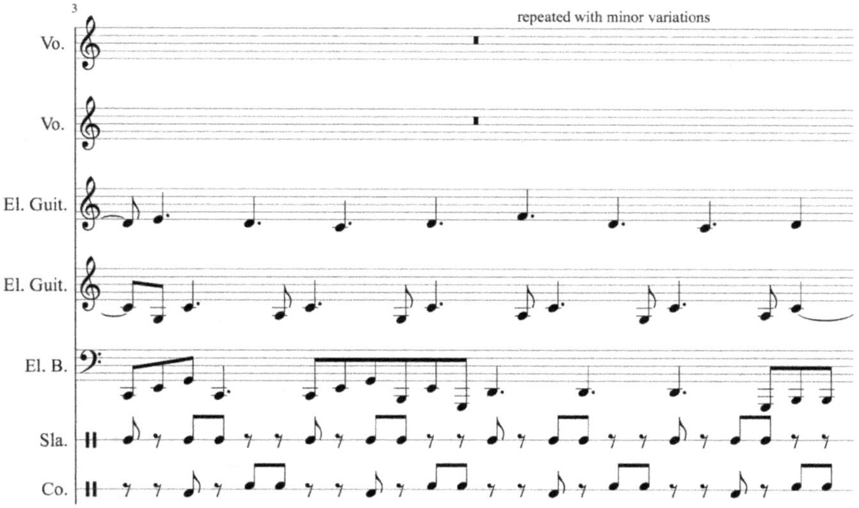
3
repeated with minor variations
Vo.
Vo.
El. Guit.
El. Guit.
El. B.
Sla.
Co.

4
Vo.
Vo.
El. Guit.
El. Guit.
El. B.
Sla.
Co.

5
basic chorus voice
Vo.
Vo.
El. Guit.
El. Guit.
El. B.
Sla.
Co.
6
solo voice
Vo.
Vo.
El. Guit.
El. Guit.
El. B.
Sla.
Co.

Figure 5.2: Transcription (in part) of the song 'Bekono Nga Nkonda' (SAF 1501, Sonafric) by Los Camaroes. Tempo: 132 bpm.

The "Balafon Guitar": The Role of Sound Imitation

The main innovation attributed to Messi Martin that contributed to him being inscribed as the "father" of guitar-based bikutsi in Cameroonian music history was his move to imitate xylophone playing on the electric guitar. It is common knowledge in Cameroon that Messi Martin used a piece of sponge or folded paper to obtain the sound of a məndzáŋ on the electric guitar. He threaded the material between the strings, at the edge of the corpus, right at the bridge. This gives the guitar a slightly muted and absorbed sound, described in French by Mvondo Ateba Albert, called Atebass, as "son sec", as a "dry sound" (Mvondo Ateba Albert, interview, October 30, 2012), perceived to be similar to the sound of the local Beti məndzáŋ, if not "balafon" music in general. The guitar-sound of Messi Martin and Los Camaroes came to be known, consequently, as "balafon guitar".

The move to imitate a xylophone on the electric guitar is commonly traced simply to musicians being inspired when listening to Beti xylophone music. Məndzáŋ ensembles were widespread in the 1960s as popular urban entertainment, they were recorded and played on the radio, and they had entered Christian religious contexts. Being of Beti background himself, Messi Martin was probably familiar with this xylophone music, but nevertheless, it might also have been Congolese dance music that inspired Messi Martin: a trend to draw inspiration from xylophone players had long been on the agenda among Congolese dance music musicians in the 1960s (cf. Mukuna 2001: 292). The guitarist of Los Camaroes at the time 'Bekono Nga Nkonda' was composed, Mbambo Simon alias Johnny Cosmos, remembered that the idea of preparing the guitar came to the group while watching a Congolese dance music group during a concert in Chad. Los Camaroes had been invited to play at a festival in the Chadian capital of N'Djamena, not far from the group's hometown of Maroua. Watching a group from the Democratic Republic of the Congo perform, Mbambo Simon and his bandmates observed the guitarist fixing something to the guitar to create a different, xylophone-like sound. Messi Martin started to experiment and after a while succeeded in producing a sound akin to the məndzáŋ (Mbambo Simon, interview, August 29, 2008).

Although sometimes mentioned as being a main feature of the song 'Bekono Nga Nkonda' and an important reason for the song's success as the "first" bikutsi song, I had difficulty identifying the guitars in the recordings available as sounding like a xylophone. Listening to the song with musicians in Yaoundé and then discussing the "balafon guitar" phenomenon, I could confirm this observation: in the two recordings released by Sonafric and Africambiance, Los Camaroes had not used the muted guitar. The special sound can, however, be heard in other songs recorded in the 1970s, for example Los Camaroes' 'Messi Mbala' and Aloa Javis et Les Idoles' 'Subugu Mu'. The practice might have been introduced later, after the early recordings of 'Bekono Nga Nkonda', or it was used for live performances, but not on the recordings. That said, the xylophone is still evoked in the song 'Bekono Nga Nkonda', but on a different level, namely in the guitar patterns and the rhythmic foundation.

The "Balafon Guitar": Guitar Patterns

As discussed in the previous chapter, all the instruments in a məndzáŋ ensemble have an equivalent in a modern guitar-based band. In the logic of a məndzáŋ ensemble, the lead guitar is the olɔ̀lɔ̀ŋ, the "solo" voice, the accompanying guitar is the oŋvəg, and the bass guitar replaces (to some extent) the èndùm. The role of the m̀bɛ is transferred to the congas, while additional percussion, like bells and rattles, remains unchanged. In later years, the drum set takes over the role of the m̀bɛ. When listening to 'Bekono Nga Nkonda' with bass guitarist Atebass, he confirmed these roles and compared the playing of the rhythmic guitar to a xylophone: "If he took a balafon, he would play this phrase with the balafon" (Mvondo Ateba Albert, interview, October 30, 2012). He continued that the fourth xylophone, the akuda-oŋvəg, would be a guitar "mi-solo" as Congolese musicians used it, but this has not taken hold in Cameroonian guitar music. The accompanying guitar line as shown in the transcription (see Figure 5.2) thus can be interpreted as the oŋvəg, the one providing the basis for the song. It provides a 24-pulse pattern that is maintained throughout the song and "holds the song" (*fr.*: "tient la chanson"), as Atebass put it. The second guitar line, the solo guitar, is not continuous throughout the song, but stops when the vocals start and only joins in again at the end of the song, when it is heard simultaneously with the singing. This correlates with the function of the olɔ̀lɔ̀ŋ as replacing or supporting the melodic lines of the song. In the relation of the solo pattern to the accompanying guitar, an interlocking structure becomes obvious: the solo guitar notes fall not on, but between the accents of the accompanying pattern. In contrast to the guitar playing in merengue and soukous pieces, this interlocking relation of the patterns points to the imitation of məndzáŋ playing. In contrast to the solo and rhythmic guitar patterns, the bass line does not relate much to the bass xylophone èndùm. Rather, it stays in line with typical bass playing in contemporary guitar-based dance music, playing typical arpeggiated tri-ads common in Congolese modern music. This might have to do with the fact that at the time, the ɛ̀ndùm did not yet have the adequate tonal range. Its role was still less melodic than the bass line in 'Bekono Nga Nkonda'. But even with the bass remaining in the Afro-Caribbean tradition, it is clear that a main feature of Beti music as played by modern dance bands was the adoption of a xylophone-like guitar-playing style, sometimes in its sound but even more so in the adoption of playing patterns and rhythms. Los Camaroes and other modern dance bands in Yaoundé aimed at imitating məndzáŋ play-ing, thereby – returning to Regev's terminology – creating an ethno-national musical practice using the available elements of the global field of pop-rock.

'Bekono Nga Nkonda' as an Elak Piece

Besides the "balafon guitar", the rhythmical foundation has been identified as being a significant marker in the shift towards Beti traditions in modern guitar-based music in Yaoundé. In contrast to the binary rhythmic foundation of merengue and soukous pieces, songs using rhythmic foundations of Beti dances, like 'Bekono Nga Nkonda', typically make use of ternary subdivi-sion of the main dance beat. Thus, one of the main changes that led the way to bikutsi becoming a popular music genre is an increasing turn to music in which the beat is divided into three pulses. The specific rhythm of 'Bekono Nga Nkonda' is one of the features behind its identification as the "first mod-ern bikutsi song". This rhythm was described on the record as being the Beti dance genre elak.

Elak is a popular dance genre throughout the region and was at least since the late 1960s increasingly being used in guitar-based music. Gerhard Kubik described it as "local dance in a fast 12-pulse rhythm" that was played by modern xylophone ensembles (Kubik 2001: 877). Traditionally, elak is a dance genre performed by adolescents for entertainment purposes. In nightly gatherings, boys and girls dance together, for fun, entertainment, and as a form of playful interaction between the sexes. There is no need for specially trained dancers; everybody is allowed to dance elak. A detailed description of the dance elak is given by Agnès Marie Mbala épouse Nkili in her work on bikutsi (Mbala 1985: 71–78). She describes elak as being accompanied by two mìǹkúl, that is, Beti slit-drums, and danced in a big open space. Up to several dozen dancers form a big circle. One male dancer enters the circle, takes up the typical hand clapping of elak and starts singing. The others join in for the chorus. After performing a few dance steps, he chooses a girl out of the circle to be his dancing partner. The couple then dances together in the circle for a while. Before returning to the circle they choose two new dancers, the boy a girl and the girl a boy, who enter the circle and dance together.

Like the improvisation of lyrics in female bikutsi songs described in Chapter 3, elak also allows for the spontaneous expression of thoughts and opinions in song. As bikutsi is the space for female criticism, elak can be seen as the same space for the youth to express themselves. "Freed of social constraints in the form of the oppressive superego of adulthood, with its burdens of the forbidden and the taboo, limiting the aspirations of the adolescents, the youth express by way of these songs without scruples their feelings and their ambitions" (Mbala 1985: 75).[3] Elak dances provide among other things a forum for ironic comments and complaints about the rules imposed by elders, the behaviour and authority of mothers-in-law, or the Christian church and its imprint on society, according to Mbala.

Elak was not approved of by Catholic missionaries due to its dancing style. The dance as performed by the couples in the centre of the circle could include bawdy and obscene gestures and movements: "Two young people dedicate themselves occasionally to expressive and revealing gestures that every now and then came close to being salacious. They often imitated situations of their amorous adventures" (Mbala 1985: 73).[4] Possibly, it was elak that led Philippe Laburthe-Tolra to say of the dances of the Mvele, a Beti group, that "[t]here is no question that certain dances had intentional sensual import" (Laburthe-Tolra 1977: 699).[5] This sexual aspect in elak dancing led the first Christian missionaries in Cameroon to forbid their followers this dance, which the youth duly ignored. Writing in the early 1980s, Mbala found that elak performances were nevertheless clearly becoming less common as the youth were turning increasingly towards other music trends like disco and Afro-Cuban dance music for entertainment (Mbala 1985: 77). Mbala might have been right concerning elak performances organized as large village parties with adolescents as their main audience. Elak itself, as a dance genre, however, had by that time been adopted as a dance to be performed with xylophone ensembles and modern dance bands in urban settings.

Pieces designated as elak are built on 12-pulse patterns and are characterized by a time-line pattern. It is the five-stroke time-line pattern described for example by Gerhard Kubik (Kubik 2010: 55–58), that provides five strokes within the 12-pulse pattern. The beat relation common for elak is illustrated in Figure 5.3. When clapped, as is very often the case in elak performances, most often only the first part is realized (see Figure 5.4). During my field research in Yaoundé I did not hear any elak pieces accompanied by other typical time-line instruments like bells. Hand clapping was the main medium for realizing the (half) time-line pattern of elak. When the professional drummer Abanda Man Ekan played elak on the drum set, he played the time-line pattern on the hi-hat while the beat was realized on the bass drum. Additionally, he played a part on the snare drum, as shown in Figure 5.5. Therein the second stroke on the snare drum could be slightly before the pulse (off-pulse).

Beti dance music includes many more dances than the elak, such as the mbali (or *ewonga* in the southern parts of the area inhabited by Beti), which is similar to the elak. Musicians described it as being "in the same family". It is faster than elak, at around 200 bpm, but has the same time-line pattern. The dance movements accompanying mbali are highly acrobatic and physically demanding of the dancers (cf. Mbala 1985: 77–78) and it is sometimes compared to the hip-hop derived break-dance. Mbali is commonly accompanied by mìnkúl, m̀bɛ, and a metal plate and it is mainly danced in the region Centre (Jules Akoudou, personal communication, November 2012). But not all Beti dances are time-line based: the women's bikutsi, for example, which finds its rhythmical foundation in the constant stamping of the feet and the hand clapping as well as in the relation to melody accents. The same can be said for the dance koé, which is usually accompanied by mìnkúl.

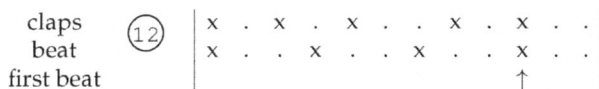

```
claps      (12)  | x . x . x . . x . x . . |
beat             | x . . x . . x . . x . . |
first beat       |                  ↑      |
```

Figure 5.3: Basic elak rhythmic formula: relation to beat.

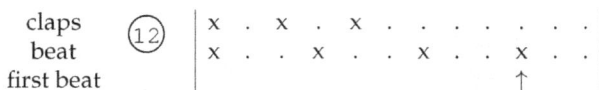

```
claps      (12)  | x . x . x . . . . . . . |
beat             | x . . x . . x . . x . . |
first beat       |                  ↑      |
```

Figure 5.4: Elak formula as commonly realized by hand clapping.

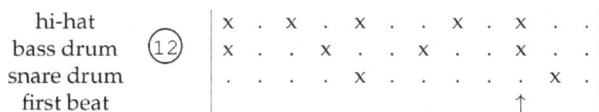

```
hi-hat           | x . x . x . . x . x . . |
bass drum  (12)  | x . . x . . x . . x . . |
snare drum       | . . . . x . . . . . x . |
first beat       |                  ↑      |
```

Figure 5.5: Elak formula on a drum set, as played by the professional drummer Abanda Man Ekan.

The five-stroke time-line pattern used in elak is neither unique to this dance nor to Beti music; it can also be found in neighbouring regions as well as in other, more distant regions of Sub-Saharan Africa. Kubik observed it in the neighbouring Bassa region, where it also starts with three strokes, and the dancer's steps are also similar (Kubik 2010: 64). The pattern is also used – even reproduced in hand clapping – in different songs documented in the Arc Musica archive founded by Joachim Oelsner, for example in songs of the Douala. The elak pattern, then, is a regionally common dance that is known under different names elsewhere. The pattern itself had already been in use in modern dance music in Cameroon before 'Bekono Nga Nkonda'. Mbambo Simon, the guitarist of Los Camaroes nicknamed Johnny Cosmos, used the term *bolobo* when describing the rhythm as it is played in 'Bekono Nga Nkonda' (Mbambo Simon, interview, August 29, 2008). The trumpeter and composer Ted Mekoulou said that this same structure was called bolobo in the Littoral, the region around Douala (Ted Mekoulou, interview, August 22, 2010). In the book *Secrets de basse africaine*, aimed at introducing bass players to African rhythms, bolobo is described as "one of the most common folklore styles in the coastal regions in Cameroon" and notated as a ternary rhythm in 6/8 time (Touré 2005: 28). Cheramy de la Capitale had already played bolobo in the 1960s, according to Mbambo Simon, and it was therefore nothing new to guitar-based music. Both the five-stroke time-line pattern and the three-stroke hand clapping typical for elak thus not only existed among other ethnic groups in Cameroon but had already found its way into (electric) guitar-based music by the 1970s. Together with the obvious references to Beti xylophone music in repertoire, structure and sound, and in describing the song as "elak en langue ewondo", the musicians clearly intended to position their music as being part of a Beti musical tradition.

What, then, makes the song 'Bekono Nga Nkonda' an elak piece? The five-stroke time-line pattern is not clearly realized, nor is the hand-clapping part. The bells play a different pattern more reminiscent of merengue pieces. Nevertheless, Beti people recognize the song as elak, and many immediately start clapping the typical three-stroke rhythm when listening to the song. When I asked musicians about what makes the song elak, the answer was always the same: the elak pattern could be found in the conga pattern. Mvondo Ateba Albert explained that the conga player "holds the base of the percussion; everybody is hooked on him. If he goes out of time, everybody will go out of time" (Mvondo Ateba Albert, personal conversation, November 13, 2012). As the congas on the recording were difficult to detect, I worked with the conga player and percussionist Jules Akoudou in Yaoundé in order to transcribe the conga pattern. Akoudou had no difficulty reproducing the conga pattern in the song, including the variations in the conga solo part. The pattern used in the song 'Bekono Nga Nkonda' and played by Akoudou is shown in Figure 5.6 in its most basic version. The main beat is not distinctly realized on the two congas, but Jules Akoudou sometimes added it in more complex versions as a muffled, soft stroke in the middle of one of the drums.

```
      main beat            | .   x   .   .   x   .   .   x   .   .   x   . |
high pitch, open tone (12) | .   .   x   x   .   .   .   (x) x   x   .   . |
 low pitch, open tone      | x   .   .   .   .   x   .   .   .   .   .   . |
```

Figure 5.6: Basic conga pattern used in 'Bekono Nga Nkonda', as performed by percussionist Jules Akoudou. The transcription begins at the first note of the conga pattern, not on one of the dance beats.

In terms of the beat position, the melodic accents in məndzáŋ playing often fall off-beat. When I tried to clap the beat to pieces without a clearly audible beat, I was often corrected by the musicians, as I instinctively used the main accents I heard in the melody. The main beat was instead just before or just after these accents. While in later bikutsi pieces played by modern dance bands, especially since the 1980s after the introduction of drum sets to the ensembles, the main beat is clearly marked by the bass drum, this was not the case in the early 1970s. Locating the beat, then, became an immediate challenge, especially because of the risk of misinterpreting the beat structure by only listening (Kubik 2004: 78). After having worked with different musicians on the song 'Bekono Nga Nkonda', it became clear that the main beat of the piece is in the bell pattern, supported by the bass line.

As for the rhythmic structure, the tension created by ternary vs. binary patterns needs to be highlighted, especially in the guitar patterns. While the solo guitar line is a 24-pulse pattern comprising six beats subdivided by four pulses (see the fourth line in transcription in Figure 5.2), the accompanying guitar line is a 24-pulse pattern with eight beats subdivided by three pulses (see third line in transcription in Figure 5.2), similar to the main dance beat. The other instruments, the bells, congas, and the bass, also divide the beat by three. Compared to rumba, soukous, and merengue pieces with essentially binary structures, therefore, the song combines a ternary and a binary structure, whereby the ternary is the main anchor. Both guitar patterns fall off-beat, with their accents on the pulses between two beats, while the main bass notes fall on-beat and provide orientation for the dancers.

'Bekono Nga Nkonda' was not the only song played and recorded in the early 1970s by modern dance bands and circumscribed on the record sleeve as being elak. Los Camaroes, for example, also had the song 'Messi Mbala' in their repertoire, which they described as "elak, chanté en langue Ewondo" on the record. The song 'Chérie Marie' by Mama Ohandja, described as being "elak" on the record, even used the typical clapping that was realized clearly on the bass drum throughout the song while the rattle played on all pulses. Aloa Javis released the elak songs 'Subugu Mu' in 1974 and 'Originale Edin Bondo Be Sukulu' in 1976. These pieces point directly to the transformations taking place in the 1970s in music played by modern dance bands in Yaoundé that were primarily a change in rhythmic foundation with a turn towards a popular traditional dance genre as well as the imitation of xylophone ensembles. It should be clearly stated, however, that this was not a one-to-one transformation of xylophone pieces to guitars. Məndzáŋ music was instead used as a conscious form of inspiration that was then reflected in a guitar-based music that was recognizable as Beti music. While the innovation of producing the sound of a xylophone on the guitar was of some relevance, the rhythmical adaptations of Beti dance music were of much more importance for its identification as Beti music. Further, as will be shown in the next section, the denomination of the pieces using Beti names was of immediate relevance in categorizing it as modern Beti music. It should be added at this point that Beti musical traditions were of course not only present in dance music performed in Yaoundé. Other music groups also had the occasional Beti music piece in their repertoire, such as for example the jazz musician Manu Dibango, who in the 1970s was already popular for his song 'Soul Makossa' and recorded the song 'Mouvement Ewondo' based on Beti music probably in 1976. Within the general trend to adapt and transform aspects of various local music traditions, Beti music simply came into focus.

The music itself remained based to a large extent on a merengue and soukous foundation, and these genres remained dominant in the repertoire throughout the 1970s. The mentioned songs, drawing on Beti musical traditions, were part of the increasing interest in Beti musical elements in "modern" Yaoundé music, leading finally to the establishment of bikutsi as an identifiable popular music genre some years later, even though the songs were at the time not – at least not in a widespread way – labelled "bikutsi". This denomination only emerged in the early 1980s, when people engaged in the media and music market increasingly started to use the term "bikutsi" to refer to Beti guitar-based music in general (see Chapter 6). The elak pieces of the 1970s only became bikutsi songs retrospectively, with elak becoming one of numerous dances that could be included under the umbrella "bikutsi". This is how 'Bekono Nga Nkonda' came to be classified as the first "bikutsi" song.

Bikutsi in Music "Made in Yaoundé"

In the 1970s, bikutsi was still seen as a dance genre like elak and not as a superordinate concept. As such, the term also appeared in descriptions of guitar-based music in Yaoundé for songs that are reminiscent of the women's tradition of bikutsi. Like with elak, there were pieces entitled "bikutsi chanté en Ewondo" on the records. One of them was the song 'Mado', released on a single in 1971 by musician Patrice Emery Akono. The shift in the symbolic classification system concerning Beti music and the rise of the term "bikutsi" as a superordinate concept becomes obvious in an incident in 1990 wherein this song had an important role. Patrice Emery Akono visited the offices of the *Cameroon Tribune* and challenged the dominant narrative that had emerged that 'Bekono Nga Nkonda' was the "first" bikutsi song. According to the newspaper article that reported the incident, the musician claimed that he had been the first to have played "modern bikutsi" (Owona 1990d). He presented his single released in 1971 to the journalists which included the song 'Mado'. Its denomination as "bikutsi", according to the musician, made him the first to have played bikutsi, the song 'Bekono Nga Nkonda' in truth being elak. The journalist reporting on the incident, Roger Owona, did not hide his amusement and quoted a singer who defined bikutsi as "a term that designates the collectivity of Beti rhythms: bol, ékan, ékomot, metsion, olamtsa, koé and even élak, etc. The list is not complete. These rhythms have one common denominator: the pounding of the earth by the dancers" (Owona 1990d).[6] Thus, the journalist continued, bikutsi is a generic term. The journalist conceded that Akono merely was the first to have written the word "bikutsi" on a record. What becomes clear in this incident that was still remembered by musicians almost two decades later when I did my research, is not only the stable historical role of 'Bekono Nga Nkonda' and Messi Martin in the medialized history of bikutsi music, but also the process of establishing bikutsi as a generic term for Beti music performed by modern music groups. While in the early 1970s bikutsi was still one of many Beti dance genres that inspired musicians and as such was put on records as a form of classification, by the 1980s the term had come to be widely used as a general denominator for a specific musical genre played on modern instruments. Of relevance in this process was not only the increasing turn towards Beti music in general by modern musicians, but also that bikutsi itself – in its narrower sense – was played and integrated into the repertoire of music "made in Yaoundé".

Ewondo	English
ǹnóm á dzǎ ǹgál á dzǎ zamata zamata a kuí	The husband eats, the wife eats, the big disorder arrives
chorus:	
ndə mə ayi *wú ndə́ mə ayi* bɔ yá eh	*Will I die? What will I do*
bə́bə́lá nǎ ǹnóm elɛ́ ǹgál elɛ́ zamata zamata ayi kuí	The husband has the drinking glass, the wife has the drinking glass, the big disorder settles in
chorus	
bə́bə́lá nə á ǹnóm elɛ́ ǹgál ìlɛ́ zamata zamata á nə̀ oh	The husband holds the drinking glass, the wife holds the drinking glass, the big chaos, my mother
chorus	
bə́bə́lá nə á ǹnóm elɛ́ ǹgál ìlɛ́ zamata zamata á nə̀ oh	The husband holds the drinking glass, the wife holds the drinking glass, the big chaos, my mother
chorus	
[...]	[...]
eh ngɔ̌ mə mén eh dzí bén mə ayi eh	I am sorry for myself, who will remember me
chorus	
oh zə́ m̀fə́ á ndə́ oh zə́ m̀fə́ á dzǎl eh á ǹnóm]	Who else in the house, who else in the village, my mother
chorus	
oh ǹgál elɛ́ ǹnóm elɛ́ zamata zamata ayi kuí	The husband holds the drinking glass, the wife holds the drinking glass, the big disorder will come
chorus [repeated]	[choir repeated]
[instrumental solo]	[instrumental solo]
ǹnóm elɛ́ ǹgál elɛ́ dùm ayi kù e á nə̌	The husband holds the drinking glass, the wife holds the drinking glass, a big miracle will come
chorus	
bə́bə́lá ǹgál ǹkɔ̌ ǹnóm ǹkɔ̌ zamata zamata ayi kuí	The husband holds the palmtree trunk, the wife holds the palmtree trunk, the big disorder will come
chorus	
ǹgál ǹtɔ́g ǹnóm ǹtɔ́g zàmàtà zàmàtà ékwé:]	The wife wears a hat, the husband wears a hat, the big disorder will come
chorus	
ngɔ mə mén eh dzé bén mə ayi eh a nə	I am sorry for myself, who will remember me, my mother

Figure 5.7: Lyrics of the song 'Zanta Akui' by Elamau et son orchestre Les Grands Esprits in Ewondo and English. Transcribed from the recording and translated into French by Jules Akoudou, translated into English by Anja Brunner. I thank Olivier Moussa Loumpata and Prof. Dr Louis Martin Onguene Essono for their help with the Ewondo orthography.

Besides Patrice Emery Akono's 'Mado', other songs were labelled "bikutsi" on their recordings in the early 1970s: 'Sogolo befam' by Gaston Olinga and Echo Jazz de la Capitale released in 1975; 'Eding Bongo Be Sikulu' by Los Camaroes and 'Zanta Akui' by Elamau et son orchestre Les Grands Esprits, both released in the early 1970s and both described as "bikutsi chanté en Ewondo" on the records. The song 'Zanta Akui' is a good example of the features that became common to all music "made in Yaoundé" in the 1970s. The song starts with a short guitar intro, after which all instruments join in together. The instrumentation includes rhythm electric guitar, solo electric guitar, electric bass, congas, and rattle; a solo singer alternates with a two-voice male choir. The guitar lines resemble xylophone playing, with a continuous accompanying pattern throughout the song, over which a solo line is played that varies slightly. While the choir repeats the same lyrics with no change in melody, the solo melody is altered when needed, in accordance with the changing lyrics. The solo melodic phrases as well as the choir part have a length of 24 pulses, divided into eight beats; the rhythmical foundation is therefore ternary, as is common. In contrast to 'Bekono Nga Nkonda', the continuous beat is clearly realized in this song; it is best heard in the rattle pattern. The double-beat is also further realized on the lower conga drum. The tempo is faster than merengue/soukous or elak pieces at around 148 bpm.

Three aspects point at women's bikutsi pieces as described in Chapter 3. The first is the alternating short melodic phrases of solo and choir that are also widely used in the female tradition. The song does not provide a verse-refrain structure. Second, the content is similar: women's bikutsi songs are frequently about marriage and partnership problems, and in 'Zanta Akui' the singer describes a marriage or partnership that gets into a state of disorder when the couple argues about rights and power and the hierarchy of traditional roles are ignored (see lyrics in Figure 5.7). It is thus a piece of strong moral advice to maintain traditional gender roles. While 'Zanta Akui' is written on the record, the phrase in Ewondo is "zamata ay kui", which means something like "the disorder arrives". Thirdly, there is the clearly marked beat. The rattle replaces the typical on-beat hand-clapping accompaniment typical of women's song-and-dance pieces. This steady beat, carried out on the bass drum in pieces which use a drum set, is ubiquitous in later pieces in the popular music genre bikutsi. In 'Zanta Akui', it is mainly played by the rattle, supported by the conga pattern (see Figure 5.8).

```
main beat (rattle)          x  .  .  x  .  .  x  .  .  x  .  .
high pitch, open tone  (12)  .  .  x  x  .  .  .  .  .  .  .  x
low pitch, open tone        x  .  .  .  .  .  x  .  .  .  .  .

main beat (rattle)          x  .  .  x  .  .  x  .  .  x  .  .
high pitch, open tone  (12)  .  .  x  x  .  .  .  x  x  x  x  x
low pitch, open tone        x  .  .  .  .  .  x  .  .  .  .  .
```

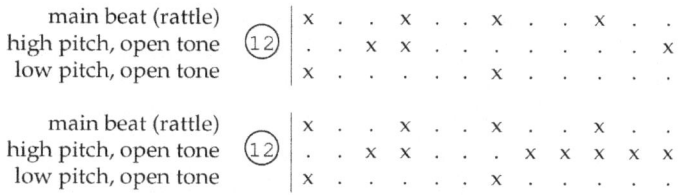

Figure 5.8: Conga patterns played alternately in 'Zanta Akui', transcribed from the recording by Anja Brunner.

In the song 'Sogolo Befam' from 1975,[7] sung by Gaston Olinga, the inspiration taken from women's bikutsi songs is even more evident. Again starting with a short instrumental introduction, the song uses short solo melodies answered by a uniform choral phrase sung by three voices. The instrumentation is as described above, but includes brass accents every now and then and a drum set. In the structure of the song, a first part with the melody in the vocals is followed by an instrumental part where the solo guitar takes over the solo vocal melody; the rhythm guitar continues its pattern. In the next part the guitars are restrained, only one guitar tone marks every second main dance beat. Instead, the solo and choral vocal alteration recommences, with the beat clearly realized by wooden sticks or hand clapping (not clearly audible on the recording) and the conga pattern. This reduction of the instrumentation to the *kób* (hand clapping) as the main accompaniment to the vocals clearly cites the women's bikutsi tradition. This part lasts around 1:30 minutes; the song then ends with an instrumental finish. Besides the kób as a feature pointing to women's bikutsi songs, at one point the singer also uses the typical cry in women's bikutsi, the oyə́ŋá. The basic pattern of the song is one of 18 (or 36) pulses, and this phrase length is used for an ambiguity concerning the beat. In the first part of the song, the binary feeling predominates; in the part with the clearly realized hand-clapping beat and reduced instrumentation the audible beat changes to be clearly ternary; the tempo is around 140 bpm.

In short, these songs of the 1970s entitled "bikutsi" clearly show features that point to women's bikutsi songs: a steady marked beat, subdivided triply, with similar content, short vocal phrases in solo and choir, and a fast tempo of at least 140 bpm. Although the differences between bikutsi and elak pieces might not be easily defined, in modern dance music in the 1970s, the distinction was nevertheless significant and meaningful. In various media reports in the 1970s different Beti dances were mentioned, even if simply in a list. The medialized process of establishing the term "bikutsi" as the main denomination for the popular guitar-based Beti music and the musical changes associated with it had not yet taken place. Only in the following decade, with the next generation of modern dance bands in Yaoundé, did the boundaries become more and more blurred, and the tendency to simply describe all Beti dance varieties as "bikutsi" arose. At the time of my research, especially in electronically produced guitar-based bikutsi, the differences between Beti dances, like elak or bikutsi, no longer played a role; it was all simply bikutsi.

The changes occurring in the 1970s in Yaoundé's dance music can be interpreted along two complementary lines. On the one hand they were an expansion of popular dance music of Afro-Caribbean influence and provided a welcome change in the usual repertoire. On the other hand, they consti-tuted a step towards creating new Beti music within existing Beti traditions: the musicians extended the known Beti musical repertoire and integrated the instruments of a modern dance band into the universe of Beti music. These complementary views on the development exist in Cameroon side by side, with the music itself, as electric guitar-based Beti music, provid-ing the connection. In Motti Regev's concept of aesthetic cosmopolitanism this development can be seen as occurring at the intersection of two merg-ing fields of musical practice: one of ethno-national musical practice, in this case Beti musical traditions, and the global and diverse field of pop-rock music, of which Cameroonian urban dance music was a part. The musicians in Yaoundé in the 1970s were part of both fields, and their inspiration and innovation in developing a distinctly Beti electric guitar-based dance music was due to this specific position. Beti dance music in Yaoundé's bars and nightclubs in the 1970s was a broadening of what was possibly interpreted as Beti music, and at the same time added a new aspect to Cameroonian popular music in general.

Chapter 6

Performing Beti "Village" Music: The Bikutsi of Les Vétérans

In the first half of the 1980s Beti dance music played by modern dance bands reached a new level in terms of performance, recording, and marketing as compared to the 1970s. More than before, it became commodified. Additionally, in connection with new musical, social, and economic possibilities, the image of the music shifted in line with changing societal values and habits. While in the 1970s urban "modern" entertainment rarely presented any openly ethnic or rural connections, this aspect became more important in the "urban modern" lifestyle in the 1980s. City people (re)discovered what they imagined to be "rural" life – and the group Les Vétérans consciously fostered a "village" image in music and performance, meeting this demand. Les Vétérans was one of the most popular bands of the 1980s in Yaoundé. In his overview of bikutsi musicians and groups, Jean-Maurice Noah described the contribution of Les Vétérans to the development of bikutsi as "fundamental" (Noah 2004: 110). The group is mentioned in the expository article of *World Music: The Rough Guide* as a "long-established bikutsi/rumba big band" (Nkolo and Ewens 1999: 443). Les Vétérans occupy a central position in the establishment of bikutsi as an identifiable popular music genre in the 1980s not only because they were one of the rare groups to persist in a musical world focused on individual artists. That Les Vétérans became popular, then famous, and that the Escalier Bar, the nightclub in which they played regularly, became one of the most in-demand cabarets in Yaoundé, catering for a middle- and upper-class public, was due to the interplay of different factors that came together in the early 1980s: the interest of a journalist, the financial means of a producer, the demand for novel music and entertainment in Yaoundé, the new recording facilities on-site, and of course excellent musicians able to adapt to and exploit these conditions. Les Vétérans was one of the first groups, if not *the* first group, whose music was marketed specifically as "bikutsi".

Promoting Bikutsi in the Early 1980s: Cultural Intermediaries and the Bikutsi Label Ebobolo Fia

The increasing turn towards Beti music by modern dance bands in Yaoundé in the 1970s has been described in the previous chapters. That said, in 1979 this music still did not have a distinct name. At the end of a long article in the *Cameroon Tribune*, Adala Gildo complained about this situation and called on the musicians to find one (Gildo 1979). Over two or three years, "bikutsi" slowly emerged as a general term for this "new" Beti music played by modern dance bands. In the media and on records the term was used increasingly to describe the music as a musical genre. The main factors in this development were, however, not the musicians that Gildo had addressed but, instead, people working in music production and marketing, and journalists who were engaged in promoting this music and forced this new, specific terminology.

In this case of the promotion of music "made in Yaoundé" (Gildo 1979), two main agents helped the music to become popular: the producer Claude Tchemeni and the journalist Jean-Marie Ahanda. Claude Tchemeni founded a label called Ebobolo Fia that was the first to focus specifically on Beti music as played by Yaoundé's dance bands. Jean-Marie Ahanda, himself of Beti origin, worked at the national newspaper *Cameroon Tribune*, writing articles on cultural matters, often on contemporary musical events, musicians, and developments. He started, due to personal interest, to focus increasingly on Yaoundé's music. Merging their different skills, or in Bourdieu's sense their various forms of capital (cf. Bourdieu 1984), Tchemeni and Ahanda managed to successfully establish bikutsi on the Cameroonian music market.

The role these two individuals played in the development of bikutsi in the 1980s was one of "cultural intermediaries". Cultural intermediaries are individuals with a specific position in the field of cultural production, which enables them to mediate between the production and the consumption of cultural goods. The concept of cultural intermediaries is associated with Pierre Bourdieu's theory of taste and aesthetic judgement, as illustrated in *Distinction: A Social Critique of the Judgement of Taste* (Bourdieu 1984). Therein he used the term for people engaged professionally in bridging the gap between producers and consumers. Although there is some debate about the scope of the concept (see Hesmondhalgh 2006; Negus 2002), in general,

cultural intermediaries, following Bourdieu, are people working in profes-
sions concerned with the presentation and representation of symbolic goods.
Jennifer Smith Maguire and Julian Matthews provide a useful definition of
cultural intermediaries:

> They construct value, by framing how others – end consumers,
> as well as other market actors including other cultural inter-
> mediaries – engage with goods, affecting and effecting other's
> orientations towards those goods as legitimate – with "goods"
> understood to include material products as well as services, ideas
> and behaviours … In the struggle to influence others' perceptions
> and attachments, cultural intermediaries are differentiated by their
> explicit claims to professional expertise in taste and value within
> specific cultural fields. (Smith Maguire and Matthews 2012: 552)

Cultural intermediaries therefore have the authority to influence the presentation of symbolic goods. The most common conception of cultural intermediaries in music points to journalists in any media, as well as to producers
and marketing personnel, as these brokers or intermediaries are often highly
influential in establishing new trends in the music market. As Nixon and du
Gay describe, "these groups of workers are able to exert, from their position within the cultural institutions, a certain amount of cultural authority as
shapers of taste and the inculcators of new consumerist dispositions" (Nixon
and Gay 2002: 497).[1] Due to their specific professional position, but especially due to their personal interest and engagement, cultural intermediaries
often play an important role in commodifying existing musical practices and
establishing new trends within the field of musical production. They act in
professional and private life in different sub-fields of cultural production,
and due to this flexible positioning in different musical environments, they
cross symbolic boundaries of aesthetic judgement and taste. Using their
specific knowledge based in different professional and cultural fields, or in
Bourdieu's sense their cultural capital, they are able to convincingly engage
in promoting new trends and help a musical practice known in one area of
the field of musical production to become adapted and succeed in another.
It is in this sense that the journalist Jean-Marie Ahanda and the producer
Claude Tchemeni acted as central cultural intermediaries in the establishment
of bikutsi as a musical genre on the Cameroonian music market.

Jean-Marie Ahanda's position in having influenced and promoted bikutsi
in the 1980s is widely uncontested, although it is usually connected with

him being the founder of the group Les Têtes Brulées in the mid-1980s. However, his involvement and influence started years earlier. Born sometime in the 1950s, Jean-Marie Ahanda received musical training during his school education. He went to the Collège Vogt, where he learned to play the trumpet. However, after graduation he did not initially follow a musical career, instead going into journalism. Around 1980 he began to work for the national newspaper *Cameroon Tribune*. Then in his twenties and writing mainly about cultural matters, he started to focus on "the particularities of Yaoundé", on groups that "played the music of the village, amplified, with electric instruments" (Jean-Marie Ahanda, interview, December 11, 2007).[2] Ahanda wrote about Yaoundé's music that had increasingly come to include Beti musical traditions. Ahanda was a regular visitor to the bar-dancing Escalier Bar, where the house band Les Vétérans played almost every evening. Although popular locally, they were unknown beyond their specific small community. The music as well as the audience was mainly of Beti origin. That he started writing about this music was, according to Ahanda, due to his interest in promoting Beti music. He was impressed by the transfer of Beti musical traditions onto electric instruments, which gave ordinary working people "who were separated from their villages the possibility to regain a bit of their identity, to have fun among themselves ... there was an atmosphere there that existed nowhere else" (Jean-Marie Ahanda, interview, December 11, 2007).[3] With his regular reviews of contemporary Beti musicians and music Ahanda played an active role in the development of the term "bikutsi". In his own recounting he was one of the first to consequently use the term "bikutsi" to describe the music genre in general. He explained that he used "bikutsi" as a generic term, in order to simplify the matter, as there were many different nuances in Beti music, and the same rhythms and dances had different names among different Beti sub-groups – "because I can't go into technical explications".[4]

Besides his activities promoting bikutsi as a journalist, Ahanda also played a role arranging pieces for and managing bikutsi groups and singers, specifically Les Vétérans and the singer "Ange" Ebogo Emerent. Both were very successful in the early 1980s. Jean-Marie Ahanda had a gift for meeting the musical taste and spirit of the time with his musical arrangements and choice of people to work with. Using his experience with Les Vétérans, he then founded his own music group Les Têtes Brulées in the mid-1980s, which gained international attention in the late 1980s. Jean-Marie Ahanda was in a perfect position to promote bikutsi with his access to the media on the one hand and his expertise as a musician himself. His influence on bikutsi's establishment and musical properties can thus hardly be overestimated.

In contrast to Jean-Marie Ahanda, Claude Tchemeni – the other relevant "cultural intermediary" – was not of Beti origin himself; he belonged to the ethnic group of the Bamileke. However, he had lived in Yaoundé since he was ten, so he spoke Ewondo quite fluently. In his own words, he "lived very much in the Beti culture" (Claude Tchemeni, interview, August 9, 2008).[5] Born in 1954, Tchemeni was trained as an electrician. He was in his late twenties when he founded a business for repairing refrigerators and opened a record shop. The shop was in downtown Yaoundé near the cinema Capitole and was called "Disco Clo Clo" – Clo-Clo was his nickname. Soon he abandoned his technical activities and concentrated on the music business. Besides his shop he also worked as a representative for European labels like Patché and Phonogramm, which released records by Cameroonian musicians (Ndachi Tagne 1985; Claude Tchemeni, interview, August 9, 2008). It was for him the next natural step to expand into the production business: "I worked for some Cameroonian artists who were produced by the Europeans. So I said to myself, why not me too? That's when I started the production of records" (Claude Tchemeni, interview, August 9, 2008).[6] In the early 1980s then, probably 1982, he founded the label Ebobolo Fia. For the musicians he would eventually have under contract he produced and organized promotional events and concerts; and he continued with his record shop. With his experience in the music business and access to financial capital, he was perfectly positioned to act as cultural intermediary for "new" music on the Cameroonian music market.

During my research stays in Yaoundé, the story of the "discovery" of Les Vétérans, which in turn led to the founding of the label, was told to me several times with little variation. Due to Claude Tchemeni's sudden and early death in 2009, it was also retold in various press obituaries.[7] The story goes that Claude Tchemeni asked Jean-Marie Ahanda, whom he knew as a journalist, if he could tell him how to get rich. Jean-Marie Ahanda told him about Les Vétérans and that he believed that this group had much potential and needed someone to produce them. Tchemeni was willing to try, and Jean-Marie Ahanda acted as an intermediary between the group and their future producer. Ahanda was then hired as musical arranger. At that time, nobody knew whether this music would transcend further than in Yaoundé's bar-dancings. To start a label on the basis of this "new" Beti music was a risky financial venture. The Beti singer Ebogo Emerent said to me that nobody wanted to hear bikutsi, not even the established producers, only Claude

Tchemeni (Ebogo Emerent, interview, August 23, 2010). Onana Zacharie, guitarist in Les Vétérans, recounted with obvious respect that producing Les Vétérans was "like a lottery" for Tchemeni (Onana Zacharie, interview, September 12, 2008). Tchemeni had the winning numbers and his dream of becoming rich, one of his main motivations for starting the music label, became true to some extent. Les Vétérans' first LP published in 1983 was a commercial hit, especially the song 'Kulu'. It was nominated "disque d'année" at the end of the year, a title awarded by a jury of journalists from the state-run print and radio media. Onana Zacharie smiled when thinking back: "When he [Tchemeni] had published 'Kulu', three months later, he bought his Peugeot 204" (Onana Zacharie, interview, September 12, 2008).[8] A Peugeot 204 was at the time a common marker of wealth. That said, Tchemeni's success was not long-lived. In my interview with him in 2008 he recounted that he had ended his involvement in the music business years ago, after having a hard time in the 1990s, mainly due to musical piracy (Claude Tchemeni, interview, August 9, 2008).

The label that Tchemeni founded was called Ebobolo Fia. The name came about, Tchemeni remarked, in a rather funny conversation in the bar-dancing Escalier Bar, with musicians and other people present. The two words are Ewondo; "fia" is the word for the avocado, while "ebobolo" means "bâton de manioc". A manioc baton is a common side dish in Cameroon made of cooked manioc paste rolled in leaves and dried. The label's logo, consequently, was a drawing of a manioc baton and an avocado. This combination signifies, according to a newspaper article, a frugal habit (Ndachi Tagne 1985), in others it is sexual: the avocado is symbolic for the female genitals, while the manioc baton stands for the male genitals. Taking into account the often ambivalent lyrics of bikutsi music and the rather suggestive dancing in the Escalier Bar, the logo of Ebobolo Fia probably has an intentional sexual connotation.

When Tchemeni started his label in the early 1980s, 7-inch singles were falling out of demand, so Tchemeni immediately started producing LP records and, soon after, cassette tapes. The necessary financial means for the production, so he recounted in my interview with him, came to some extent from European friends. One of these was Guy Maurette, who also contributed cover photographs for the LPs. Tchemeni estimated that he had needed around one million CFA (around 1500 EUR at the time of writing, a small fortune in 1980s Cameroon) to finance the whole production process for his first Les Vétérans album.

Ebobolo Fia quickly acquired a name for itself and the popular music genre bikutsi in the 1980s. Beside producing Les Vétérans in the 1980s, Tchemeni also produced other artists, such as Georges Seba, Anne-Marie Nzié, "Ange" Ebogo Emerent, and the group Golden Sounds/Zangalewa. Most records produced by Ebobolo Fia were by Beti musicians and/or contained Beti music. The starting point, however, was Les Vétérans, which will be examined more closely in the following in order to explain why it was this group that Ahanda and Tchmeni started to promote and – especially – had success with. Even if cultural intermediaries have a big share in promoting and establishing musical trends, they nevertheless depend on the immediate output of the creative individuals themselves, in this case the musicians.

Les Vétérans: The Peculiarity of Persisting as a Group

Les Vétérans was founded in 1974 by guitarist Ndo Lévy de la Lune (also written Delalune), who acted as band leader, following the break-up of the group Les Titans. Common practice at the time was to add the name of the city the group was based in, so the entire name of the group was Les Vétérans d'Ongola, "Ongola" being the Ewondo term for Yaoundé. Their first records, all 7-inch singles, bore this name; it was only on later publications that the group was presented as Les Vétérans alone. The name was apparently a reference to the fact that the band members were all musical veterans and had played in other groups before (Essame 1974). Les Vétérans eventually inherited Les Titans' status as house band in the bar-dancing Escalier Bar, located in the popular Mvog Ada quarter, which was mainly inhabited by Beti people and well known for its weekend entertainment scene. The founding of Les Vétérans was probably supported and even initiated by the bar owner, who was again looking for a band for his bar-dancing.

Les Vétérans published several 7-inch singles with compositions by its members in the 1970s with the bar owner acting as producer, but according to later band leader René Ahanda they did not sell very well (René Ahanda, interview, August 23, 2008).[9] Every now and then, the group was engaged as a session band for the recordings of solo singers, as was the case with group members Meyong Ambroise and Ondoua Akono Gaston, but also with singers who were not part of the group, such as Yongoua Ngoubissam (e.g., Boyomo Assala 1976a). The music of Les Vétérans in the 1970s was in line with the music "made in Yaoundé": mainly soukous and merengue sung in

Ewondo, with a few pieces inspired by Beti music. The instrumentation used included electric guitars, congas, a drum set, and maracas.

After disbanding due to internal disputes, Les Vétérans reformed around 1980. Ndo Lévy de la Lune and several others in the band did not join the new formation, which came to include the original members: guitarist Angoué Joseph Kwamy, singer Tchimo Paul, drummer Ondoua Martin, and percussionist Anyou Philippe. New to the group was the singer Meyong Ambroise, with whom the group had already recorded. A list of members on the record cover sleeve of an album from 1983 included the percussionist Mengue Alexandre, the bassist Pigla Zachée, the bassist Bomba Essomba, the guitarist Onana Zacharie (alias Onana "Chantal"), and the drummer René "Cosmos" Ahanda (cf. record cover of *Me Ne Ngon Oyap*, 1983). It was with these members that the group gained wide popularity in Yaoundé and beyond. Only small changes in the formation occurred in the 1980s, with the ten musicians making up the core of the group. On the 1985 recording, two more group members were mentioned, the guitarists Edzoa Dieudonné and Ondoua Gaston. Compared to the groups of the 1970s, Les Vétérans was rather large. They had several singers, some of whom also played an instrument, and all instruments were played by two musicians. However, they still did not have any wind instruments in their fixed line-up. As with other Yaoundé-based groups working with Beti music, the members did not necessarily all have an ethnic Beti background. The band leader René Ahanda and Meyong Ambroise belonged to different Beti subgroups, Pigla Saché was Bassa, Tchimo Paul came from the region East Cameroon, and Angoué Joseph was Ntumu.

What is remarkable about Les Vétérans is that they persisted at all as a group in the 1980s. Such fixed formations were rare in Yaoundé, and in Cameroon in general, a general trend in popular music in Africa at that time (Bender 2000). In 1982, Jean-Marie Ahanda wrote that Les Vétérans was the only functioning music group in Yaoundé to perform regularly. The state-maintained dance bands the Berets Verts and the Golden Sounds existed over a longer period, but they were not part of the bar and cabaret scene. Others, like the Tulipes Noirs playing with Mekongo Président or the Makossa-oriented band Black Sounds, had disappeared. The reasons were manifold: divergent career plans, different interests within the group, emigration of musicians. Furthermore, most bar-dancings had introduced hi-fi systems since the late 1970s, and playing recorded music was much cheaper than hiring a dance band, who not only needed to be paid, their travel expenses often had to be paid, and instruments sometimes needed to be provided for them as well (cf. J.-M. Ahanda 1982b). The trend in the 1980s was thus that most musicians were not generally members of fixed groups, but were hired individually by bar-dancing owners or other musicians and singers for events and concerts. While some musicians had their own music groups, which they founded and maintained, like, for example, the young singer Ebogo Emerent, in these cases the singer stood in the foreground and the band sometimes did not even have a name. But not so Les Vétérans: they were to my knowledge the only band in Yaoundé in the early 1980s to present themselves as a music group over a long period.

How was it that Les Vétérans managed to survive as a group, when other bands struggled and regularly failed? The reason is clearly the continuing business relationship between the owner of the bar-dancing and the group. Being aware of the value of a good music group for his bar-dancing, the owner, Ngomba Effoudou J.P., reacted by providing them musical instruments and paying them a regular wage of around 40,000 CFA each. This was not a large sum and only allowed for a modest lifestyle, but at the time, to receive a salary on a regular basis at all was an exception among musicians in Cameroon. Furthermore, Ngomba Effoudou J.P. acted as a producer for his house band, presumably with the idea in mind to promote his bar-dancing. The 7-inch singles produced in the 1970s appeared under the label Ngomba Productions. In short, the main reason for Les Vétérans still existing as a group in the early 1980s was their economic ties to the cabaret Escalier Bar. In a newspaper interview, band leader René Ahanda recounted that the arrangement worked like an enterprise where the musician was "l'enfant chéri", the "favoured child" (Bissi 1983), meaning that the musicians found themselves in a financially and materially secure situation. With their success following their cooperation with Ebobolo Fia, there was no reason for any of the musicians to leave the band to seek something better – there was nothing better around.

The "Temple of Bikutsi": The Escalier Bar in Yaoundé

Besides the economic privileges that the musicians enjoyed as members of the house band in the Escalier Bar, the reputation of the venue rubbed off on them. "Escalier", that is "stairs", referenced the long staircase that led from street level down to the entrance of the bar-dancing. The locale had been a simple bar since the 1960s, becoming a bar-dancing with music played on a record player, until, in the early 1970s, the owner, Ngomba Effoudou

J.P., himself of Beti origin from the region around the town of Akonolinga, invited the group Les Titans to perform as house band. Les Titans were later replaced by Les Vétérans in 1974.

While in the 1970s the Escalier Bar was a cabaret like many others in Yaoundé, not attracting any particular attention, this changed in the early 1980s. At least in part, if not in general, this was again due to Jean-Marie Ahanda who wrote a short article about the cabaret in the *Cameroon Tribune* in March 1982, which led to a veritable jump in its popularity. The article was a boxed text accompanying a dossier on the decline of the music scene in Yaoundé. Entitled "Le dernier refuge", it can be read as a promotional text for the bar-dancing and the band Les Vétérans:

> Those who prefer to turn their nose up at it speak of jostling, punch-ups and a stifling atmosphere. Those who like it create this atmosphere and do not stop to praise the location at this time of the last living dance band in the capital ... In fact, the Escalier Bar experiences a trance on Friday going into the weekend. For a modest entrance fee and drinks practically for free, the visitor will have an astonishing night. (J.-M. Ahanda 1982c).[10]

The Escalier Bar had not been mentioned before in the newspaper, and it is likely that this article led to some curiosity among the readers and to rumours that made people come and look – and come again. This text was published just before Jean-Marie Ahanda entered into his cooperation with Claude Tchemeni, and the promotion via newspaper was probably part of his strategy to position the Escalier Bar as something exceptional.

In terms of music and programme, an evening in the Escalier Bar most likely resembled my description of such an event in Chapter 4: after a prelude with lesser-known singers, the stars of the evening took to the stage. However, unlike in the 2000s, in the 1980s, the main band at the Escalier Bar was on stage all night, joined by guest singers or a guest opening band. That is why most instruments were played by at least two musicians in Les Vétérans: it provided them the possibility to have a break during a long performance night. A typical night at the Escalier Bar was described by Onana "Chantal" Zacharie as follows:

> When we arrived, we started with the preludes, a bit of gentle and mellow music, bossa nova, cha-cha-cha, you see, a bit of prelude for an evening. Later, around 21:30, that's when it gets

interesting. That is, we start with pieces like merengues. Around
23:00 then, the bikutsi begins, and that goes on until the morning.
(Onana Zacharie, interview, September 12, 2008)[11]

There was thus a clear order concerning the choice of music during the
night: starting with slow dance music, followed by merengue and similar
genres, and the pieces drawing from Beti musical practices were always last.
While the repertoire included merengue and soukous pieces and what Onana
Zacharie called "mellow music", the heart of the evening was dance music
with a clear connotation to Beti musical traditions – in short, music called
bikutsi. Highlighting this focus on bikutsi, the Escalier Bar earned the nickname "Temple of Bikutsi".

Les Vétérans played from Tuesday night to Sunday night. The entrance fee
varied from 300 Franc CFA on weekdays to 500 Franc CFA on weekends and
sometimes even 1000 CFA. Weekends were busier than weekdays, Friday
night being the busiest, as René Ahanda recounted laughing: "Because Friday
was the big day, it was the Friday of the bankers. Friday was insane" (René
Ahanda, interview, August 23, 2008; cf. J.-M. Ahanda 1982c).[12] A regular
visitor of the Escalier Bar, Jean-Marie Ahanda lived behind the cabaret in
the 1980s. He remembered that the bar had a special area for VIPs which he
called "the side of the bankers": "It was divided into two areas: one part for
all the ordinary people, the mortals so to say, and at the back a part reserved
for those who had the means" (Jean-Marie Ahanda, interview, August 16,
2008).[13] These "bankers" were the wealthy people of Yaoundé, businessmen
probably, who used Friday nights in the Escalier Bar to display their wealth
and to spend a lot of money, as various interviewees remembered. Especially
on Friday nights, the cabaret was crowded and the atmosphere stifling.
Citing the locale's nickname "Temple of Bikutsi", René Ahanda said, tongue
in cheek: "On Fridays, everybody came to church service" (René Ahanda,
interview, August 23, 2008).[14] Curiously enough, according to a newspaper
article in 2005, a church was in fact built on the site of the Escalier Bar in the
early 2000s (Binyam 2005).

These Fridays are the reason that, for musicians and visitors alike, evenings
in the Escalier Bar in the 1980s are still associated so vividly a quarter-century
later with pleasure, pride, and affluence. Writing in 2005, the journalist
Junior Binyam said that "everyone who was 'in' had to be seen there"; and a
former regular visitor recounted that "it was nearly a mark of shame to hear
that this or that one did not come to the Escalier" (Binyam 2005).[15] When
Claude Tchemeni re-issued the songs of Les Vétérans on CDs in 2008, he

wrote "Escalier Bar" on the cover sleeves in an attempt to capitalize on these memories of good times gone by. The Escalier Bar has, over time, become a mythical icon for bikutsi in the early 1980s. The atmosphere, the music, the content of the songs, the dancing and the entertainment, provided a kind of experience not available anywhere else at the time.

But what made the Escalier Bar so attractive in the 1980s, be it for the "bankers" or the "ordinary" people? Reports on the group or the locale repeatedly recalled various images of a "village". The evenings at the Escalier Bar were repeatedly described as a "fête au village"; an article and interview with the group in the magazine *Bingo* was entitled "A circle in the village"; and still in 1989, a picture of the group in the newspaper had the caption "Les Vétérans: like in the village" (Bissi 1983; Ayissi-Essomba 1984; Owona 1989). When the group left the Escalier Bar to play another bar-dancing in Yaoundé, the title in the newspaper read "The village resorts to Tailleur Bar" (J.-M. Ahanda 1988a). This "village" connotation was also consciously maintained by the musicians, when they shouted "Au village!" during their songs. Their third album was consequently even entitled *Au village* (1985). The link to an imaginary village that was associated with the nights at the Escalier Bar is clear.

The "village" is an important place in Africa and is loaded with great symbolic power. In Cameroon, everybody has their "village", be it in a rural area or a quarter of a town, where they come from. Even if someone is born somewhere else and has lived there all their lives, they still identify with "their" village; the connection to the village, to the extended family and the ancestors remains. A village or natal region thus serves as a strong identity marker. Among the Beti, for example, belonging to a village can be equated with belonging to a specific family. Similar to how Turino describes the situation in Zimbabwe (Turino 2000: 24), the village provides a real place that can be visited and where one might want to be buried, and at the same time it can also be a spiritual home.

Francis Nymanjoh wrote that the significance of such links to a village have increased since the 1980s:

> The home village in Africa has retained its appeal both for those who have been disappointed by the town, and for those who have found success in the town. It seems that no one wants to stay in town permanently; even corpses are subject to competing claims for burial by kin in different rural localities … And even those who have no ties with village kin and are permanently trapped

in urban spaces often reproduce the village and localist styles in subtle and fascinating ways. It appears that no one is too cosmopolitan to be local as well. (Nyamnjoh 2005: 37)

Especially for the residents of the growing towns and cities, the "village" served as an imagined, symbolic place. It became a metaphor for a way of life that in the 1980s was connected to ideas of community and a connection to land and nature as well as certain cultural traditions. It tended to be seen as ahistorical and constant, but also as being related to some kind of way of life in the past, sometimes also something lost beyond recall. This image of a "village" was positioned in opposition to people's "urban way of life", modernity, technology, and Western habits, seen as progressive and forward-looking. What shines through here is one possible facet of the predominant dichotomy of "tradition" and "modernity" so common in the late twentieth century, not only in Africa, but also in the interpretations of African development by Western scholars.

That said, how the village is interpreted as a symbol for rural lifestyle as opposed to living in an urban environment can vary greatly. In the case of the ascribed "village" image of Les Vétérans, René Ahanda remembered that their music was known in Yaoundé as "musique de sauvages", that is, as "music of the savage". This colonial term of the "savage" is the opposite to "civilized" people, and its use for describing the music is openly pejorative. On the other hand, the popularity of Les Vétérans came about specifically due to this image of being "wild" and "uncivilized" that was paired with a glorified image of raucous "village parties", dancing, and exciting traditional events. While some rejected the music because of its "village" image, others were drawn to it especially because of this image. The music and performance of Les Vétérans had the potential to be associated with aspects of rural village life, either in a positive way as entertaining, exhilarating, and humorous, or in a negative way as rough, uncivilized, and lewd.

The reasons for these images that the group itself consciously provided and maintained and used for marketing and promotion become even clearer with a detailed look at their music, its content, and its performance. It has to do with evoked Beti traditions performed in an urban environment. Les Vétérans had done something that others before had not dared: they carried specific elements already present in the music "made in Yaoundé" in the 1970s further, thereby reenforcing and at the same time reinterpreting "tradition".

The Music of Les Vétérans: The Making of New Bikutsi Trends

Les Vétérans were initially not a musical exception in Yaoundé; they had merengue and soukous pieces in their repertoire as well as pieces of Beti music that on record covers were marked as being "bikutsi". But already then, bikutsi pieces outnumbered merengue/soukous pieces, and since their success with the song 'Kulu' in 1983, bikutsi became their main focus, as René Ahanda stated: "If you talk about Les Vétérans, that's bikutsi" (René Ahanda, interview, August 23, 2008).[16] Like other musicians in Yaoundé at the time, however, Les Vétérans were deeply rooted in their Congolese-derived musical heritage, and they did not give up those roots easily, even with their success with Beti-derived music: every album had at least one piece that was not bikutsi, but merengue or soukous.

The available acoustic sources for the group's music in the 1980s are their commercial releases, a total of five albums published by the label Ebobolo Fia. The first album released in 1983 was *Me Ne Ngon Oyap* ("I have a girl far away") and included the song 'Kulu' ("The turtle"), the group's first commercial success. According to René Ahanda, the first printing of 3000 copies was sold out within days (quoted in Bissi 1983). This first LP was awarded "disque d'année" of the year 1983. Within the same year, the group released the LP *Wa Dug Ma* ("You cheat on me"). "No. 1 du bikutsi" already marked the cover, clearly representing the musical orientation and at the same time referring to the success of the first album. In 1985, the next album was released, adopting the common connotations of village life and wildness ascribed to the music and entitled accordingly: *Au Village*. The fourth album, released in 1986 and also available on cassette tape, was entitled *Traditions*, but is often called "Man Kalba" which is a song on the album. The last album, *Envuvut Man Minga* ("Chubby pretty girl") was only released in 1989, although it had already been recorded in 1987. This was due to the problems the group had at that time with the owner of the Escalier Bar, which activated them to find a new home bar-dancing to play at. The album was released on LP and on cassette tape, and the title song 'Envuvut Man Minga' was, according to Onana Zacharie, the group's last success before Les Vétérans dissolved (Zacharie, interview, September 12, 2008).

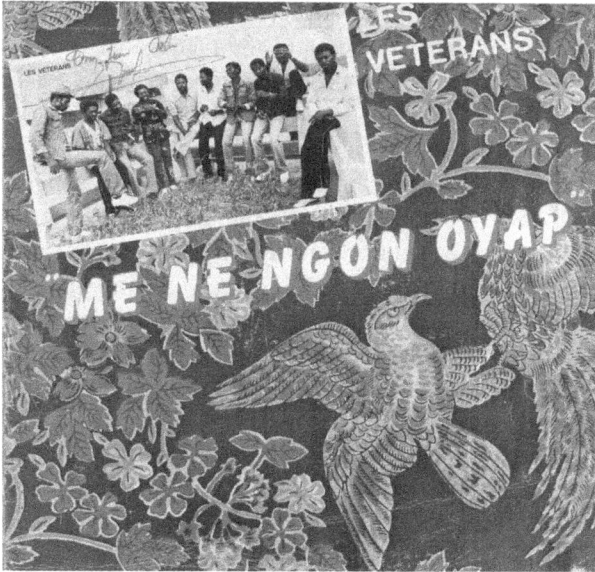

Figure 6.1: Record cover of the first LP of Les Vétérans: *Me Ne Ngon Oyap*, Ebobolo Fia, 1983.

Figure 6.2: Record cover of the second LP of Les Vétérans: *Wa Dug Ma*, Ebobolo Fia, 1983.

The choice of the pieces that were recorded for the albums was, according to Zacharie, based on the success of the pieces that were played in the Escalier Bar. The songs were composed and rehearsed in the late afternoons without writing them down and played in the bar-dancing by heart. The recorded versions of the songs were a variation of the original versions performed nightly. First, they were shortened significantly. A song played live at the Escalier Bar could last up to about 20 minutes; the songs on the LP have a duration of around six to ten minutes. Second, there were alterations in the lyrics, especially in what came to be known as *animation* (see next section) by the singers in the bar-dancing. These were kept on the recordings to some extent, but their crude and suggestive character was toned down. And thirdly, there were changes made in arrangements and instrumentation in part due to the recording conditions, to which I now turn.

On the route from the bar-dancing to recording for the commercial market, the music of Les Vétérans was not only processed as is common in all music production, it was in part also newly arranged for the recordings. The new arrangements for the first two albums, that is, the music that made Les Vétérans popular in the early 1980s, were mainly done by Jean-Marie Ahanda, the music journalist and "discoverer" of the commercial potential of the group, with some parts done by musicians based in Paris. In an interview, Ahanda recounted: "I told them [the musicians] that if you put exactly what you play in the bar on the record, you will only reach the audience of the bar, and the rest will not listen" (Jean-Marie Ahanda, interview, December 11, 2007).[17] Ahanda was competent in writing music and was responsible for the arrangements, especially the parts for wind instruments that were added in Paris. By the time the third album was being produced, Ahanda had already founded the group Les Têtes Brulées and had stopped working with Les Vétérans. Thus, for the album *Au Village*, the arrangements for wind instruments and keyboards were done by Mbida Douglas, an active bikutsi musician himself. On the cover of the fourth LP *Traditions*, the arrangements for the wind instruments' parts were credited to Essono, Mabenga (also written Mebenga), and Georges Seba. The arrangements on the last two LPs, cited as being "arrangements rhythmiques", were credited to Les Vétérans. So, while additional sound parts on wind instruments and keyboards were added by other musicians, the main musical foundation remained the group Les Vétérans.

This musical foundation was, according to Zacharie, maintained from the primary recordings carried out in Yaoundé. These were the vocals, the guitars (rhythm, solo, and bass) and the percussion, also called "rhythmique" by Zacharie (interview, September 12, 2008). These parts were recorded at the recording studio of the National Radio Station in Yaoundé, which had been opened in 1982. It provided modern equipment to record a maximum of 16 different tracks, and at the time was top standard among African music studios. The studio was easily accessible and thus used by most musicians in Yaoundé throughout the 1980s and beyond. According to Claude Tchemeni, the studio provided a drum set and various percussion instruments; all other instruments had to be brought in (Tchemeni, interview, August 9, 2008). The studio could be rented on a daily basis for an affordable amount of around 80,000 CFA. The master tape recorded in Yaoundé was then sent to a studio in France. There, instrumental parts were newly recorded and added, and badly recorded tracks were redone, or rather, replayed.

Listening to the albums of Les Vétérans, for a regular visitor of the Escalier Bar, one alteration was immediately evident: the addition of wind instruments. Wind instruments were played in live music in Yaoundé; however, as singer Ebogo Emerent explained, they were used primarily in Congolese-derived music, for soukous and merengue, but less in Beti music (Emerent, interview, August 23, 2010). According to guitarist Onana Zacharie, Les Vétérans sometimes included wind instrumentalists in their live performances, "borrowing" musicians from the group Zangalewa, the successors of the Golden Sounds, who were also under contract with the label Ebobolo Fia. But this only became common after their first successful commercial releases on which additional wind instruments were added. Wind instruments and keyboard were not recorded in Yaoundé, but were added in Paris, because of the better technical possibilities and greater availability of trained musicians. As Claude Tchemeni put it, the recordings had to be "reinforced" (in his words: "renforcé"). In this process, badly recorded tracks were also re-recorded in the studio in Paris; Tchemeni specifically mentioned backing vocals as an example. Wind instruments were clearly seen as a necessary musical element and were, in turn, where possible, integrated into live performances. The music based on string instruments and percussion had been extended with new sounds according to their availability, and the recorded versions could include more instruments than the live versions in the bar-dancings.

The mixing of the music could also not be done in the local studio in Yaoundé because of a lack of technical equipment and more importantly lack of experienced technicians (see press interview with Claude Tchemeni in Ndachi Tagne 1985). The best sound engineers for mixing Cameroonian popular music did not work in Yaoundé, but in France, due to the concentration of active Cameroonian musicians in Paris, in and around the "équipe nationale du Makossa". This group of musicians had emigrated from Cameroon to Paris, where they engaged in the composition and production of most makossa music at the time. Most prominent among them were the guitarist Toto Guillaume and the bassist Aladji Touré. These two musicians, who were part of the "équipe nationale du Makossa" were, according to Noah, "the musts for creating a makossa hit" (Noah 2010: 68). Noah estimated that in the 1980s around 95 per cent of makossa releases were recorded in France, and the remaining five per cent were recorded in Cameroon and then mixed in France (Noah 2010: 67). Producers for bikutsi music also worked increasingly with Cameroonian musicians in Paris. Ambassa Moustick, for example, was most popular for bass guitar parts and also contributed to Les Vétérans' music. The saxophonist Jimmy Mvondo Mvélé, called "Jimmy Sax", and the trumpeter "Fredo", who also worked as a duo under the name Jimmy et Fredo, were both well-renowned and frequently booked studio musicians in Paris and were responsible for the wind instrument parts on releases in the 1980s, not only on Les Vétérans recordings. Jimmy Sax was further involved in the mixing of music. The processes of arranging the music, re-recording badly recorded instrumental parts, and mixing the music were largely in the same hands and went hand in hand.

The changes and alterations to the music due to the production process did not pass unnoticed in Cameroon. René Ahanda, leader of Les Vétérans, stated in an interview in the daily newspaper *Cameroon Tribune* that the recording conditions in the studio of the National Radio station in Yaoundé were good and sufficient. In a letter to the editor, a reader openly disagreed and illustrated the path of the master tape from Yaoundé to Paris. He reckoned that the listeners were being betrayed:

> From time to time, certain instruments whose recording had completely failed were deleted and re-done by other musicians in France, an example being the bass on the last album of the Vétérans re-played, I think, by Michel Alibo. Anybody who has set foot in the Escalier Bar knows the mastery of the typical bass

of the musician that plays it in said bar, however, he is betrayed by the sound recording of the multitrack studio in Yaoundé. The same can be said for the wind instruments, for the work of musicians like Essono and Mebenga (trumpet and saxophone) was systematically eliminated, despite their playing well, because the recordings did not meet the standard quality for the album "Traditions". (Ondigui 1986)[18]

This comment indicates that for the album *Traditions*, the wind instruments had been recorded in Yaoundé; on the record cover, however, the musicians Essono and Mebenga were solely credited as arrangers for the wind instrument parts. In his reaction, René Ahanda defended the recording procedure, pointing to the conditions of the instruments and declaring that the re-recording in Europe was common for Cameroonian music production. Further, he stated that the recording time for an album in the studio in Yaoundé was not more than three days, and that in this short time utmost proficiency was not possible and a partial re-recording and mixing in Paris was therefore necessary (R. Ahanda 1986). Obviously, the musicians themselves agreed to the process, even though they did not have any final control of the music that was then put on the market under their name. In the 1980s it was not possible to send a sound file across continents within seconds, so the musicians had to rely on the musical choice and competence of their producer and the musicians working on and with their music in Paris. When the final musical product then came back to Cameroon, the outcome was not only new for the audience, but also for the makers of the music themselves. That this "surprise" was accepted by the musicians, had to do with yet another factor of Paris-based productions: an album recorded or mixed outside Cameroon, at best in France, was regarded by the paying public as more attractive than others. Recording and mixing in France had a positive connotation, so it was for many producers out of the question to record and mix anywhere else, especially not locally. Of course, this reputation was not unearned and the paying public had enough experience to value the specific quality of the recordings. The music's international "voyage" was thus not only necessary in terms of technical quality and the Paris-based musicians' mastery of the instruments, but also for prestige and status reasons. While the musicians of Les Vétérans played their role in the studio in Yaoundé and the main parts were kept on the final recording, obviously there were significant differences between the playing in the bar-dancing and the music on the records. This is not surprising and the rule rather than the exception. However, as the recordings are the only acoustic source left for obtaining a glimpse of the music Les Vétérans played at Escalier Bar in the 1980s, there is a need to keep this in mind when taking an overall look at the music itself on the basis of the available recordings.

Although wind instruments and keyboards were added to the recordings, the foundation of the music remains in the other instrumentation: the electric guitars, the electric bass, the then obligatory drum set, and additional rhythm instruments. The vocals are usually a solo voice and choral parts in a call-and-response scheme, but continuous two-voice pieces or solo parts of the melody can also be heard. In the call-and-response parts, the answer could also be realized by instruments (wind instruments or guitars). In one song, 'Au village', an accordion is used, which is a typical instrument for "bol", a bikutsi variant associated with the Bulu regions south and south-west of Yaoundé. Especially in the last two albums, the use of reverb, keyboards, and synthesizers becomes evident. Compared to the songs discussed in Chapter 5, the recorded songs became longer in the 1980s. On the LPs of Les Vétérans, every song lasts at least five minutes, which only became possible with the introduction of LP records. The song 'Kulu', discussed in detail in the next section, lasts over ten minutes.

The songs of Les Vétérans were generally called either "bikutsi" or "meringué". The distinction between different Beti dances had at that time already become less relevant for both modern musicians and their audience; bikutsi was slowly becoming a catch-all term for this kind of Beti-derived dance music played by modern music groups. No matter whether elak, ekaŋ, bikutsi, or mbali, or combinations thereof, the general label on the records and in journalistic articles became "bikutsi".[19] These changes in denomination went hand in hand with changes in the music.

Besides the instrumentation and recording procedures, the overall tempo of the songs had increased. The bikutsi songs of Les Vétérans have a tempo of around 160 to 170 bpm and are slightly faster than the 1970s ones. The soukous/merengue pieces remain at a tempo of 120 to 130 bpm as before. The beat/pulse-structure remains the same: the bikutsi songs of Les Vétérans provide 12-, 18-, or 24-pulse cycles divided into ternary beats. Concerning the rhythmic instrumentation, the obvious change is the confirmed status of the drum set that is used in every song. It provides the main rhythmic foundation. The bass drum clearly marks the main beat, the hi-hat plays continuously on the pulses, while the snare drum can be used to mark certain accents.

Sometimes, for example in the song 'Wa Dug Ma', on-beat hand clapping is added. The main rhythmic foundation on the drum set is then supported by the bass, which plays on-beat patterns and often provides the harmonic fundamentals in I and V alternately, especially in earlier recordings. In later songs, the bass playing becomes more playful and experimental, as a whole becoming increasingly important during the 1980s. In all songs, the guitars are prepared in the style of the "balafon guitar" as discussed previously: they sound slightly muffled. Most often, two guitars play simultaneously. In some songs, three guitars are heard playing complementary melodies, at times taking over the melody of the vocals, at times entering into a dialogue of melodies. The playing style is fast; there is a guitar sound on every pulse. The melodic phrases played by the guitars do not stay the same throughout the songs; they can change several times throughout a piece.

In short, a common bikutsi song of Les Vétérans is built on a mostly 12- or 24-pulse structure with a continuous marked ternary beat, supported by a repeated on-beat bass pattern usually in I–V harmonic structure. The guitars in balafon guitar style are busy, with fast, continuous melodic phrases, supporting the melody and changing throughout the song; the solo guitar provides additional colouring and melodic ornamentation. With these changes the music contributed to the mentioned "village" image of the group. Les Vétérans took elements of Beti musical practices further than groups before them, such as the continuous marked beat as well as the guitar imitating məndzáŋ. Although played on guitars in an urban bar-dancing setting, the music was clearly perceived as Beti, as local, as traditional – as in the village, even if on different instruments. In contrast to other urban music, it did little to meet Western, urban, upper-class musical tastes. Rather, the musicians specifically addressed an urban Beti public that wanted to hear their own music. This can now be seen by taking a closer look at the songs, using the example of the song 'Kulu (La Tortue)', which features an additional element of immediate relevance, the concept of *animation*.

The Song 'Kulu (La Tortue)' and the Concept of *Animation*

In stories about the music scene in Yaoundé in the early 1980s and reports on the popularity of Les Vétérans in general, one narrative stands out, namely the success that the group had with one specific song, which sold extremely well, surprising everyone. It is the song 'Kulu (La Tortue)', released in 1983 as the second song on the A-side of the first LP with the label Ebobolo Fia. As Onana Zacharie recounted in an interview, the focus for the marketing of the LP was in fact on the song 'Si Ndon', a merengue piece, and the success of 'Kulu (La Tortue)' took them all by surprise. However, as the musician noted, "it's because of this that it all started".[20] According to Jean-Marie Ahanda, who lived behind the Escalier Bar and was a regular visitor, this was the song the audience waited for during performances: "Everybody was always waiting for 'Kulu', because it only came around two o'clock in the morning. Everybody was impatient. But when 'Kulu' began, the room was filled. No one was left seated, when 'Kulu' was played".[21] The song 'Kulu (La Tortue)' became Les Vétérans' first commercial success and cemented their position as a bikutsi band.

The song uses the usual instruments and is set in E major. Wind instruments were recorded in the studio in Paris and often answer in a call-and-response scheme to the guitar pattern or the vocal melody. The song starts with a solo electric guitar intro built on phrases of 12 and 24 pulses. In the first section, when the lyrics are in the foreground, the guitars are rather laid back; they get more attention and specific solo parts in instrumental passages. The electric bass, on the contrary, drives the music forward from the beginning, providing on-beat notes in I–V alteration. Additionally, the drum set provides the rhythmical foundation, with the typical beat in four, subdivided triply, on the bass drum. Accents are set on the snare drum as shown in Figure 6.3. A clapping pattern is clearly audible from about 5:00 onwards: the drummer changes to mainly playing the pulses on the hi-hat, the bass changes its pattern and drops into the background. The vocals encouraging the audience to dance and the rhythm section step into the foreground. While sung parts, especially choral phrases, occur also in this phase of the song, they sound thrown in more than being carefully placed. The solo guitar changes its patterns several times (see, e.g., Figure 6.4), the rhythm guitar seems to pause or only play a rhythmical pattern on one note. The tempo increases slightly from 166 bpm to 170 bpm. This second section of the piece is referred to as *animation* (*fr.*, [*animasjɔ̃*]), a section dedicated to elated dancing, where the lyrics take a back seat and the singers turn to animate the audience.

```
bass drum       x . . x . . x . . x . .
hi-hat    (12)  . . . . x . . . . . . x
claps           x x . . x x . . x x . .
```

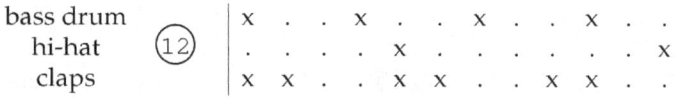

Figure 6.3: Basic drum set rhythm in the song 'Kulu (La Tortue)' by Les Vétérans (with variations in the hi-hat pattern throughout the song), transcribed from a recording by Anja Brunner.

René Cosmos Ahanda described the song 'Kulu (La Tortue)' as "pure bikutsi" (R. Ahanda, interview, August 23, 2008). The percussionist and balafon player Jules Akoudou from Balafon Star on the other hand described it as a mixture of elak and bikutsi (see the basic pattern played on the drum set in Figure 6.3; for basic elak patterns see also Figures 5.3 and 5.5). These different explanations show that with the transformation of Beti music into modern dance music, formerly relevant categories and rhythmical distinctions lose their importance and become blurred. For the musicians as well as the audience, a clear classification beyond the general label of "bikutsi" was not necessary or maybe even no longer possible. The distinct traditional cultural contexts of dances were not significant for an audience looking for entertainment in an urban club. However, the link and allusion of a tie to Beti traditions nevertheless remained relevant, especially in terms of lyrics.

Figure 6.4: Transcription of guitar lines in the song 'Kulu (La Tortue)' (TC 0001 / MAG 82014, Ebobolo Fia) by Les Vétérans, transcribed from approx. 6:45 and 7:33 minutes by Anja Brunner.

Translated as "turtle", 'Kulu (La Tortue)' cites a popular figure in Beti children's folk tales, proverbs, and mythology in its title. The turtle is regarded as wise and clever, but also a possibly deceitful and insidious animal. Its role in mythology is to highlight the importance of wisdom and cleverness (Mba 1981: 53; cf. Tsala 1985: 14; for tales about Kulu see Beling-Nkoumba 1985: 37–50). It is impossible to escape stories around Kulu in Beti communities, so when Les Vétérans chose this famous mythological animal as the title of their song, the reference to Beti culture was evident. In the song itself, however, it is actually not so easy to find Kulu. The lyrics only pick up on this topic briefly at approximately the halfway point of the song, and it is by far not the only content touched upon.

The structure of the song 'Kulu (La Tortue)' is not evident. It is a mosaic of topics and phrases, of thoughts and jokes. There is no section that could be called a refrain or a verse, and the different text sections do not seem to refer to one another in content (see song lyrics in Figure 6.5). The song consists of four different sections of various length and content. The first section (A), repeated with some variations, is the longest sung part and the one corresponding most to what might be called a verse. Set apart by spoken interjections, two short sections follow (B and C), each repeated. Then, another section (D) starts around the 5:00 minute mark, in line with the change in music mentioned above, when rhythmical and vocal parts come into the foreground in the *animation*. The following phrases are spoken, not sung, and the singer addresses the audience directly. There is no message-like content; the focus is on creating an ecstatic atmosphere. Especially in section D, but also during short instrumental interludes beforehand, the singer shouts what sound like random words of encouragement and phrases to promote the *animation*, such as "dansez dansez dansez" or "ça ça ça" (not included in the transcription, Figure 6.5). These phrases do not have a specific literal meaning, but are used to cheer the audience on and to entertain. The song structure and the lyrics were developed out of the live playing in the cabaret. Except for the first section, it is a conglomerate of pieces of text, of short tales and jokes that give the impression of being recounted to entertain the audience, and not to fit into an overall thought-through song structure.

Ewondo	English
chorus:	*chorus:*
mə nə ngɔn yə oyab tə wə a we mə́	I am a girl from far away, don't kill me
chorus	*chorus*
eh mə awú mə awú məwúla ǎ ǹnóm wama dzí wə a bɔ mə dzí	Eh, my husband, what are you doing to me?
chorus	*chorus*
bə́bə́lá nə á mɔ́ngɔ́ yə́ ǹnám abaŋ ǎ ǹnóm wama tə wə a wé mə́	I am a child of the village of Abang, my husband, don't kill me
chorus	*chorus*
bə́bə́lá nə á jósəb kwamí ǎ ǹnóm wama tə wə a wé mə́	Really, Joseph Koami, my husband, don't kill me
chorus	*chorus*
mə a kám nə ábím étɔ bǐ wə bǐ tɔbə yə ǎ ǹnóm wama tə wə a wé mə́	I'm surprised that you want to kill me after so many years of marriage
chorus	*chorus*
mə a dzó nâ ngə́ mə́ daŋ yə á bɔ bibɔn ǎ ǹnóm wama dzí wə á bɔ mə dzí	Even if I have many boyfriends out there, my husband, don't kill me
chorus	*chorus*
eh mə a wú mə a wú məwúla oh ǎ ǹnóm wama dzí wə á bɔ mə dzí	Eh, my husband, what are you doing to me?
chorus	*chorus*
bə́bə́lá nə á jósəb kwamí ǎ ǹnóm wama dzí wə á bɔ mə dzí	Really, Joseph Koami, my husband, what are you doing to me?
chorus	*chorus*
eh tə wə á wé mə́ eh tə wə á wé mə́ eh mə á mə bílí fə ǹguma ndə́ bod ǎ ǹnóm wama tə wə à wé mə́	Eh, don't kill me, don't kill me, I have a family at home too, don't kill me, my husband
chorus	*chorus*
kə́ mə́ fə́ mə bílí ísiə́ kə́ mə́ fə̀ mə bələ́ nyiə́ mə á mə bilí fə̀ ǹguma ndə́ bod ǎ ǹnóm wama tə wə à wé mə́	I have a father, I have a mother, I have a whole big family, don't kill me
chorus	*chorus*

[guitar solo]

chorus	*chorus*
chorus	*chorus*

[first part repeated with minor variations]

asss	Asss! [local exclamation of animation]
a bod dzé a	How are you, guys!

population, ooh	people, ooh

bon mə a dzó miá nâ *ça, c'est au village* Bon, I will tell you that, here, that's in the village

ndo á mə á dzó miá nâ *pour mieux danser ça* I will tell you that so that you dance better
owé mə a wóg Yes, I listen

man ŏnɔn a dzó yə́ What does the little bird say?
man ŏnɔn a dzó yə́ What does the little bird say?
man ŏnɔn ǎ kɔ́bɔ́ nə á The little bird says this
man ŏnɔn ǎ kɔ́bɔ́ nə á The little bird says this
sí eh sí eh sí é nə zəzə The ground, the ground, the ground, it's all in vain

sí eh sí eh sí é nə zəzə The ground, the ground, the ground, it's all in vain

[part before repeated]

kúlu a ngá líg məngɔŋ mə́ kələ́ Kulu (the turtle) has left his bells hanging
kúlu a ngá líg məngɔŋ mə́ kələ́ kúlu a ngá líg When Kulu has left his bells, he has left them
məngɔŋ mə́ kələ́ kúlu a ngá líg məngɔŋ mə́ – why?
bɔ yə́
[part befoe repeated]

bon, vous allez danser comme ceci Well, you will dance like this

ngə́ mĭ ayi nâ *disque* á wúlú mvɔ́ɛ If you want this disc to work well
obɔ á nə́ u é bɔ́rəbɔ obɔ á nə́ u é nyigəbi Bend yourself, twist the backbone
o kələ si kələ si o kələ yób kələ yób go down, go down, go up, go up
à gauche, à gauche, à droite, à droite Go left, go left, go right, go right

ásə́gə́lé assekele [term of animation]
ǎ bòd dzé a ásə́gə́lé How are you guys, assekele!

eyɔŋ té bia zu dzə́m *rapidement* This time, we will dance fast
eyɔŋ té bi a zu dzə́m *population* biningá ai When we dance, everybody, we dance men
bəfám bə́sə̀ fŭfulu and women together
ah oui, je commence d'abord par les femmes Oh yes, I start with the women, we will dance
eyɔŋ té bi á zu dzə́m ai *population* biningá now with the population of the women,
bə́ nə vé *population* biningá oh where are they, population of the women
ŏwé mə ayi nâ ǎ bə́bə́dzáŋ ai bəkál báma Yes, my brothers and sisters, I want this
màjì nâ
ngə́ ó bəgə́ *corsage* ovǎ *corsage* ngə́ obəgə́ If you wear a blouse, take it off, if you wear a
soutien òvǎ *soutien* ngə́ obəgə́ étun kaba *tu* bra, take it off, if you wear a kaba,[1] take it

me laisses ça en place parce que c'est pour moi	off, and leave it all here, because it's for me
ndo á mə áyi nǎ mə́ wɔg anə́ məbɛ́ mə́ ábími á ǹkug á kpàb kpàb kpàb kpàb	And now I want to hear how your breasts hit your chest, flap flap flap
kúlu é tour nyí ǹdzo á é nə́ nâ bə̆bə́lá nâ *c'est pour les hommes*	Kulu, this time, it's the moment of truth, that's for the men
kúlu é mén á soya fə zá mén ánə́ kúlu anə é wə mén ónə fám	Kulu himself is already here, who is Kulu?, Kulu, that's you, the man, we will dance like this
ngə́ obəgə́ *pantalon* ovǎ *pantalon* eyɔŋ té wə á kə bɔ́d étun sanda	If you wear trousers, take them off and rather take a loincloth
eyɔŋ o kə yə a tindi sanda *écartez moi des jambes* 10 cm mi á yəm nâ bǐ ǹtɔ́ mìnə̆m bi á dzə́m otə̆tə́g	When you have fitted your loincloth, distance between the legs of ten centimeters, because we are already old, we dance slowly
eyɔŋ té wə á fógə̆ nyiə́ modo otə̆tə́g á ndə́ŋ ndəŋ ndə́ŋ	Now you move slowly your lower belly, deng deng deng
alors, maintentant tout le monde à la piste mòd ásə̀ *à la piste*	So, now, everbody to the dance floor Everybody to the dance floor
population, excusez-nous avec ça, vous allez vite comprendre. C'est toujours Kulu, la tortue. Et alors, c'est Kulu, mon beau, tu connais Kulu? Un type qui marche comment, tu entends comment il marche? Gbwé gbwé gbwé...	People, excuse us with that, you will soon understand. That's still Kulu, the turtle, And so this is Kulu, my beautiful, you know Kulu? A guy that walks how, you hear how he walks? Gbwé gbwé gbwé...
ah oui, ca revient tout de suite	Oh yes, it's coming back now
ăbólə yə a	It crashed

[fade out]

[1] A *kaba* is a locally specific wide dress for women.

Figure 6.5: Lyrics of the song 'Kulu (La Tortue)' in Ewondo and English. Transcribed from the recording and translated into French by Jules Akoudou, translated into English by Anja Brunner. I thank Olivier Moussa Loumpata and Prof. Dr Louis Martin Onguene Essono for their help with the Ewondo orthography. French words used in the Ewondo text are set in italics.

The main message of the song is in the first part, and it is about the mistreatment of women in marriages. The song tells the story of a woman who has left her village to marry and is treated badly by her husband. The vocals – chorus and solo voice – are from the viewpoint of the woman, who complains to her husband and cries out her suffering. The repeated chorus phrase "I am a girl from far away, don't kill me" illustrates the physical violence.

After this section, the song does not return to this topic, but merges themes referring to tales and proverbs, not really expressing a clear message. Rather, the lyrics work via allusion and are often ambiguous or metaphorical. The next short section, where the singer asks "what does the little bird say", might refer to the importance of bird songs in Beti traditions that are often said to be the inspiration for Beti songs. It could, however, also just be seen as the singer pointing to a bird somewhere and asking himself what it says. In the next part, the turtle comes into focus for the first time. This section refers to a tale in which Kulu, the turtle, is on the hunt with other animals, without the tale actually being told. The animals have bells with them so that they can inform one another when they have been successful, but Kulu leaves his bells on a tree to fool his companions, because he does not want to share his kill. At the same time, however, the word "bells" can – and is – interpreted as a metaphor for testicles, although the story then no longer makes sense. These described sections – starting with marriage problems, followed by the allusion to a secret sung by a bird, and then the short piece on Kulu – are the sole pieces of the song that might be called verses. What follows clearly falls under the category of *animation*.

After about five minutes, approximately in the middle of the (recorded) song, the next section starts. The singer switches from singing to shouting to the audience and animates them to dance. He shouts "go down, go down, go up, go up", instructing the dancers to do squats. He then addresses the women and then the men, calling them to take off their clothes. Important aspects in this *animation* are onomatopoetic expressions, for example for the style of a turtle walking, like Kulu. The character Kulu is mentioned repeatedly during this section of *animation*, but alone as a mythological figure and not in the context of any specific story or message.

In summary, about half of the song 'Kulu (La Tortue)' is dedicated to ecstatic dancing, animated by the singer. As Onana Zacharie explained, the song 'Kulu' was meant purely as *animation* and not as a song with a specific task, with a message or advice, which he saw as a completely different kind of song. Réné Ahanda described the structure of a typical Les Vétérans song as follows:

> We settled for a certain tempo in the beginning so that the people who were interested could follow the lyrics. Then we had a[n instrumental] "break" to set the mood, the point when the people, with the "boom" … that's then the beginning of the end. That is,

you get up, you take off, everybody is up, until the end! (René Ahanda, interview, August 23, 2008)[22]

What bandleader Ahanda points to in this statement is the common song structure of bikutsi songs that Les Vétérans used throughout, including in their merengue or soukous songs, and is a feature common for most bikutsi songs even today, namely a pairing of a song section and a dance section, although these are not always clearly distinguished. The improvisational character of the music increases during the course of the song, and while the main point of the first section is still to get a certain message across, the second section is dedicated to dancing.

The latter section of these songs dedicated to dancing has acquired a specific (French) denomination, namely *animation*. In French, this term literally means to enliven or to stimulate. However, in the context of Cameroonian dance music, the meaning of the French term goes beyond that sense and includes what Bob W. White described for Congolese "musique moderne": "(1) the fast-paced dance sequence of each song; (2) the action of encouraging people to dance and have a good time …; and (3) the emotional state that results from this action, a kind of liveliness or excitement often described as joy or ecstasy" (White 2009: 54). In Congolese music, this *animation* section is called "seben", but there is no equivalent term in Ewondo. Elements of *animation* can occur throughout the song, but increase in frequency towards the middle and the end of the song. Even in songs that repeat one verse throughout and do not have a clearly distinguishable section especially for ecstatic dancing, aspects of *animation* are important features. The *animation* part is commonly done by the main singers or instrumentalists who invite and animate the audience to dance by calling them to the dance floor, making jokes, naming important people, or giving specific instructions for dance moves. Examples of exclamations include "au village!", "dance! dance! dance!" or the neologism "sekele" (also "assekele"), which is used repeatedly and does not have a meaning beyond being used for encouragement during *animation*.[23]

In the early 1980s, *animation* emerged as an obligatory aspect of Yaoundé's Beti dance music played by modern music groups – or rather, it was intensified, because earlier bands had also used such elements in their live performances but usually left them out of their recordings. In part, this increasing relevance of *animation* in the late 1970s and early 1980s is due to the developments in Congolese modern music, where the "seben" section was extended considerably in the 1970s (White 2009: 55).[24] Bob W. White also shows a connection between the flowering of *animation* in modern music and state-sponsored musical singing and dancing under the regime of president Mobuto, called "l'animation politique et culturelle" (White 2009: 64, 67–82). I am not aware of a similar development having taken place in Cameroon. However, besides Congolese modern music, another possible source for this structure lies in Beti music itself, namely in women's bikutsi songs. As described in Chapter 3, these songs have a message part and a dance part, and the latter is dedicated to demonstrating dancing abilities and having fun in dancing and movement. While the movements are slow and laid back during the singing part, they change to quick, ecstatic moves and rapid dancing, encouraged by the lead singer's shouts. It seems that in this historical period around 1980 cosmopolitan influences and local influences met productively. Their confluence triggered the intensification of *animation* as a specific part of bikutsi music.

Looking at the lyrics of the songs of Les Vétérans, relationships between men and women treated from different angles dominate. While the violence in a partnership is the focus of 'Kulu (La Tortue)', the song 'Wa Dug Ma' (which means "you cheat on me") is about the act of betraying one's partner. In 'Marie Loulou', the Escalier Bar owner's girlfriend is praised as the most beautiful girl around. And in 'Jobajo', the singer promises to marry a girl even if she cannot let go of her "jobajo", which is the Ewondo term for the beer Beaufort. In their choice of topics, Les Vétérans' songs were not unique; love and relationships were and continue to be central themes for lyrics. However, being sung in Ewondo and often citing Beti traditions or cultural motifs, the songs were identified as Beti songs. The songs take up aspects of traditional mythology, and references are made to specific places in the Beti region or to certain people. The songs that are sung from the perspective of a woman can easily be interpreted as bikutsi songs taken from or referring to the female song practice. This is the case for the first part of 'Kulu (La Tortue)' which points in the direction of female bikutsi songs due to its topic and the female speaking voice. Les Vétérans worked with Beti songs they knew and that were part of a certain repertoire of women's bikutsi. For Onana Zacharie, the inspiration for the compositions came from "village songs": "We really made an effort; with us, it was folklore".[25] With "folklore" he was referring to traditional Beti songs in general, which for him, like for René Ahanda, was identical to bikutsi. Ahanda explained further that they used traditional songs and developed and arranged them, "but not really like the women, like our grandparents sang, but further than that, it was a composition, like editing".[26] Probably due to this practice, the group was accused of collecting their songs in the tontines, the meetings of Beti women.[27] In an interview, when the issue of copying existing music was raised, Les Vétérans' band leader Ahanda did not object to the admonition, but argued it to be a universal issue because "all musicians get inspired by somebody or something, but essentially, our pieces come from ourselves" (quoted in Ateba Ndoumou 1986).[28] While a composer is stated on the records for every song, the recordings of Les Vétérans do not provide any information on possible sources of inspiration or copied songs. This was not common at the time. However, it is relatively clear that one main source of inspiration for Les Vétérans came from Beti traditions (and they were not alone). This possibly includes individual songs that were little more than rearrangements for modern guitar-based music.

The repeated references to Beti traditions in the lyrics of their songs contributed to the "village" image of the music of Les Vétérans. The songs and their contents were associated with rural traditions rather than with modernity and urban life. Allusions to mythological figures such as Kulu add to this image of rurality, contrasted and at the same time linked to a modern, Western style of urban life with new stories and ways of doing things. The songs of Les Vétérans evoked a romanticized rural life, usually not in a sentimental way, but – in line with the idea of *animation* – with a good deal of ironic humour. This is demonstrated by the hidden and openly displayed sexuality and eroticism in the lyrics and the acclamations during live performances and on recordings.

The Issue of (Im)Morality: The Suggestive Character of the Songs of Les Vétérans

One issue connected to bikutsi as a popular music genre that one can hardly escape and that is also intrinsically linked to Les Vétérans is the discourse over moral issues and the sexual innuendo in their lyrics and in the dance. Descriptions of bikutsi pieces as "pornographic" and "obscene" are common in the media and were present in everyday conversations during my research. The Cameroonian philosopher and music scholar Jean Maurice Noah defined some bikutsi as being a "pornographic spin-off" (Noah 2004: 55–61). As part of a large-scale attack on music with immoral content, the Cameroonian philosopher Mono Ndjana coined the term "Cameroon Sex Music (CSM)" in his appropriately titled book *Sodomme et Gomorrhe* (Mono Ndjana 1999). During my fieldwork, the perceived immorality of bikutsi was criticized repeatedly in conversations about contemporary bikutsi, as allusions to sex and eroticism appear regularly in bikutsi songs and performances, although not all performers made these allusions explicitly.

Tracing this aspect of suggestive eroticism historically, Mono Ndjana found its source in the 1950s and 1960s, for example in the songs of Max Minkoulou. These songs, according to Mono Ndjana, took up topics of sexuality and the erotic, but in a "sociological" sense, not in a "biological" one, which for him was morally acceptable. In the 1970s the practice of throwing in raunchy words with no link to the content of the song became an important element, for example by musicians such as Messi Martin, who Mono Ndjana mentions explicitly. It was only with Les Vétérans that songs with immoral content and openly suggestive comments became the main model for bikutsi music – with some rare exceptions (Mono Ndjana 1999: 11–23). Following Mono Ndjana, then, erotic and sexual topics have long been discussed in song, but the character of dealing with it has changed – and Les Vétérans had a significant share in this development. Even in the rare case when a song was not about male-female relationships, a humorous allusion to sex seems obligatory. The song 'Osun' is about a species of mosquito (called *osun*) that annoys a man in a village. It bites him on different parts of the body, but the first mentioned are his genitals, which they call his "village" (Ewondo: *nnam*).

The practice of throwing in more crude and immoral words is connected intrinsically with the growing relevance of *animation* in the songs and in the new practice of recording the *animation*. As seen with 'Kulu (La Tortue)', phrases during the *animation* could be maintained on the recordings even if they had a (hidden) suggestive character. This is also the case with other songs, like 'Au village', which starts with the shouted declaration that "the underwear is annoying". In 'Jobajo', the singer asks during an *animation* part, "sweetheart, do you know how to turn your backside?" and shouts phrases like "You have white hair on your head and white hair down there". With more time dedicated to the *animation* in the songs, the allusions to sexuality and the erotic increased. The reason for this increasing turn towards more suggestive and crude lyrics and dance is usually explained with reference to the demands of the audience, as stated by Réné Ahanda: "It's business, it's the market, that's what interests them [the audience], we were obliged to do it".[29] This statement reiterates Mono Ndjana's (1999) argument that the public asks for such music and that it sells better.

Claude Tchemeni was of the same opinion. Compared to the live versions, however, the songs and the *animation* had already been balanced and cleaned up for the recordings. Live performances in the Escalier Bar included sexual and erotic comments as well as openly suggestive movements by the dancers. The atmosphere in the Escalier Bar described above owed much to this aspect of the evening. Claude Tchemeni recounted that people came to the nightclub "to let off steam", to freak out, and this evolved into an atmosphere with verbal comments that one could not put on disc. Tchemeni explained that the music on the recordings is cleaned up significantly: "When they recorded, they limited the content, because the message had to be suitable for the public".[30] René Ahanda described the differences: "In the club, it was straightforward. That is, we got directly to the point. We said directly what needed to be said. But when recording, there was need to play 'hide and seek'. No, in the club it was bad, I tell you, it was direct, crude".[31] Onana Zacharie recounted those times in a similar manner, laughing: "Yes, it was there, [the obscenity]. But it was a bit hidden on the recording. But in the Escalier, it was open".[32] Trying to find out in what way this aspect was different and more open in live performances compared to the recordings, I encountered very reluctant reactions. Although the issue was omnipresent, the answers in interviews on this question were evasive.[33] Only once was I told an example of a phrase that was common in the Escalier Bar as *animation*, spoken in Ewondo and translated to me by a friend afterwards: "give me your vagina", which considering the reactions of the people present, was extraordinarily direct and crude. Phrases in this direct mode could not be recorded. This example gives a glimpse of the mood and atmosphere in the clubs in the 1980s, where the play and performance of sexuality, eroticism, and humour reigned supreme.

My questions on sexuality and eroticism in bikutsi often led to statements comparing the old 1980s bikutsi, called "ancienne bikutsi", to contemporary bikutsi. There was general consent that the language of the songs of the 1980s was much more restrained and that things were not said as openly as is common today. Réné Ahanda said that "instead of talking about sex, we had little expressions to name the things, there were certain expressions, and only we, the Beti, understood what we wanted to say".[34] The importance of this hidden meaning was highlighted repeatedly in many of my conversations. Denis Rathnaw pointed out that "[w]hile it is true that themes can be intensely suggestive and downright lewd, the best singers are said to be oblique, poetic, and masters of Ewondo linguistic codes and references" (Rathnaw 2010: 51). It is this mastery of words that people referred to when insisting that bikutsi in the 1980s – or Les Vétérans especially – was not as open as in the 2000s, but rather used a hidden language only intelligible to people with knowledge of Beti culture and language. The music is thereby positioned on the positive side of a discourse accompanying bikutsi ever since, a discourse around the aesthetics and quality of lyrics and poetics in general that highly values metaphorical, hidden, and oblique language.

As Auguste Owono-Kouma has shown in a detailed analysis of the language used in bikutsi lyrics, different metaphorical names for male or female genitalia (e.g., "baton de commandement", "biberon", "le mortier") or metaphorical and suggestive accounts of sexual intercourse have been common in bikutsi (Owono-Kouma 2004). Especially since the 1990s, openly sexual movements and content leaving no doubt about the singers' intentions have increased in bikutsi, with female singer K-Tino being the most cited example (Mefe 2004). The rare discussions on this "pornographic" aspect of contemporary bikutsi concentrate on the political framework of (female) empowerment and the reclaiming of public space (Rathnaw 2010; cf. Mbembe 2001) or the cosmopolitan aesthetics of popular music (Brunner 2012). The linguistic aspect of bikutsi and the differences between 1980s bikutsi and contemporary bikutsi in terms of the mastery of the language and the openness of sexual and suggestive lyrics, however, remain to be studied in detail.

For the wild and savage "village" image of Les Vétérans, the playful handling of immorality and uncivilized topics was extremely relevant. The suggestive comments and sexual allusions allowed the public to live out something that they could not do in their day-to-day lives. The atmosphere in the Escalier Bar provided a space where "uncivilized" behaviour was not only possible but desired and encouraged. Here the evoked image was one of "wild" behaviour, contrasting the need to otherwise act in a civilized and morally correct way. Suggestive elements were not part of every single recreational event, but sexuality and eroticism did and do play an important part in traditional Beti entertainment dances. As a counterpart to "civilized" modern lifestyle and as a new form of one's "own" music, the *animation* in Les Vétérans' performance had an important role in the "village" image of the music.

***

Les Vétérans played at the Escalier Bar until 1986 and, despite being happy with the monetary rewards for years, they stopped playing the Escalier Bar for financial reasons. Apparently, the musicians found out that the owner had earned much more from the popularity of Les Vétérans' music than he had let on and could easily have paid them a lot more. After he refused to do so, the group did not return to the cabaret after a concert tour in Gabon but instead was hired as a house band at another cabaret in Yaoundé, the Tailleur Bar in the Nkoldongo quarter and later in Super Mirama. But their peak of success had passed and the group soon dissolved. Some of the group's members continued in other formations, others ended their musical careers and made a living elsewhere. The "Temple of Bikutsi", the Escalier Bar, hired other musicians after parting ways with Les Vétérans, but to little success, and the cabaret closed at the end of the 1980s. In the 1990s, it was re-opened under the name Escalier New Look for a time, but it could not reach its previous levels of popularity (Binyam 2005). New musicians and new locations had entered the then already clearly constituted field of bikutsi as a popular music genre.

What lasted from the period of Les Vétérans was a distinct name for the new music genre and certain perimeters – social and musical – from other music genres. In collaboration with Jean-Marie Ahanda and Claude Tchemeni, Les Vétérans created with their musical arrangements, marketing strategies, and live performances a specific, commercially successful popular music genre that came to be known as bikutsi and made a radical and lasting change in the field of dance music in Yaoundé, in Cameroon, and in Beti music traditions.

Chapter 7

Bikutsi in the 1980s: Political Change, Diversification, the Use of Television, and Les Têtes Brulées

Beginning with the commercial success of Les Vétérans, bikutsi steadily gained ground on the Cameroonian music market in the 1980s. Following the pioneering work of Les Vétérans, the group Les Têtes Brulées popularized bikutsi music, making use especially of their visual presentation, promoted via the newly introduced technology of television. With Les Têtes Brulées, bikutsi also went international. At the same time, the group musically developed guitar-based bikutsi further, placing more importance on solo guitar and funk and rock sounds. The background for further popularizing bikutsi as a popular music genre was a political shift, that is, the taking over of power by a Beti and the subsequent political developments. Additionally, more musicians started to gain a foothold in Yaoundé's bikutsi dance music scene in the 1980s, and guitar-based bikutsi music diversified. In contrast to the immoral and sexually laden, ecstatic music of Les Vétérans and Les Têtes Brulées, bikutsi music with more morally acceptable lyrics gained ground that fostered a soft, romantic love song tradition. All in all, in the 1980s bikutsi was consolidated as a distinct, identifiable popular music genre.

Changes in State Politics: A Beti President

Cameroon saw an important political change in the 1980s: president Ahmadou Ahidjo unexpectedly stepped down and appointed his prime minister, Paul Biya, to the presidency in 1982. Biya consolidated his power over the next two years and won the election in 1984. In the same year, he foiled a coup d'état, presumably organized by the former president Ahidjo who had been – according to rumours – tricked into stepping down from office.[1] Paul Biya

has been Cameroonian president ever since. For the Cameroonian population, the change in power brought about much hope, especially in terms of
a softening of the rigid system of state control. Biya announced a political
reform under the title "Régime du Renouveau national" when he took power.
To mark a difference from the former president, he stated that Cameroonians
would be able to speak their mind freely and that he would work towards a
more democratic society (Nyamnjoh 2005: 133). Nevertheless, for the next
decade, political practice remained to a large extent the same as the time
under Ahidjo. "Biya's idea of freedom, it soon became apparent, was limited
to the freedom to criticize former president Ahidjo and Biya's own critics.
As soon as the media became critical of him and his government as well,
they were punished accordingly" (Nyamnjoh 2005: 135). Changes in media
politics were only introduced in the 1990s. In 1990, freedom of the press was
anchored in law, and in 1996 it was grounded in the constitution. However,
arrests and harassment of journalists have continued (cf. Nyamnjoh 2005:
168–80) up until today.[2]

As under Ahidjo, promoting national unity was Biya's highest priority.
Biya regarded different ethnic cultures as "national socio-cultural resources"
(cited in DeLancey 1989: 74). The awareness of ethnic and regional identity,
overshadowed in public discourse in the years of Ahidjo in favour of rhetorical phrases on national unity but bolstered unintentionally nevertheless,
came increasingly to the surface during the first years under president Biya.
While other areas of conflict remained present as well, such as the north/
south divide and the differences between Francophone and Anglophone
regions, ethnic and regional belonging became ever more relevant in the
postcolonial state, built on the "trinity of violence, allocations, and transfers"
(Mbembe 2001: 48; cf. Introduction), that is, within the established forms
of support from the state. This was also due to the economic crisis that hit
Cameroon and other African states in the 1980s. With fewer resources to
distribute, "own" communities were served first. The trust of the population
in the state and its capability to care for the well-being of all Cameroonians
consequently started to decrease, and the fair and balanced state system,
which was the legitimization for violent state suppression, started to falter.
Paul Biya himself is of Bulu origin, a group associated with the Beti. He
regards himself and is regarded in media representations as being a Beti in
the broader sense. With the highlighting of ethnic identity and origin in general, these ethnic groups increasingly gained influence and power within the
state (cf. DeLancey 1989; Mehler 1993). The 1980s thus saw a rise in the
politic influence of Beti people, in line with ethnic consciousness in general.

And with fewer resources to give and generally less wealth in the country, the Beti ethnic groups – due to their access to power – were being increasingly perceived as being privileged by the state system.

This change in power and the increased ethnic awareness that followed is significant for the development of bikutsi in the 1980s. It is no coincidence that the music of the ethnic group of the Beti gained relevance in the music market during the regime of a Beti president. Many Cameroonians believe that the political power of the Beti played a big part in this development. As state control over any societal and cultural matters was still very tight, especially via the media, this is most likely the case. Beti had more access to power than before, and this helped bikutsi gain fame in the country. However, an explanation of bikutsi's rise in the 1980s to becoming a distinct and commercially successful – albeit politically contested – popular music genre solely on the basis of political support is too one-dimensional. Bikutsi as a popular music genre had already started its path towards commercial success in the national music market before the political changes, and it did not become one of the most popular dance music genres in Cameroon solely due to politics, but also due to changes in music production and distribution – that is, with the introduction of the music cassette and active musicians working on its development, such as those that will be featured in this chapter.

Moral Bikutsi: The Singer Ebogo Emerent

While the bikutsi played by Les Vétérans was characterized by extensive use of sexual allusions and clear messages, especially in live settings, another form of bikutsi was also gaining ground in the early 1980s. These songs were romantic love songs, songs about everyday life and problems, songs with moral advice, concerning societal issues and commenting on social problems. In contrast to morally "incorrect" bikutsi, sometimes called "bikutsi brute", these bikutsi songs are defined as being "bikutsi soft" or "bikutsi morale" (cf. Noah 2004). Of course, the boundaries between these two categories are blurred, but many musicians have increasingly positioned themselves distinctly against the "pornographic" or "immoral" content that bikutsi has often been associated with since the 1980s.

One of these was Ebogo Emerent. In the 1980s, the young Ebogo Emerent was a rising bikutsi singer of morally correct bikutsi. Because of his angelic voice, Emerent was nicknamed Ange Ebogo. He sang in different groups in the 1970s, releasing some 7-inch singles, and in 1979 he released two LP records (J.-M. Ahanda 1982a). He won the "disque d'année" a year after Les

Vétérans in 1984 with his song 'Okon Makon' (see "Hit Parade de C.T." 1985: 27). This success, the musician recounted to me, made it possible to get a loan from the bank to buy instruments and to form the group Ozima (Ebogo Emerent, interview, August 23, 2010). In contrast to Les Vétérans, Emerent and his group did not have a fixed place to perform. Instead, they were booked by different cabarets or bars, in Yaoundé, but in other towns as well.

While Emerent's repertoire was still mainly in line with the soukous and merengue trend in the 1970s, in the following decade he turned increasingly toward Beti music. Emerent's LP *Sita Mengue*, his third album released in 1982, included one song marked as "bikutsi" called 'A Nti Kama'.[3] On the next album entitled *Expérience* all the songs went in the direction of bikutsi. In my interview with him he recounted that previously nobody really wanted to hear bikutsi: "Even when invited to play at an event, a wedding for example, the people did not allow bikutsi to be played; they said that it was too provincial".[4] In this respect Emerent had a similar experience to the musicians of Les Vétérans. A positive connotation of this music beyond some dispersed city residents only emerged with the producer Claude Tchemeni and his label Ebobolo Fia (Ebogo Emerent, interview, August 23, 2010).

Ewondo	English
ókɔ́n mə á kɔ́ eh mə kə̌ mɔ́ bálá mɔ́sə	With the disease I have, I already tried all remedies
mə kə̌ mə à ndə́ŋ á bə́ dɔ́bə́dá təgə yə e dɔ́ŋ	I was in every hospital, without success
bə á kad mə nâ ókɔ́n té ó nə ediŋ	They told me that this desease, that's love
koo nâ é miningá mə á diŋ	And that the woman I love
nyǎ yənə mə sié oh	Has to cure me
ediŋ e nə m̀kpálí	Love is crazy
ediŋ e nə m̀kpálí	Love is crazy
ediŋ e nə m̀kpálí	Love is crazy
á miningá mə á diŋ eh	Woman of my love

Figure 7.1: First verse of the song 'Okon Makon' by Ebogo Emerent in Ewondo and English. Transcribed from the recording and translated into French by Jules Akoudou, translated into English by Anja Brunner. I thank Olivier Moussa Loumpata and Prof. Dr Louis Martin Onguene Essono for their help with the Ewondo orthography. French words used in the Ewondo text are set in italics.

That said, while still initially being "trop village", Ebogo's music did not go in the direction of immorality and sexual allusion. He positioned it consciously as morally correct, often with proscriptive, educational elements. One of his most popular songs was 'Okon Makon', a popular bikutsi song from the early 1980s. The title can be roughly translated as "I am ill". The song is a love song that describes loving a woman as a disease that can only be healed by the reciprocated love of this woman (see lyrics of first verse in Figure 7.1). It was recorded in the newly opened studio at the radio station in Yaoundé, post-produced in Paris, and released on the LP *Expérience* with the label Nso-Ngon Musik (N.N.M. 184). The instrumentation included bass guitar and two electric guitars, drums, synthesizer-piano, and wind instruments; the last two were probably only recorded in Paris. The song itself, lasting 7:40 minutes, has a tempo of 157 bpm with three repeated verses. It is set in E major and starts with one bar of the accompanying guitar pattern before the other instruments join in. The drums play the already typical on-beat bass drum comprising three pulses, alternating with stick slaps on the closed hi-hat. Additionally, there is an off-beat pattern realized by wooden sticks or claps. The bass guitar supports the main harmonic structure on I and V with an on-beat pattern (see pattern in Figure 7.2). The solo guitar generally plays a simple pattern accompanying the voice, but sometimes leaves the pattern to improvise. The accompanying guitar, starting the song, is hardly audible on the recording after the introduction; however, it maintains a steady pattern throughout the song. From 4:40 minutes onwards, a break introduces a new section that is marked by on-beat hand clapping, introducing a short *animation* part. Ebogo Emerent uses some acclamations, but mostly guitar playing dominates, with different repeated patterns over the drums and bass patterns. In a way, it is a long, extended solo of the lead guitar; the singer starts with the verses again at approximately 6:30 minutes. The song shows typical characteristics of bikutsi in the early 1980s: a tempo of around 160 bpm, the metric structure of three pulses within a beat and four beats to form a phrase, and the on-beat bass drum as necessary features for bikutsi as modern guitar-based music. Even if not played in a "balafon guitar" manner, the repeated guitar pattern is clearly reminiscent of an accompanying pattern in xylophone playing and is characteristic of bikutsi songs.

Figure 7.2: Pattern in the song 'Okon Makon' by Ebogo Emerent, taken from the LP *Expérience*, transcribed from the recording by Anja Brunner. The main beat is on the bass drum.

The *animation* so prominent in Les Vétérans' bikutsi does not play much of a role in Emerent's early bikutsi songs. The song 'Okon Makon' lacks the extended ecstatic section of *animation* at the end, which was part of many other bikutsi songs at the time. The short *animation* part in the middle alone is meant for dancing and is introduced by hand clapping evoking the female bikutsi dance tradition but it is markedly more subdued than in the music of Les Vétérans. 'Okon Makon' features instrumental parts between the verses, but the acclamations of the singer only involve the shouting of the word "expérience", the title of the album, and the invitation to open and close their jacket ("serrez, ecartelez la veste"), addressed at men and citing a specific dance style. Emerent's bikutsi songs were more for listening to the contents of the lyrics than for ecstatic dancing, avoided sexual or erotic allusions, and focused on a moral, emotive, and engaged message.

The album *Expérience* was arranged and produced by Jean-Marie Ahanda, who already had a big share in the rising popularity of Les Vétérans, as discussed in Chapter 6. According to Ahanda, he encouraged Emerent's move in the direction of bikutsi because he was convinced that this would be the way to success (Jean-Marie Ahanda, interview, December 11, 2007). Ahanda was consequently not only at least in part responsible for the "disque d'année" in 1983, but also for the one in the subsequent year. His position in the process of establishing bikutsi in the Cameroonian music market remained significant throughout the 1980s. In 1986 he launched his own group Les Têtes Brulées, and bikutsi gained an audience unheard of before. Of immediate relevance was a change of media: the introduction of television in Cameroon and its conscious use by Les Têtes Brulées.

Introducing Bikutsi to Television: The Unique Strategies of Les Têtes Brulées

Television was introduced to Cameroon in 1985, three years after Paul Biya took over the presidency. It was one of the last African countries to do so. According to Eonè, the project of establishing audio-visual media in Cameroon was already envisioned by president Ahidjo in the early 1960s when he announced the importance of establishing television as soon as the infrastructure for radio was sufficient. Apparently, this was not the case until the early 1980s. In 1985, the first event to be broadcast on television was the congress of the presidential party in the town of Bamenda. The images could be received in five towns only, including Yaoundé and Douala (Eonè 1986:

33–34). Seven years after its introduction, in 1992, there were an estimated 288,000 TV sets in Cameroon (XIX Article 19 1997); by 2004 this number had grown to include about 23 per cent of all households (Alobwede 2006: 16). The national TV station CRTV remained the only one available until the early 2000s, when due to the legalization of private media the number of commercial and privately-owned TV stations grew rapidly.

Before television was introduced in Cameroon, video tapes and VCR recorders had already been available since the late 1970s. Eonè argues that the delay in the introduction of television in Cameroon led to a broad interest in video (Eonè 1986). Too expensive for the majority of households, VCRs were set up in cafés and bars to attract clients in the late 1970s and 1980s, and it is likely that music videos of international artists were played alongside Cameroonian ones. The cinema was also very popular in Cameroon in the 1970s and 1980s, mainly in urban centres. Eonè cited about 60 movie theatres with around 4000 seats in Cameroon, and their popularity can be seen in the numerous announcements in the *Cameroon Tribune* (Eonè 1986: 32; cf. *Cameroon Tribune* 1974–1990). The popularity of the cinema declined during the 1990s, when other film media, such as video, TV, and DVD became widely available at a low cost.

When first introduced, television was received enthusiastically, and television programming became immediately relevant for music promotion. Music was part of the initially sparse television programming right from the beginning, which included one programme in particular: the music show *Télé-Podium*, presented by Elvis Kemayo, a renowned and popular musician active since the 1970s. In this show, Cameroonian musicians or music groups were invited to present themselves and their music. Through this platform, musical artists could successfully obtain followers and fame. Bikutsi musicians, in particular, were promoted and supported:

> The advent of national television in 1985, with a Beti as the general manager, brought bikutsi to the living rooms of viewers even in regions originally dominated by makossa and other music forms. The fact that the management of the national television corporation CRTV has remained firmly in Beti hands since the advent of television has meant more than 20 years of privileged attention for bikutsi. (Nyamnjoh and Fokwang 2005: 257–58)

While the rise of bikutsi as a distinct popular music genre was thus intrinsically connected to the introduction of television in Cameroon, one group was especially clever in using the new media for themselves: Les Têtes Brulées.

Les Têtes Brulées first performed in the Liberté Bar in the Mvog Ada quarter of Yaoundé before they began to perform regularly in the Chacal Bar in the Nlongkak quarter in 1987/88. Their instrumentation corresponded to what was common for modern music groups at the time – a drum set was then already a must. As evidenced in early media reports on the group, after some changes in the group's membership, a core group of musicians emerged to form Les Têtes Brulées within a couple of months in 1986. According to a special three-page report on the group in the *Cameroon Tribune* in 1987 ("Decouvrons les Tetes Brulees": 18), the group included Epeme Théodore alias Zanzibar (solo electric guitar, vocals), Ango Michel alias Apache (rhythmic electric guitar), Mvondo Ateba Albert alias Atebass (electric bass, vocals), Afata André (drums), and Owona Joseph alias Jojo (vocals). Other musicians joined the group every now and then, such as the singer Sala Bekono or the guitarist Gibraltar Drakus. Bass player Mvondo Ateba Albert, called Atebass, also remembered Essono George on the piano (Mvondo Ateba Albert, interview, October 30, 2012). It is worth mentioning that according to Atebass, all the musicians were of Beti origin. Although he said that this was a coincidence, it nevertheless shows that the field of guitar-based bikutsi was becoming a field of a more or less exclusive Beti musical practice.

The promoter behind Les Têtes Brulées was Jean-Marie Ahanda, its manager and creator. He only performed on stage with the band during a tour in Europe (Mvondo Ateba Albert, interview, October 20, 2012). As manager and mentor, he actively used his position as a journalist at the *Cameroon Tribune* to promote the band (J.-M. Ahanda 1986a, 1986b, 1986c). In January 1987, just months after the founding of the group, Ahanda wrote a short portrait of the already popular guitarist Zanzibar, who had just released an album with the label Editions Rainbow by the producers Foty and Lanceleaux (J.-M. Ahanda 1987). Ahanda described Zanzibar as at "the firmament of the bikutsi giants",[5] highlighted his guitar playing and stated that nothing like this had been seen in bikutsi before. Ahanda consciously combined his artistic engagement and ideas with a positive presentation of the group in state media, to which he had easy access. That Jean-Marie Ahanda was considerably embedded and involved in the presentation of musical matters in Cameroonian state media was a position he had already been able to use with Les Vétérans before, and now did so again with Les Têtes Brulées.

Ahanda remained the driving force behind the group, especially concerning their media representation and visual image, which have made them the most popular bikutsi group ever since.

In 1987, the group was invited to perform on *Télé-Podium*, which gave them the opportunity to present themselves to a greater public. The band decided to perform not in their regular clothing, but to surprise the audience with a special look. Corresponding to their name Les Têtes Brulées, that is, "the burnt heads" or "the hotheads", which implies a somewhat crazy, unpredictable lifestyle, the group created a look that is still remembered today as being characteristic for them. Atebass described the developing of the look as a collective process:

> It was Foty, [the producer,] who suggested that we leave modernity, that we rip our jackets and our trousers. I then proposed that we shave our heads, like the [Native American] Indians, as the group was called "the burnt heads", that's where the inspiration came from; everybody should find a look for their head. And that was settled. Jean Marie Ahanda invited us to his home, and when the shaving of our heads was done, he rose, he went to his room, he took some paint and a brush, and he put it on my head, and really, that was beautiful. Everybody applauded, and that's how we started to use paint. (Mvondo Ateba Albert, interview, October 30, 2012)[6]

In the end, the musicians painted white patterns on their body and their faces for their performances, they had partly shaved heads with Mohawk haircuts, and they wore torn clothes. This look was accompanied by sunglasses and sneakers. Ahanda recounted laughingly: "Having arrived at the television station, I hid the Têtes Brulées, and when they were announced, 'and here come the Têtes Brulées', not even the presenter had seen them. So, even for him it was a terrible surprise" (Jean-Marie Ahanda, interview, December 11, 2007).[7] The reactions to the unusual look of the group were mixed. While for some it was funny and amusing, others found it rather flagrant (Mvondo Ateba Albert, interview, October 30, 2012). Nevertheless, the coup was complete – they attracted attention and their popularity soared. The group, with Ahanda as manager and creator, had succeeded in using the new media format of television exactly how it was intended: to present the music group on a visual level. In the following months, the group not only appeared repeatedly on television, they were also regularly featured in the

Cameroon Tribune, including pictures showing them in their costumes. Their performances in the Chacal Bar were extremely well attended, as witnessed in a special report on the group in July 1987 (Simgba and Badjang ba Nken 1987). Les Têtes Brulées had created a dynamic visual concept which contributed immensely to their popularity.

The ambitions behind this visual concept were manifold, and aspects of publicity and media attention went hand in hand with vague socio-political messages and statements. One objective was to present a look on stage that was different to other musicians, namely clothes made of matching African fabrics or suits and ties. Ahanda mentioned makossa musicians and the need for musicians to conform to an official and politically correct image. Les Têtes Brulées wanted to position themselves differently: "For us, it was a way to present poverty, even wearing tattered clothes voluntarily, the deprivation, with – how can I say that – paradoxically clown-like trousers, with sneakers that were a bit military, and backpacks" (Jean-Marie Ahanda, interview, December 11, 2007).[8] Ahanda highlights the contradictions at play, the playful handling of different symbols, and also the economic aspect, since to dress five people in proper stage clothes could be very expensive (Jean-Marie Ahanda, interview, December 11, 2007). Denis Rathnaw suggests a reading of the visual representation of Les Têtes Brulées as highlighting the integration of Beti traditions:

> The shaved heads and body painting can represent the scarification from traditional Beti ceremonies, immediately providing an alternative to the cosmopolitan flash of makossa musicians. The torn clothing speaks to the real economic situation of the public, rather than the escapist scenario offered by most mainstream media images. Finally, the backpacks worn during performance, while perhaps giving rise to speculation regarding the baggage of modernity, or the white man's burden, is a reference to the babies tied to the backs of women as they danced traditional bikutsi. (Rathnaw 2005: 191)

While bikutsi was at the time of Les Têtes Brulées' popularity already ethnically coded as thoroughly Beti music, I could not verify during my research that the group consciously cited specific Beti traditions in their performances. Instead, as Rathnaw further describes, the performance strategy of Les Têtes Brulées must be read as strategic minstrelsy, as an active and conscious action of communicating the ambivalence of African life in general: "In terms of the transnational music industry, the media, and issues such as the commodification of black bodies, white or black pleasure, and the culture industry at large, Les Têtes Brulées offer self-mockery as well as subversion, blackness as well as racial domination, commodification as well as contestation" (Rathnaw 2005: 198). Les Têtes Brulées used images connected to "savagery" and "wildness" that were widely popular at the time, such as references to North American indigenous peoples with their distinctive haircuts and the nickname "Apache", thereby also subversively challenging (but not openly discussing) colonial attributions of various kinds. Taking into account Ahanda's previous engagement with Les Vétérans and others as well as his position as a journalist for a state newspaper, the idea to create a specific look was a conscious handling of new media opportunities. With the television as a new visual media gaining ground in Cameroon, Ahanda was one of the first to realize its potential for music and the need to provoke and draw attention not only on a musical level, but also on a visual level.[9] In doing so, Les Têtes Brulées were a provocative and spectacular political statement, playing with and uncovering colonial representations of blackness.

The look of Les Têtes Brulées, with their painted faces, shaved heads, and torn clothes, has remained their trademark, long after the group dissolved. Any pictures of the group show them in their costumes. Noah chose a photo of this group to be the cover of his book about bikutsi (Noah 2004), and in a widely popular overview of world music a special boxed commentary was dedicated to the group (Nkolo and Ewens 1999: 444). Their specific look is as intrinsically linked to the group as the group is linked to bikutsi. While their look was their entry point to fame, it went hand in hand with innovative developments in their music.

The Bikutsi of Les Têtes Brulées: Playful Lyrics and Extensive Guitar Solos

Les Têtes Brulées were, more than any other groups before them, an exclusively bikutsi group. Merengue and soukous hardly played a role in their repertoire. In their international releases their influence went in the direction of rock and funk. They brought some changes to the way in which guitar-based bikutsi was played in Yaoundé in the mid-1980s, especially in the improvisational playing style of the lead guitar. The guitar playing of guitarist Zanzibar is still remembered for its exceptionality. Other popular elements of bikutsi were maintained and popularized further.

Les Têtes Brulées existed for about a decade, until the mid-1990s. Their peak in popularity in Cameroon was in the late 1980s, before they went on a European tour. The group released several albums as a group and as an accompanying band for solo artists, such as Sala Bekono or Abanda Kys Kys. Their first album under the name Les Têtes Brulées appeared on cassette as well as on LP in 1987, after their TV performance, and was called *Révélation Télé-Podium* accordingly.[10] In Cameroon, Les Têtes Brulées worked mainly as a live band. According to Atebass, the group Kassav gave a concert in Cameroon, and Les Têtes Brulées were invited to play as well. It was here that they were discovered by a European promoter, who then contracted them for a concert tour. The subsequent album released in 1989 was recorded during this French tour in 1988 and accompanied the Claire Denis documentary *Man No Run*. The album shared this title. Later releases were all aimed at the French and international markets and were promoted sparingly in Cameroon. After the death of their guitarist, Les Têtes Brulées released an album called *Ma Musique à Moi* in 1990 followed in 1991 by *Bikut Si Rock*, and *Be Happy* in 1995, all produced by the label Dona Wana. In 2000 a "Best Of"-CD was released entitled *Bikutsi Fever* with the label Africa Fête. By that time, however, the popularity of the group had declined, other artists had taken over the charts in Cameroon, and the group itself had broken up. From their album output it is evident that after their first album on the local market, the group immediately went international – and for various reasons they could not gain ground again in Cameroon, as will be discussed in the following.

The two most popular Les Têtes Brulées songs in Cameroon were from their first release, *Révélation Télé-Podium* from 1987, both of which had long been part of their performances (Simgba and Badjang ba Nken 1987). These were 'Essingan' and 'Nnam' (see, e.g., Noah 2004: 109; Mvondo Ateba Albert, interview, October 30, 2012). According to Atebass, the success with these songs led to the invitation to perform on *Télé-Podium* (Mvondo Ateba Albert, interview, October 30, 2012). While 'Essingan' was written and composed by guitarist Zanzibar, 'Nnam' is a piece by bass player Atebass. These two songs will now be used to discuss the music of Les Têtes Brulées in its specifics and peculiarities.

152 *Bikutsi*

Ewondo	English	
tə téle tə téle mənə́g éban	Don't put your calebasse	*Part One*
ziliang	ziliang [war cry, animation]	
tə téle tə téle mə a bɔ éban	Don't put your foot	
ziliang	ziliang	
tə téle tə téle mənə́g éban	Don't put your calebasse	
ziliang	ziliang	
tə téle tə téle mə a bɔ éban	Don't put your foot	
ziliang	ziliang	
éyə́ŋ éban yə á mvɔŋ bod bətadá é ngá líg	On the strange/foreign heritage/ground that the ancestors of our fathers have left	
ziliang	ziliang	
ébán éyəŋ jə á mvɔŋ bod bətadá ngá líg	The strange/foreign heritage/ground that the ancestors of our mothers have left.	
ziliang	ziliang	
o tsogo məmá eh bə́bə́lá o tsogo məmá eh o tsogo məmá eh mə mə á dzɔ́ nǎ o tsogo məmá eh	Remember your papa, remember your mama Remember your papa, remember your mama	*End of Part One*
	instrumental solo *Part One repeated* *instrumental solo*	
International zubáki	International Zoubaki [cry of animation]	
zubáki zubáki ...	Zoubaki zoubaki ...	
yé yé yé yé yé ngǎŋ ai wə	Ye, ye, ye, ye, ye, I thank you	*Part Two*
ësingaŋ	Essingan	
yé yé yé yé yé ngǎŋ ai wə	Ye, ye, ye, ye, ye, I thank you	
ësingaŋ	Essingan	
ěsingaŋ ěsingaŋ ěsingaŋ	Essingan, essingan, essingan	

ĕsingaŋ	Essingan
abím m̀bəŋ o ngá bɔ mə ngǎŋ ai wə	I thank you for all the good that you did to me
ĕsingaŋ	Essingan
ó ŋgá vǝ́ mə kúb o vǝ́ mə ékɔn mə dzǎ m̀bəŋ	You gave me a chicken and a bunch of plantain and I had a good meal
ĕsingaŋ	Essingan
eh mə dzǎ m̀bəŋ esingaŋ ngǎŋ ai wə	I had a good meal, again thank you
ĕsingaŋ	Essingan

End of Part Two

instrumental solo

biá tám láŋ mǝ́fúlú moê	We will count your faults
ĕsingaŋ	Essingan
esingaŋ a daŋ dzam abé	Essingan is very mean
ĕsingaŋ	Esssingan
Un, zero	One, zero
esingaŋ a bonde mədzó	Essingan creates problems
ĕsingaŋ	Essingan
Deux, zero	Two, zero
esingaŋ a wode mə fón	Essingan eats my maize [he teases me]
ĕsingaŋ	Essingan
Trois, zero	Three, zero
esingaŋ a daŋ minal	Essingan lies to much
ĕsingaŋ	Essingan
Quatre, zero	
okídí mə ayi wə kŭs mercedes	Tomorrow, I buy a Mercedes
ĕsingaŋ	Essingan
Cinq, zero	Five, zero

instrumental solo

International zubáki zubáki zubáki ...	International Zoubaki Zoubaki zoubaki ...

	Part Two repeated	
Silence !	Silence!	
esingaŋ a man bidzí á ǹnam	Essingan finishes the food of the village	*Part Three*
ĕsingaŋ	Essingan	
eki tə́ dzí nyag və kúb	He never eats beef, he only eats chicken	
ĕsingaŋ	Essingan	
bikɔ́rɔ biá man á bafia	He finishes the yam of Bafia	
ĕsingaŋ	Essingan	
Three note [original English]	Three note	
eh mə dză kəpέn yə á Bertoua	Even the couscous de Bertoua	
ĕsingaŋ	Essingan	
Mbongo tchobi àjón Edéa	The mbongo-tchabi de Edéa	
ĕsingaŋ	Essingan	
Allo !	Hello!	
eh tɔ bə kangá yə á akónolinga	Eh, even the Kanga [sort of fish] of Akonolinga	
ĕsingaŋ	Essingan	*End of Part Three*
esingaŋ a man bidzí á ǹnam	Essingan finishes the food of the village	
ĕsingaŋ	Essingan	
Un, zero		
	instrumental solo	
	Part Two repeated	
	Instrumental solo	
	animation, including imitation of animals	
	Part III repeated	
eeeeh	Eeeeh	
oyəngá fám	Oyenga of the men	

Figure 7.3: Lyrics of the song 'Essingan' by Les Têtes Brulées in Ewondo and English. Transcribed from the recording and translated into French by Jules Akoudou, translated into English by Anja Brunner. I thank Olivier Moussa Loumpata and Prof. Dr Louis Martin Onguene Essono for their help with the Ewondo orthography. Grey type signifies the singing of the background singers.

'Essingan' is one of the most popular of Les Têtes Brulées' songs, even at the time of research, especially due to the long guitar solos played by Zanzibar, but also due to its ambiguous lyrics. The title of the song is the Ewondo word "èsìngàŋ" which describes a species of tree known in English as "bubinga" or guibourtia tessmannii, after the German anthropologist Günther Tessmann, whose wood is often used for high-quality, luxury items. The tree grows very tall and has a dense crown, reaching heights of up to 40 metres and with trunks of up to 1.5 metres in diameter. Among the Beti, "Essingan" is the strongest and most lasting tree, and it is therefore also perceived as sacred. Metaphorically, the word is also used to refer to a powerful or influential man or one who is old. The President of Cameroon or the head of a village can, for example, be called an "Essingan", due to their power, strength, and influence. In the transcription of the song lyrics, I refrained from translating the word "Essingan" as it intentionally remains unclear in its exact semantic meaning. This is because the song has yet another twist: in the original version played in the cabaret, the title of the song and the word sung throughout the song was not "Essingan" but "èsùsòlì", the term for penis. According to Atebass, the word was only changed to "Essingan" in the studio since the original term could not be put on record because it was not respectable (Mvondo Ateba Albert, interview, October 30, 2012). That said, "Essingan" can also be understood to mean penis, so the original meaning has not been completely eradicated with the change of terms. Depending on which interpretation one chooses for the term "Essingan", the song changes its possible message.

The song consists roughly of four sections, some of them repeated (see Figure 7.3 for the lyrics), which are interrupted by extensive instrumental sections, wherein the solo guitar or the interplay of solo guitar and bass guitar are in the foreground. The song is the longest in the group's repertoire, the version recorded for the "Best Of"-CD *Bikutsi Fever* being 11:45 minutes. Live versions were usually even longer. Like the songs of Les Vétérans, the structure of 'Essingan' is difficult to identify. It is, rather, a mosaic of different loose sections woven together. The first section of the song (Part One) is, according to Atebass, part of a children's tale about an animal that had planted a field of plantains and wanted to protect it from intruders and thieves (Mvondo Ateba Albert, interview, November 13, 2012). The animal asked a friend, a mussel living in a pool next to its field, to help. The mussel composed a song that it sang when intruders came. This song is the first section of 'Essingan'. The interjection "ziliang" does not have a literal meaning; it is a call of confirmation and answer, a form of *animation*. In the following section (Part Two), the singer thanks Essingan, and here the double meaning becomes relevant. Either a powerful man that helped the singer and gave him food is being addressed, or it is a penis, which would imply that the speaker is a woman thankful for a sexual experience or service. The rest of the song can be interpreted in the same way – counting the faults of Essingan, accusing him/it of lying, of teasing. In the last section (Part Three), Essingan is presented as taking all the food in the village, that is, as greedy, but also spoiled, taking something good to the detriment of others. Considering that in Beti society it is common for women to be obliged to cook for their partners – married or not – this section takes on another meaning: the man has eaten everything in the village, he got all the goods; or he has had sexual intercourse with many different women, or with only one, but numerous times. Overall, the song 'Essingan' provides in its lyrics manifold possibilities for interpretation and "immoral" or sexual implications. As such, it existed not only in the already popular tradition exemplified by Les Vétérans; it also met the demand in Beti songs for a mastery of language.

The music of 'Essingan' seems to be composed as one long piece of *animation*.[11] As seen in the lyrics, the song has no strophic structure; on the contrary, it is a conglomeration of sung and spoken lyrics and extended guitar solos. Although the lyrics were important for the success of the song, they play a rather minor role within the piece. The main objective of the song was not to transmit a distinct message, but to provide a context for dancing and having fun. In tempo and metric foundation, the song is typical for bikutsi; it has a tempo of 164 bpm and is built on the common 12/8-meter. In other words, the basic pattern length is 12 pulses divided into four beats. On top of the on-beat bass drum every third pulse, typical for bikutsi at the time, the hi-hat provides fast playing on virtually every pulse in only slightly differing variations throughout the piece, while the snare drum plays off-beat accents (see Figure 7.4). At various points throughout the song a bell is added, playing rhythmical phrases often used in bikutsi, for example the time-line formula of the elak dance (cf. Chapter 4). A dominant feature of the song is clearly the fast and continuous guitar playing throughout. From the start of the song, it only takes about 30 seconds before the first lead guitar solo starts. The lead guitar dominates throughout the piece, with solos played over a steady percussion pattern realized on the drum set. It is the fast and – when compared to other bikutsi songs – rather free and improvised guitar playing that played an important part in the popularity of Les Têtes Brulées and especially their guitarist Zanzibar. This focus on solo guitar might have been drawn from the common sound aesthetics in international rock music in the 1980s, which was made explicit on the band's album *Bikut Si Rock* in 1991. The rock and funk aesthetics, however, were clearly more elaborated on the international releases than on the ones in the 1980s recorded for the Cameroonian market.

```
    hi-hat          |  x  x  x  x  x  x  x  x  x  x  x  x
 snare drum   (12)  |  .  .  .  .  .  x  .  .  x  .  .  .
  bass drum         |  x  .  .  x  .  .  x  .  .  x  .  .
  first beat        |  ↑
```

Figure 7.4: Drum pattern played in the song 'Essingan' by Les Têtes Brulées. Transcribed by Anja Brunner. Note that different variations are performed on the hi-hat, for example, by leaving out single strokes and altering the sound with open/closed cymbals.

In contrast to the improvised character of 'Essingan', Les Têtes Brulées' other popular song entitled 'Nnam' has a strophic form and features the structure of message part and *animation*. It provides three repeated verses of similar structure, followed by a section for dancing with instrumental solos and acclamations of the singer that also includes a sung *animation* part, wherein the singer calls on all the members of the band. The main structure is the typical bikutsi song structure of the 1980s as described for Les Vétérans and Ebogo Emerent. Les Têtes Brulées did highlight the improvisational character of bikutsi songs as well as the use of guitar solos with the song 'Essingan' and others, but they never lost sight of the established song structures and characteristics of 1980s guitar-based bikutsi.

'Nnam' comments on a central political issue in the 1980s using a humorous approach. The title of the song simply translates as "village". The inspiration of Atebass to write this song came from a mid-1980s political campaign in Cameroon, launched by the president, that aimed at stopping and reversing the rural exodus and convincing people to return to the countryside and till the fields. The song is structured as a dialogue between a husband and wife, arguing over the need to go to the village and work in the fields. While the husband explains that he has no money and therefore wants his wife to go to the village, as it is planting season, the wife refuses, referring to the need to maintain her beauty and status (see Figure 7.5). What becomes evident in this song is the gap between village life and life in town, including some of the associated images: hard work and low standard of life, but income possibilities on the one side; beauty, luxury, and a cosmopolitan lifestyle albeit with limited job opportunities on the other.

Ewondo	English

ábóg bá bɔ bisié abog té á dí ǎ ǹgál wáma
mayi nâ ó kə ǎ ǹnam mè nə á m̀fə̀g təge e dɔ́lɔ̀ wayen yá
mə sígi dzáma kə á ǹnam a mú nâ mə á mbára mə ze á yombo abé ǎ ǹnom wáma
ye mod a kad yombo m̀bəŋ á míní:ngá yə wayi vǝ́ *jobajo* ekpǝ́klǝ́

The time of the work on the fields has come, my wife
I want you to got to the village, I don't have a penny in my pocket, what do you think?
I can't go to the village, because I am afraid to grow badly old, my husband
Is growing old any good at all, madame, you only want to drink your *jobajo* [beer], you are making fun of yourself

abog bǝ́ abo bisié abog te á dí ǎ ǹgál wáma
mayi nâ o bi ebag mə nə á m̀fə̀g təge e dɔ́lɔ wayen yá

mə sígi dzáma namba ébag amú nâ bǝ́ zá mə loé *villageoise* ǎ ǹnóm wáma
ye *villageoise* a kad kə ábum ai dzóm dzi ndə obóya fɔ́ mbutúku

The time of the work on the fields has come, my wife
I want you to work with the hoe, I don't have a penny in my pocket, what do you think?
I can't touch the hoe, because I risk being treated as a villager
What has the stomach to do with this issue of village, so, you are ignorant

abog bǝ́ abo bisié abog te á dí ǎ ǹgál wáma
mayi nâ o bi fa mə nə á m̀fə̀g təge e dɔ́lɔ wayen yá

mə sígi dzáma bi fa amú nâ mə ámbáda mə zâ bí mǝ́tólóg á mɔ́ máma ndɔ̌ fə bié bízǎ mə manǝ́ tsígi esié mɔ́ mə ebadá bɔ̌ nyángá ai dzé ǎ ǹnóm wáma

The time of the work on the fields has come, my wife
I want you to hold the machete, I don't have a penny in my pocket, what do you think?
I can't hold the machete, because I am afraid to get blisters on the hands
Plus, I risk to break my fingernails due to this work, I could not look after my beauty, my husband

I di wanda [pidgin]

I wonder

Na wara wara woman [pidgin]

What a woman

á tege, tege ǹkug

Move the loins

a nyəngəle chef a nyəngəle small a nyəngəle

[animation for dancing]

atéba akə óyɔ́, mvondo atéba wə abə́lə ke óyɔ́ etom dzé me síki dzamá kə óyɔ́ mə atám wə kud bass	Ateba, are you sleeping? Mvondo Ateba, you are really sleeping, why? No, I cannot sleep, I beat the bass.
Bernard akə óyɔ́, Essomba Bernard wə abə́lə ke óyɔ́ etom dzé me síki dzamá kə óyɔ́ mə adzə́m musique	Bernard, are you sleeping? Essomba Bernard, you are really sleeping, why? I cannot sleep, I dance to the music
yə john akə óyɔ́, Jean Marie Ahanda wə abə́lə ke óyɔ́ etom dzé me síki dzamá kə óyɔ́ mə adzə́m məzíg	Are you sleeping, John? Jean-Marie Ahanda, you are really sleeping, why? I can't sleep, I dance to the music
Nylon akə óyɔ́, Nylon wáma wə abə́lə ke óyɔ́ me síki dzamá kə óyɔ́ mə abom batterie	Nylon, you sleep, my dear Nylon, you are really sleeping I can't sleep, I play the drums
yə Epeme akə óyɔ́, Zanzibar Epeme wə abə́lə ke óyɔ́ me síki dzamá kə óyɔ́ kudánə mə məzíg	Epeme, you sleep, Zanzibar Epeme, you are really sleeping I cannot sleep, beat the music for me
Allez ! *Chaud ! chaud ! ...*	Go! Hot! Hot!
Delphine akə óyɔ́, Delphine Nkou Celes wə abə́lə ke óyɔ́ me síki dzamá kə óyɔ́ mə adzə́m məzíg	Delphine, you sleep, Delphine Nkou Celes, you are really sleeping I cannot sleep, I dance to the music
Apache akə óyɔ́, Apache wáma wə abə́lə ke óyɔ́ me síki dzamá kə óyɔ́ mə abom solo	Apache, you sleep, my dear Apache, you really sleep I can't sleep, I play the solo
Tete Brulée, ake óyɔ́, Tetes Brulees wáma wə abə́lə kə óyɔ́ mə atam kə óyɔ́ mə nə fatigué	Tête Brulée, you sleep, my dear Tête Brulée, you really sleep I sleep, because I am tired

Figure 7.5: Lyrics of the song 'Nnam' by Les Têtes Brulées in Ewondo and English. Transcribed from the recording and translated into French by Jules Akoudou, translated into English by Anja Brunner. I thank Olivier Moussa Loumpata and Prof. Dr Louis Martin Onguene Essono for their help with the Ewondo orthography. French words used in the Ewondo text are set in italics.

The song 'Nnam' has a typical bikutsi tempo of 154 bpm and is organized metrically into patterns of 12 pulses. Although not as dominant as
in 'Essingan', the particular role of the solo guitar is also evident in this
song, wherein two guitars interact with each other. The solo guitar is louder
and plays solo parts. The bass guitar unfortunately is hardly audible on the
recording available for analysis.[12] The lyrics are sung by a male solo voice,
answered by a male chorus, in this case the rest of the band. The chorus sings
the part that is written from the perspective of the wife, and also joins in with
the answer of the husband sung by the solo voice, which is vocalized by the
bassist Atebass. In the part dedicated to dancing, the strophic part is over, the
animation starts, and the musicians of the band are all introduced by name. In
terms of rhythmic structure, again the bass drum plays the regular beat divid-
ing the 12 pulses into four. The hi-hat and the snare drum provide the rhythmical patterns and variations, while at some points in the song a bell is used,
playing an off-beat pattern. Interestingly, wind instruments, so prominent in
the songs of Les Vétérans, are left out of both this song and 'Essingan'. In
live versions, according to the musicians, wind instruments were included.

Because of the success of Les Têtes Brulées, the role of the lead guitar
became more important in popular bikutsi. Guitar-based bikutsi with its basic
structure of 12/8-patterns, steady bass drum beat, rhythmical tension in the
percussion, and fast guitar playing was consolidated during the 1980s and
with Les Têtes Brulées. This is due to a large extent to the guitarist Zanzibar
and his famous guitar playing. Although Zanzibar preferred soukous and
merengue pieces, according to Jean-Marie Ahanda, he became popular for
his improvised and fast playing style in bikutsi songs that he developed with
Les Têtes Brulées.

The End of the Original Les Têtes Brulées: Popular Music and Local Religious Traditions

A tragic incident put an immediate end to the career of Les Têtes Brulées in
Cameroon. Shortly after they returned from their tour in 1988, their popular
guitarist Zanzibar died under unexplained and mysterious circumstances on
October 22, 1988. According to some reports on the events surrounding his
death, Zanzibar was at the cabaret in Nkomo where Atebass was playing. He
returned to his home early in the morning and went to bed. Later he was found
in a distressed state and brought to hospital, where after some questioning, he

declared he had taken some pills (Mpessa Mouangue 1988). Although every possible action was taken, the musician died soon afterwards.

The loss of a central member of the group was only one aspect of many that ended in the dissolution of Les Têtes Brulées. More influential were the subsequent public discussions and the rumours concerning the reasons for Zanzibar's death. Since the incident, the events have remained uncertain and have led to suspicions. From an outsider's perspective, especially from a Western background, and for many Cameroonians, the most probable explanation for Zanzibar's death is that the musician committed suicide, as there is no reason to believe otherwise. In his obituary in the *Cameroon Tribune*, Jean-Marie Ahanda alluded vaguely to the possibly unstable state of the guitarist by referring to a song Zanzibar had written entitled 'Qui me regrettera', wherein he asked who would miss him (J.-M. Ahanda 1988b). Three fellow musicians reported on the incident in short statements that seem like testimonies, including information on the musician's statement about having taken pills. Further, Zanzibar appeared to be having trouble with his girlfriend (Owona 1988). However, in Cameroon another perspective on the incident has emerged, namely that the musician was killed. Suspected first and foremost were his fellow group members, motivated by jealousy due to his popularity. Rumours about conflicts during the tour in Europe abounded as well (cf. Owona 1988). These suspicions remain (cf. Fumtim and Cillon Perri 2013). While one reason for these suspicions most probably lies in the influence of Catholicism on Beti society in the late twentieth century, another is grounded in Beti tradition itself.

In Beti tradition, blaming someone for another's death is not unusual and can under certain circumstances be part of funeral rituals. This is the case if the deceased has passed away due to reasons believed to be unnatural. Any death before a certain age, for example, is considered dubious, and soon suspects are found that are accused of having killed the person. It is not necessarily a person that is suspected of being the murderer since belief in black magic is widespread; unnatural deaths are often explained by black magic that had been sent by someone. Often, it is close family members that are accused of having provoked deadly events or an illness. During a Beti funeral ritual, the accusations are made public and form an important part of the ritual (for more on this matter see Abega 1987). Taking this tradition into account, for people thinking along this traditional logic, the death of Zanzibar was without question provoked by somebody else. He was only 25 years old and therefore not of an age to die naturally. With his family not close by, the most obvious suspects were his fellow musicians; the suspected motive was jealousy. As Atebass put it bluntly, "[t]he Cameroonians accused Les Têtes Brulées of having killed Zanzibar" (Mvondo Ateba Albert, interview, October 30, 2012).[13]

In traditional Beti contexts, after long laments and accusations, the accused step forward to defend themselves and then the body is buried. In a similar manner, Jean-Marie Ahanda and the other musicians have reiterated that nobody in the group had provoked Zanzibar's death and that at the height of their success this would have been a rather stupid thing to do, as Zanzibar was vital to their popularity. However, these arguments did little to quell the rumours, and the image of the group was damaged. Les Têtes Brulées never got back to the level they had prior to the tragedy. Moreover, in Cameroon they were openly as well as indirectly ostracized in the following years. While they played concerts in Europe and Canada and released records for the international market, in Cameroon they performed rarely. The group tried a comeback in the early 1990s. Atebass, who had left Les Têtes Brulées before the first tour to Europe to found his own group called Les Martiens, returned (Mvondo Ateba Albert, interview, October 30, 2012), but the spark was gone and the group dissolved for good. Ahanda stated simply that "our success remained in Europe" (Jean-Marie Ahanda, interview, December 11, 2007).[14]

Due to his tragic and mysterious death and his excellent guitar playing, the guitarist Zanzibar has remained a mythical figure in Cameroonian music history. His grave in his natal village of Okola is decorated with an artistic monument featuring a guitar lying on the covering plate. The year after his death, a guitar competition in memory of Zanzibar was organized in the cabaret Escalier Bar. The song 'Essingan' with his guitar solo therein remains an ode to the guitarist and bikutsi in general.

In a way, Les Têtes Brulées still existed at the time of my research, at least as a concept that could be revitalized if necessary. The scholar Dennis Rathnaw has put them on stage again with the help of Jean-Marie Ahanda.[15] In an interview with Radio France International in 2009, Jean-Marie Ahanda announced the release of a new single and it seems that for him the group is still alive and working, even if with different musicians.[16] The original group, however, the one that created a furore with their stage appearance, dissolved in the early 1990s. But they left a lasting impact in Cameroon and still hold an important position in bikutsi history.

After Les Têtes Brulées: An Outlook on Later Bikutsi Developments

While Ebobolo Fia, as the first label to promote guitar-based bikutsi under that name, continued to record and release various artists in the 1980s (and 1990s), new young labels sprang up in Cameroon. Some of them were connected intrinsically to makossa as a musical genre, but some of the new players also entered the growing market for bikutsi music, such as the label Editions Rainbow, which also released records with Les Têtes Brulées. In addition to the founding of labels, new recording facilities emerged that provided an alternative to the studio at the radio station that had opened in 1982. The most popular was producer and arranger Albert Broeuck's recording studio called Studio Dobell 16, which he opened in Douala in the mid-1980s. There he recorded and arranged, among others, bikutsi musicians such as the young singer Nkondo Sitony. For a while he also ran a duplication business for cassettes, however apparently not for very long (Ndachi Tagne 1988; Owona 1990b). Cassettes entered the Cameroonian music market in the early 1980s, at first as blank cassettes that were used to copy music from LPs and singles (J.-M. Ahanda 1982e). In the mid-1980s, the first originally recorded cassettes with Cameroonian music were released. One of the first original cassettes mentioned in the *Cameroon Tribune* was the album by Oncle Medjo me Nsom, produced by Ebobolo Fia (Abui Mama 1985). The shift to cassettes brought an important change for consumers since it made recorded music much cheaper.[17] After a period of transition during which albums could appear on LP and on cassette, as one album of Les Vétérans did, cassettes overtook LPs due to their reduced costs and greater durability (on the impact of cassettes on a local music market see Manuel 1993). In 1990, most albums were released only on cassette tape (Owona 1990b).

With Les Têtes Brulées the tradition of music groups presenting themselves as such came to an end. The trend in the 1980s was in the direction of solo singers. In the 1990s there were still some groups in the tradition of Les Vétérans and Les Têtes Brulées, such as Les Zombies and Les Martiens, but these soon disappeared, with their members being hired elsewhere or leaving the music business. The upcoming younger generation of bikutsi musicians grew into a culture of solo artists. The extended opportunities in recording and producing by means of more studios and labels as well as the reduced costs also made it easier for willing and motivated musicians to enter the music business. With the emergence of electronic instruments such as the synthesizer, singers no longer needed to hire a whole band, but could do much on the synthesizer. This drove the trend to present oneself as a solo artist. The next generation of bikutsi musicians in their twenties at the beginning of the 1990s, composed, produced, and arranged their work in the studio, with an arranger/producer. When performing live, they hired musicians or played with the music groups provided by the cabaret, but their presentation was built on an image as a solo singer.

Connected to the new generation of musicians and the rise of bikutsi as a popular music genre are two aspects of immediate relevance occurring in the early 1990s that – at the end of this chapter and the closing of this study – should briefly be mentioned. The first is the increasing openness towards sexualized lyrics and performances that parallels the appearance of women as solo singers. The second is the ethnic conflict arising around popular music genres bikutsi and makossa. While sexual allusions and immoral content and *animation* were already present in the 1980s in bikutsi performances, at the end of the 1980s bikutsi lyrics and dance allowed more and more direct and openly communicated allusions to sexual matters. The most popular singer associated with "immoral" bikutsi at the beginning of the 1990s was Mbarba Soukous, especially because of his song 'Essamba Essamba'. The song title, which means "in single file" or "in a row", refers to the dancing style connected to the song that is still practised today when 'Essamba Essamba' is played.[18] The people danced one behind the other, back to front, very close, with slightly bent knees and slowly moved forward together – like a snake. Mbarga Soukous and his song 'Essamba Essamba' were intrinsically connected to the cabaret Eldorado La Piscine in the Nkomo quarter in Yaoundé. The locality was one of the most popular cabarets at the time and had its own swimming pool, hence the name. Mbarga Soukous performed there regularly in 1990. In an informal conversation, Jean-Marie Ahanda recalled that Mbarga Soukous' *animation* used many sexual allusions and open exclamations. For example, he had the lights turned off for about a minute, animated the women present to take off their underwear, and when the lights went on again to wave them over their heads. Like Les Vétérans in the Escalier Bar, Eldorado La Piscine is still remembered as a synonym for raucous parties, with its overtly sexual dancing.

The aspect of morality and sexuality in lyrics and performance was much debated publicly at this time. In an article in the *Cameroon Tribune* in October 1990, journalist Roger Owona took up the topic and positioned Mbarga Soukous in line with the French singer Serge Gainsbourg and his song 'Je t'aime... moi non plus', a scandalous song in the 1960s, and the US-American soul singer Marvin Gaye and his song 'Sexual Healing' (Owona

1990a). Shortly after, the newspaper dedicated a 16-page special on the lyrics of Cameroonian songs entitled "Cameroonian songs: which message?"[19] The articles discussed the issue from different angles, speaking for example of "the wave of obscene songs" (Nken 1990) and including an interview with Mbarga Soukous (Owona 1990c). Further, the song 'Essamba Essamba' and sexual content in such songs in general was taken up in cartoons. As I have discussed elsewhere (Brunner 2015, 2012), the trend towards overt sexual representations can be read as a strategy of postcolonial resistance. In an endeavour to keep public space clean, tidy, and orderly, the postcolonial Cameroonian state's representatives frequently used their power to punish people who did not visually conform to the desired image. The rising vulgarity, obscenity, and open sexuality in general and in bikutsi in particular can be read as a reaction to the state's broad interference in and control of public space (cf. Ndjo 2005; Mbembe 2001). The debate culminated in the book *Les Chansons de Sodome et Gomorrhe* by philosopher Mono Ndjana, published in 1999, wherein the author criticized these developments and coined the term "Cameroon Sex Music (CSM)" (Mono Ndjana 1999: 19).

In the early 1990s, women entered the male-dominated bikutsi field as solo artists, a development that was connected to the increased openness concerning sexualized performance. The first popular female bikutsi singer was Catérine Edoa Nkou, who used the stage name K-Tino at the time of my research but had begun her career as Katino or Catino. K-Tino gained public attention with her solo album *Ascenseur* in 1991, after having worked as an accompanying dancer and background singer. In the 2000s she was still one of the best-known and liked bikutsi singers in the country. Her lasting fame is associated with her openly performed, suggestive dancing style on stage and in videos as well as her lyrics, which are praised for their sophisticated use of Ewondo. This mastery of the language of Ewondo brought her much respect and situated her directly in line with the female bikutsi tradition (see Chapter 3). In the song 'Ascenseur: Le Secret de l'Homme', K-Tino sang in metaphorical language about having sex with a priest (see lyrics in Nkolo and Ewens 1999: 443). Called "la femme du peuple", K-Tino became a symbol for what Noah has called the "pornographic spin-off" of bikutsi (Noah 2004: 55–60). Sex, eroticism, vulgarity, and obscenity have been essential features in her representation ever since her first appearance as a solo singer, and especially in the accompanying music videos. This aspect of bikutsi has been a continuously contested and debated aspect of the genre without which the music today is hardly imaginable.[20]

Alongside the sexual connotations brought to bikutsi and the conscious turn to performances of immoral character, bikutsi's ethnic connotations have increased steadily throughout the 1980s. In public appearance and perception, bikutsi was and wanted to be Beti music. As the Beti groups included the President and many other leading political officials, this ethnicity of bikutsi led to suspicion concerning the political support of the music genre. Its media presence, in print, radio, and television, was supposed to have been possible only because Beti working in the respective state-owned institutions supported the music and the musicians' visibility. This suspicion led to increased resentment among makossa musicians and fans who felt neglected and disadvantaged. The late 1980s saw an increasing rivalry between the two music genres, their fans, and sometimes the musicians. Mathias Eric Owona Nguini analysed this in detail in his study "La controverse bikutsi-makossa" (Owona Nguini 1995). The conflicts between musicians and fans of the two musical genres intensified in the late 1980s and culminated in a violent incident during a large concert in Douala in December 1990, when the bikutsi singer Nkodo Sitony was beaten and seriously injured by concert visitors (cf. Madiba 1990). Around 1993 the tensions changed in focus to the point where the main fault line was one of being for or against bikutsi, which was seen as the musical representation of the state. Owona Nguini refers to the rival sides as "bikutsiphiles" and "bikutsiphobes" (Owona Nguini 1995: 273). Politically, these conflicts took place along ethnic and regional lines, especially involving the ethnic groups of the Beti, who had massive political influence, and the Bamiléké and anglophone Cameroonians, who had the main economic power and felt politically discriminated against and not represented.[21] The disputes were coupled with the economic crisis that had hit Cameroon in the 1980s. One of the places where the conflicts had become especially obvious since 1990 was the University of Yaoundé. Besides protest marches and campaigns, violent acts dominated university life from 1990 to 1996 (Konings 2002). Bikutsi and makossa figured as musical representatives of different world views clashing in a time of economic troubles and political unrest. Although the conflicts had ebbed by the mid-1990s, bikutsi's ethnic connotation has remained relevant, although with reduced intensity. The political unrest did not stop bikutsi from developing further and a new generation of bikutsi musicians worked on the genre in the 1990s. With the turn of the century, the popular music genre bikutsi remained a dominant player on the Cameroonian music market and in Cameroonian daily life. The developments in the 1980s establishing the music as a popular genre on the national market have had a lasting effect.

Chapter 8

Conclusion: Bikutsi Shifts

The developments in bikutsi described in this book took place primarily in the 1970s and 1980s in the southern part of Cameroon, in and around the capital Yaoundé in the heart of a region inhabited mainly by Beti ethnic groups. At the end of these two decades, bikutsi had become an established, identifiable popular music genre in the Cameroonian music market. Similar developments, that is, the emergence and popularization of new popular music genres in regional or national music markets, were taking place all over Africa in the twentieth century, from mbalax in Senegal (Brunner 2010) to highlife in Nigeria and Ghana (Waterman 1990; Amoah-Ramey 2018) and chimurenga in Zimbabwe (Turino 2000). These processes, although different in detail, all developed out of a transfer of local, often ethnically coded musical phenomena to other, usually imported instruments, often electric guitars. It is important to have an understanding of the specific historical processes behind the success of these popular music genres establishing themselves within local, national, and sometimes international markets and the shifts occurring on this basis when examining the terms and concepts around popular music in these countries today. Bikutsi in the twenty-first century can only be understood in the light of its evolution in the 1970s and 1980s as an identifiable popular music genre. These developments positioned bikutsi within the Beti and Cameroonian (dance) musical universe in a completely new way. In the following I summarize these processes in terms of relevant shifts occurring in music, political conditions, technological developments, and market positioning. One enduring aspect thereof is the semantic meaning of the term "bikutsi".

The shift in musical taste leading to the emergence of the popular music genre bikutsi has several interconnected aspects: the instrumentation used, the adoption of xylophone music, and the slow disappearance of merengue and soukous out of the dominant repertoire. Applying Motti Regev's concept

of "aesthetic cosmopolitanism" introduced in Chapter 1, the musical foundations of this shift are the double embedding of bikutsi musical practices in the
field of global pop-rock – understood in a broad sense – and local Beti music
traditions. Specifically, the development of bikutsi is positioned within the
overlapping fields of dance music such as merengue and soukous on the one
hand, and Beti musical traditions with women's song-and-dance pieces and
Beti xylophone music on the other.

The influence of global popular music trends in the development of bikutsi
is clearly visible in the instruments and their transition over time. The guitar
as a typical pop-rock instrument was from the beginning the main instrument
for interpreting Beti music in modern contexts, first as an acoustic instrument, but soon also in its electric iteration. While congas and maracas were
predominant in the 1960s as the main percussion instruments, the drum set
replaced the percussion section in the 1970s as the instrument became available and affordable in Cameroon. In the late 1970s and 1980s, keyboards
and synthesizers gained ground in modern dance bands in Cameroon. These
instruments provided, as Motti Regev argues (Regev 2007a, 2007b), a certain
sound aesthetic that was globally recognizable and readily used in different
regions of the world, Cameroon and bikutsi being no exception. In addition
to the sound layer, musical elements taken from other popular music genres
were always part of the inspiration – funk or reggae elements in bikutsi in
the 1980s, for example. Consequently bikutsi's sound aesthetics changed in
terms of instrumentation and desired sound in meeting more or less with
international trends, yet always dependent on the availability of instruments
and new electronic devices. For bikutsi, the change in the percussion section
is of immediate relevance: with the adoption of the drum set in the 1970s,
the clearly marked beat on the bass drum has become a central feature of any
bikutsi played by modern dance bands. While not as distinct in earlier Beti
music, since the 1980s virtually all popular bikutsi pieces feature a regular
marked beat.

While positioned within the context of modern dance music, the dance
band musicians in Yaoundé in the 1970s drew considerable inspiration from
Beti xylophone traditions, and to a lesser extent from the women's tradition of song-and-dance pieces. This led to the creative introduction of certain aspects of sound, rhythm, content, and structure of music performed
traditionally on the məndzáŋ (Beti xylophones used for dance music), into
their guitar-based music. In addition to the "balafon guitar" used by music
groups in the 1970s and 1980s, a clear imitation of the sound and structure of məndzáŋ playing, pieces played by modern dance bands increasingly

featured a structure of two distinct sections within songs: a message part and a dance part, the latter called *animation* (*fr.*). This two-part structure can be traced back to either women's song-and-dance pieces and məndzáŋ dance pieces, or – within the field of popular music – to Congolese dance music trends of the time. Musicians turned away from their merengue repertoire in consequence of these developments. While pieces in the 1970s, even if inspired by Beti music traditions, were still close to merengue and soukous playing styles, the genres were clearly distinct in the 1980s. Connected to the increasing popularity of Beti musical traditions in modern contexts, the repertoire slowly changed. In the early 1970s, the music being played by the respective music groups was still much in the tradition of merengue and soukous; by the early 1980s, the number of these pieces in any group's repertoire had decreased significantly.

In all these changes, however, there is one aspect that has remained constant throughout: the metric foundation, a central aspect clearly associating the music with Beti music traditions. Pieces recognized as bikutsi or related dances have a ternary structure wherein the main beat divides the pulses into groups of three each, with a common length of 12 or 24 pulses, that is, with 4 or 8 beats. Within this metric scheme, different rhythmic realizations are possible, all of them associated with bikutsi or Beti music in general. While in the 1970s the rhythms played were often those drawn from traditional dance genres, like elak or bikutsi (in the sense of a specific rhythmical pattern), over time musicians developed new rhythmical patterns and re-interpreted existing rhythms freely. A general feature therein was a continuous off-beat phrasing on at least one instrument, its accent placed one pulse before the audible beat. In addition to the rather fast tempo of 150 to 170 bpm, this off-beat phrasing produces a tension in the music that adds to its popularity as dance music.

The two rather different fields of musical practice – Beti music traditions and international dance music trends – never existed as strictly separated from each other in Cameroon. On the contrary, they had already merged in one way or another during colonial times, as evident in the adoption of the guitar across Africa and the use of this instrument to interpret various local traditions, or in the use of brass instruments. Independence and the need to construct a distinct national identity created a political demand to creatively develop popular dance music. This met with an increasing availability of instruments and recordings. Attempts by musicians to adopt ethnic musical traditions for popular dance music in order to contribute to the representation of the new nation-state and to adequately express musically the new identity of being "Cameroonian" were high on the agenda in the 1960s and 1970s.

The specific political conditions in a newly emerging and consolidating postcolonial state was significant to the musical development of bikutsi. Popular dance music of various kinds was part of official national musical representation, and supported accordingly. The quest for national representation as well as efforts to establish an ethnic and regional equilibrium in the 1970s was mirrored in the ambitions and attempts to work with one's "own", local, ethnic musical traditions. More often than previously, musicians playing popular dance music like merengue and soukous turned towards various ethnic musical traditions. This turn fit the general social and political zeitgeist prevalent throughout the continent of remembering African roots and simultaneously developing a distinct national consciousness. Furthermore, it was in line with a personal and individual creative need to develop the performed music in new directions. Musicians too were caught in this generally welcomed drive towards creating a Cameroonian identity. In the 1970s, Beti music was just one of many sources of inspiration.

The rise of bikutsi in the 1980s is connected to the increasing power of the Beti within the state and the associated state organizations, such as national radio. Bikutsi, clearly associated with Beti ethnic groups, became a dominant force on the national music market roughly at the same time as a political shift occurred with a Beti becoming president. However, this development was still grounded in the musical innovations that occurred the decade before, as well as the power of the music market and fans. But bikutsi, as Beti music, received much more attention in the 1980s in the media and was increasingly perceived as the music of the state and its authorities.

In terms of technological developments in musical production and dissemination, three important changes occurred in the period in question. First, in 1982, the state-owned multi-track studio in the newly built national radio station in Yaoundé provided new recording opportunities that were widely used especially by musicians based in Yaoundé. As these musicians were mainly performers of bikutsi, the opening of this studio had a considerable impact on the rise of the genre in the Cameroonian music market as a whole: it suddenly became easier and cheaper to produce bikutsi recordings than before. Secondly, in the late 1980s, cassette tapes started to replace vinyl records and became the dominant sound storage medium until well into the 2000s. Bikutsi was one of the first popular music genres to be marketed via cassettes and combined with the spread of cheap cassette players, bikutsi became accessible to people with less financial means. Finally, television was introduced to Cameroon in 1985, and bikutsi got considerable airplay on this new audio-visual communication medium, due to the specific political situation within the postcolonial state, the authorities largely being Beti themselves.

Bikutsi's rise in popularity in the early 1980s is further grounded in a shift in its market position. Two individuals in the music business in particular succeeded in framing the music of bands in Yaoundé in a new way that made it attractive to a wider audience. Acting as "cultural intermediaries" were the founder of a new record label focusing on bikutsi, Claude Tchemeni, and the journalist Jean-Marie Ahanda, himself a musician. Both contributed their own specific forms of social, cultural, symbolic, and economic capital (Bourdieu 1984) to the strategic positioning of bikutsi as a new popular music genre. The combination of media access, musical expertise, financial means, and music business know-how made the communication of a new musical trend in a different societal field possible. Beti music played by modern music groups, until that time a genre known only to insiders in Yaoundé, became visible, publicly negotiated, and popular with a wider audience. This new framing of an existing musical practice required specific marketing techniques, especially the introduction of a distinct name for the music under consideration. While the term "bikutsi" was already being used to designate some Beti music played by modern dance bands, it was only in the early 1980s that it was firmly established as a term for a popular music genre, with Tchemeni and Ahanda at the forefront. During the 1980s, then, bikutsi emerged as a term to describe not only the women's song-and-dance tradition but more generally any Beti popular music.

The act of naming the popular, electric guitar-based dance music played in Yaoundé bikutsi brought about an important shift to the genre, in addition to those occurring in music, social context, technology, and politics: what bikutsi meant in the 1970s is not what bikutsi came to mean from the 1980s onwards. This enduring change in the semantic field of bikutsi is what this book has set out to explain. In the 1960s and 1970s, bikutsi described either the particular song-and-dance practice of Beti women, a specific dance movement and rhythmical pattern, or a musical genre played for example by xylophone ensembles to which one can dance accordingly. In the 1980s, the term was extended to include any Beti popular music, that is, music played by modern music groups with references to Beti musical traditions. This extension had far-reaching consequences, especially since it became a marketing term. At the time of my research for this book in the 2000s and 2010s, bikutsi was used to refer to Beti music in general, to Beti music by modern dance bands in particular, to the women's dance tradition, or simply to all music that could be danced as bikutsi. The semantic layers of the term had grown and broadened even more than in past decades, a fact often leading to confusion and misunderstandings. Elderly musicians and some younger ones lamented this development, as the diversity of rhythmical patterns and dance genres and their respective names within Beti culture was in the process of being lost. Since the 1980s, any Beti dance was increasingly being called "bikutsi" and not its proper name, even if a specific and identifiable dance pattern was used.

This development, positioning bikutsi as a commodity on the Cameroonian music market, is of immediate relevance to scholars in the field of Beti and Cameroonian music. Older sources on Beti music until the 1980s do not mention bikutsi at all. In the 1990s, bikutsi slowly emerged as the core topic of studies on Beti music. This is obviously due to the rise in popularity and significance of the musical genre in postcolonial Cameroon and its musical landscape, and clearly linked to this shift in semantic layers. In order to both adequately apply earlier sources on Beti music and understand Beti musical traditions, this extension of the term bikutsi is of importance for any future scholarship on these issues.

In addition to this ever more multifaceted meaning of bikutsi, in my research I encountered two rather different views on bikutsi in terms of its positioning as a popular music genre. The first is that musicians in the 1970s created a new popular music by drawing on Beti music, consciously working on a modern urban music tradition constructed around the instruments of a modern music group that could effectively be situated on the Cameroonian music market. The second is that the field of Beti music, the totality of ethnically associated and defined musical practices, has been extended in its possible performance settings and instrumental variation. Guitar-based bikutsi is not only an urban popular music using some Beti elements but first and foremost a new version of Beti music. In Cameroon, these two perspectives exist side by side and complement one another. While being modern, urban, popular, media regulated, and embedded in, if not dependent upon, the music market, the music has not lost its ethnic connections and is inherent in a field of Beti musical practices in line with Austin Emielu's idea of progressive traditionalism: "A musical tradition can develop progressively without disconnecting from its indigenous roots, and contemporary African musics, particularly ethnic-derived dance-band musics, are simply new forms of traditional music that have been revitalized or renewed as a local strategy of sustenance and generational relevance" (Emielu 2018: 226).

At the time of my research, bikutsi was a major economic factor in the field of popular dance music entertainment. In the national musical landscape it held a well-established position. Certainly, the music had changed since the 1980s in accordance with various global aesthetic trends and possibilities. There were also signs that the ethnic connotation of bikutsi had to some extent been loosened, for example with French emerging increasingly as a possible language for song lyrics. Bikutsi remained, however, Beti music; the ethnic association persisted. At the same time, bikutsi musicians and other players in the field of bikutsi production of course continued to observe developments in popular music around the world. Any attempt to understand the popular music genre bikutsi and its musical and social embeddedness needs to take into account these complementary and interdependent aspects and recognize bikutsi as a locally and ethnically embedded player in a global field of popular music practices.

Notes

Chapter 1

1   Figures taken from CIA Factbook, https://www.cia.gov/the-world-factbook/countries/cameroon/ (accessed March 30, 2021).

2   Of relevance during colonial times in the early twentieth century for an emergent feeling of collective identity were the missionaries and the spread of Christianity. Charles Atangana, a Beti employee in the German administrative system, had a significant role in this process due to the extraordinary position of power and influence he gained in the course of his career (Quinn 1980).

3   See the classifications and denominations in Nekes 1911; Tessmann 1913; Tsala n.d.; Alexandre and Binet 1958; Laburthe-Tolra 1977, 1981b; Mviena 1970; Quinn 1980, 2006; Ngumu 1976a; Mehler 1993.

4   Cameroon is divided into ten semi-autonomous regions in turn subdivided into "départements" and "arrondissements". The Beti-Faŋ people extend further into the regions Sud and Est.

5   Laburthe-Tolra mentions that "Faŋ" means "homme" (*fr.*) or "Herr" (*ger.*) ("man"); this supports my notion of Beti and Faŋ being the major groups. The term Bulu (and others) in contrast are connected to specific attributes; Bulu, for example, is a title of honour (Laburthe-Tolra 1977: 93–96).

6   See e.g., Turino 2000; Askew 2002; Martin 2004; Englert 2008; White 2009. For Cameroon specifically see Modo 1995; Owona Nguini 1995; Onguene Essono 1996; Nyamnjoh and Fokwang 2005.

7   On Cameroon's postcolonial history under Ahmadou Ahidjo see Bayart 1979; Nyamnjoh 2005; DeLancey, Neh Mbuh, and DeLancey 2010; Schicho 2001. For the period under Paul Biya see Konings 2002; Monga 2000; Nkwi and Socpa 1997; Sindjoun 1996; Mehler 1993.

8   With Cameroon being a bilingual state, an English version was published as well.

9   *La Presse du Cameroun* was part of the group Breteuil; Charles de Breteuil founded the first daily newspapers in Francophone Africa (cf. Perret 2005).

10 For more on the problem-centred interview see Witzel 2000; Scheibelhofer 2008, 2005.

Chapter 2

1 Original French: "inspirateurs de la musique typique 'in Yaoundé', qui puise sa sève dans les racines mêmes du folklore béti-et-fang (et assimiliés ...)'"

2 For more on Anne-Marie Nzié see Ndachi Tagne (1990) and Brunner (2013).

3 Biographical information on Cheramy de la Capitale has been taken largely from a lengthy report on the singer by a journalist published on the website http://www.nkul-beti-camer.org/ekang-global-revue. php?cmd=personnage&Item=33&PHPSESSID=h4ie6a9thghk3g9559kn9sko76 (accessed June 17, 2011).

4 The brass band was founded and funded by the Beti Charles Atangana, who had gained significant influence in the German and later the French colonial administration; he maintained the brass band for representational and entertainment reasons (Quinn 2006).

5 Original French: "Dans un Yaoundé qui se voulait haut lieu d'élégance et gardait malgré tout un caractère villageois avec ses maisons en nattes, Cheramy était la vedette".

6 Original French: "Dans les receptions où l'orchestre jouait sous un abri de palmes, on buvait du champagne soda, de la bière Stoubic, Kronenbourg, Beaufort Spécial, Slavia, Heineken, du vin rouge Kiravi et Bellevie".

7 Original French: "Les artistes d'avant s'initiaient en écoutant d'autres groupes. Par exemple, on interprétait la musique congolaise, on interprétait les Cubains, le Sud-Américains, le patchanga, ces genres ... donc, on était un group de variété".

8 Original French: "Comme la pluie chasse le beau temps, la chaine chasse de plus en plus le musicien dans nos boites de nuit".

9 Original French: "Lorsque dans les années 76/77, le gouvernement organise le recrutement de jeunes gens dans les corporations du théatre, de musique et de la danse, on rêve d'un grand group à l'image du Daniel Sorano de Dakar ou de l'Orchestre national de Guinée-Conakry".

10 Original French: "Les instruments traditionnels puisque le but de l'orchestre est entre autre de les exploiter on timidement fait leur apparition sur la scène".

11 See for example Essola 1975; Sango 1976, 1977; "Les orchestres scolaires commencent à se manifester" 1976; "Musique scolaire dimanche au Capitole. Quatre orchestres au programme" 1978; Lemana 1980.

12 For more on makossa that in the 1970s became the first Cameroonian popular music genre see Noah 2010.

13 There were an estimated 1.78 million radio sets in Cameroon in 1992 (XIX Article 19 1997).

14 https://www.macrotrends.net/countries/CMR/cameroon/population-growth-rate (accessed July 19, 2012).

Chapter 3

1 The neologism "mezik", most likely derived from the French word "musique", has emerged in Beti languages and is used especially among younger musicians with a similar meaning to "music" as it is understood in Western contexts. The particle "me-" being a plural signifier, this is perceived as a plural; thus, occasionally the constructed singular "azik" is used, which would mean something like "one music".

2 Original French: "si nous regardons vivre le Beti, nous sommes vite frappés de la facilité et de la spontanéité avec lesquelles il chante. Il chante aussi bien dans les circonstances le plus graves de sa vie que dans les moments de loisir et de détente. Il chante quand il est dans un groupe comme quand il est seul, quand il est petit comme quand, la tête blanche et ployant sous le poids des années, il reste à la case à garder les petits-fils et les arrière-petits-fils. Joyeux, il chante, mais qu'il soit dans la peine, dans les larmes et dans le deuil, il chante encore".

3 One day in Yaoundé, I was in the office of François Bingono Bingono, then vice director of the national radio station. Bingono Bingono told a woman present about the death of a person she had known, and she immediately fell into a state of mourning, rocking back and forth singing syllables, words, and complaints in a low voice to herself. The melodic form always started high and descended slowly. This behaviour was pointed out to me immediately by Bingono Bingono as a common spontaneous reaction among Beti women to express grief over a deceased person.

4 Original French: "il danse seulement mais il ne sait pas bien danser".

5 Original French: "on ne peut éxécuter les bikutsi sans le chant. Les pas des danseuses vibrent à son rythme. Le chant commande également les gestes du danseur".

6 The Ewondo terms are given here and in the following in the orthography used by Mbala.

7 Another term used by Mbala is "meyebe"; according to Tsala, "yébë" means to answer a call ("reponde à un appel", *fr.*), to agree, as well as to believe (Tsala n.d.: 683). The meaning hence corresponds to the term "mekasi".

8 Original French: "Les vois les plus rauques exécutent à merveille des morceaux de bikutsi".

9 Again, a brief look at the dictionary provides yet another translation: the verb "dzomi" is translated by Tsala as "to conclude" ("conclure", *fr.*) and "to lower" ("baisser", *fr.*).

10 For examples see Mbala 1985, in particular 501–681; Betene 1973: 53–59; Awona n.d.: 88–93.

11 Original German: "obgleich ich selbst keinen rechten Überblick über das krause Zeug gewinnen kann und nur soviel verstehe, daß über die Männer das ganze Füllhorn weiblichen Spottes und weiblicher Klatschsucht ausgegossen wird".

12 Original French: "En effet le langage de ces chants est tellement énigmatique qu'il faut, au préalable, être initié pour en saisir le fond".

13 The word "abog" means both "dance" ("danse", *fr.*) and celebration or festivity ("fête", *fr.*) (Tsala n.d.: 27).

14 English translation by the author. The French translation, by Christian Tsala Tsala based on the recording, read: "Dans la vie, si tu ne prends rien au serieux, tu ne vas rien récolter de serieux".

15 Original French: "Aux claquements de mains traditionnels s'ajoutent aujourd'hui des instruments modernes tels que le saxophone et la guitare".

Chapter 4

1 Original description by Hornbostel in German: "Die (8) [sic] Klangstäbe sind auf Holzträger aufgebunden, die mit Rindenzeug umwickelt sind, und unter jedem Klangstab ist ein Kürbisresonator aufgehängt; das Instrument wird an einem Gurt um den Hals gehängt und durch einen großen Bügel, der zugleich die Holme trägt, vom Körper des Spielers abgehalten" (Hornbostel 1913: 322–23).

2 Original French: "Or, en cette date du deux Janvier 1962, c'est une véritable canonisation des instruments traditionnels qui participaient officiellement à un office liturgique et faisaient ainsi entendre leur voix pour la première fois dans la Cathédrale de Yaoundé".

3 Original French: "La danse, sombre il est vrai, vient quant à elle mettre fin à la traditionnelle dichotomie entre âme et corps et attester que dans la nouvelle liturgie l'homme tout entier, esprit, âme et corps doit désormais vaquer à la recherche de l'absolu".

4 Original French: "La Maîtrise poursuit et soutient l'instauration d'une adaptation vraie et authentique de la religion à la mentalité et à la vie africaine".

5 Original French: "Dans certains bars, on acceptaient qu'ils viennent, qu'ils se mettent dehors, ils se mettent à jouer, et bon".

6 Original French: "Vous voulez un morceau, vous payez, c'est comme ça".

7 Original French: "C'est avec beaucoup de Plaisir que le public a écouté 'Richard Band' dans son répertoire fait de vieux morceaux, tels que Meringue Mariage, Menga yen aval adzo dont on se souvient, raffolaient beaucoup de Camerounais entre 1970 et 1974".

8 Original French: "Ce que j'ai vecu en grandissant à Yaoundé, c'est le fait que avant, quand les gens se marier, ils embarquaient une sono dans la voiture, ou bien une orchestre moderne avec des guitares, et ils dansaient dans la rue en

marchant ... Et petit à petit, on a vu que ce qui avait moin de moyenne prenait les balafons, et souvent les balafons allait loin, ils venaient due village".

9   It has to be noted that the names of the individual instruments and their roles in the ensemble can vary from region to region, depending on the respective Beti subgroup and their dialectal variant. For example, the names Kubik documented (Kubik 2001: 873) were slightly different to the ones Ngumu and Mba used and that I heard myself during fieldwork. The terms used here are those used by the members of the ensemble Balafon Star, who have family ties to the region around Akonolinga, east of Yaoundé. These names correspond to those provided by Ngumu (1976b).

10 Original French: "tout comme le sifflement s'entend par rapport à la voix normale de l'homme".

11 Original French: "à la limite du bruit et du son".

12 Original French: "Le xylophone qu'il avait connu et pratiqué dans son enfance ne comportait que les neuf lames ..., pour la construction du premier instrument. Mais par la suite il avait constaté, surtout lors de son séjour en pays Etenga, que quelques groupes de mendzaŋ avaient introduit un nouveau son entre la lame 1 et la lame 6".

13 The first was called "60's Anthology"; the second, being Volume 2 to the first (as written on the cover), was titled "Couple Heureux".

14 Original French: "Dans les boites de nuit, c'est maintenant qu'il y a des gens qui paye les orchestres de balafons pour jouer".

15 http://musiki-cm.com/component/content/article/558-cet-homme-est-dangereux-pour-carrossel.html?tmpl=component&print=1&page=   (accessed May 18, 2011). Original French: "Vous êtes donc à la descente Carrossel et pourtant les nombreuses voitures qui se battent pour des mètres carrés de parking déversent des dizaines de personnes à l'entrée d'un autre cabaret, La Couronne. La concurrence de ce petit voisin, dit-on ici, serait telle que les noctambules viennent s'éclater là avant d'aller faire un tour au prestigieux Carrossel".

Chapter 5

1   Original French: "le style guitare-balafon qu'on découvre dans le thème 'Bekono Nga Nkonda' crée par l'orchestre Los Camaroes, marque vraiment le départ d'un nouveau style dans la musique 'typique' ou de variété camerounaise".

2   I thank Joachim Oelsner wholeheartedly for the information on the two earlier recordings and for providing me with copies of the original recordings for research purposes (email communication with Joachim Oelsner, June 27, 2011; personal communication, November 2012).

3   Original French: "En effet, libérés des contraintes sociales, tel ce surmoi oppressif que constituent les adultes, avec leur chapelet d'interdits et de tabou tribaux,

limitant ainsi les aspirations des adolescents, les jeunes à travers ces chants, expriment sans scrupule leurs sentiments et leurs ambitions".

4 Original French: "Les deux jeunes gens se livrent parfois à un gestuel expressif for éloquent qui frise parfois la grivoiserie. Ils miment souvent quelques scènes de leurs aventures amoureuses".

5 Original French: "Il est hors de doute que certaines danses avaient intentionnelle en tune portée sensuelle".

6 Original French: "un terme qui désigne un ensemble de rythmes beti: bol, ékan, ékomot, metsin, olamtsa, koé et même élak, etc. La liste n'est pas exhaustive. Ces rythmes ont pour la plupart un dénominateur commun: le martèlement du sol par les danseurs".

7 A more popular version of the song released by Fiesta in 1978 and which can be found on YouTube differs significantly in its structure.

Chapter 6

1 It should be noted that for Bourdieu, who developed this concept on the basis of research carried out in France in the 1960s and 1970s, this authority is connected to a specific social position: cultural intermediaries are members of an emerging class of petit bourgeoisie. Their cultural habits and tastes blur well-established distinctions like the one between so-called "high" and "low" culture which was very well defined before (cf. Negus 2002: 503). Thus, the potential of members of the petit bourgeoisie to place a higher value on certain cultural goods also makes them flexible enough to promote them and engage in their marketing, especially in professional positions. For more on cultural intermediaries see the special issue on cultural intermediaries of the journal *Cultural Studies* (Vol. 16/4), especially Nixon and du Gay 2002 and Negus 2002, as well as Wright 2005, Hesmondhalgh 2006 and Hennion 1989. The role of cultural intermediaries in the British music industry concerned with releases under the label "World Music" was analysed by Haynes 2005.

2 Original French: "pour parler un peu des particularités de Yaoundé et en boite comme Escalier, où on jouait la musique du village, amplifiée avec des instruments electriques".

3 Original French: "qui ont été deracinés du village, retrouvent un peu leur identité, et viennent s'amuser entre eux ... Il y avait une animation là-bas qui n'existaient nulle part ailleurs".

4 Original French: "parce que je ne peux pas entrer dans les explications techniques".

5 Original French: "Je suis arrivé ici à l'age de 10 ans, et j'ai vecu beaucoup plus la culture Beti".

6   Original French: "Je travaillais pour certains artistes camerounais qui étaient produit par les Européens. Je me suis donc dit, pourquoi pas moi aussi, et c'est là où je suis lancé dans la production des disques".

7   See articles in *Cameroon Tribune* (July 20, 2009) and *Le Jour Quotidien* (August 5, 2009).

8   Original French: "Quand il a sorti 'Kulu', trois mois après, il a acheté sa Peugeot 204".

9   I am aware of the following 7-inch singles from the late 1970s: Les Vétérans d'Ongola: 'Dulu Ya Awola'/'Olun Minlem' (Ngomba Productions); Les Vétérans d'Ongola: 'Maye Bo Yo?'/'Sara' (Ngomba Productions); Les Vétérans d'Ongola: 'Eyenga Osono'/'A Mama Ye Wo Yen' (Ngomba Productions); Meyong Ambroise et les Vétérans: 'Ngon Mvele'/'Identité' (Disques Cousin); Ondoua Akono Gaston et les Vétérans: 'Agnes'/'[not readable on recording] Brigitte' (Disques Cousin). My thanks to music archivist Joachim Oelsner in Yaoundé for this information.

10 Original French: "Ceux qui font la fine bouche parlent de bousculades, de rixes et d'ambiance surchauffée. Ceux qui aiment reprennent cette ambiance à leur compte et ne tarissent pas d'éloges à l'endroit de ce temps du dernier orchestre vivant de la capitale … En fait 'Escalier Bar' connaît sa transe le vendredi, aux approches du weekend. Pour une place à un prix modique et des boissons pratiquement données, le client vit un grand nuit époustouflant".

11 Original French: "Dès que nous arrivions, on commençait avec les préludes, un peu de la musique douce, la bossa nova, le cha-cha-cha, tu vois, un peu les préludes d'une soirée. Après, vers 21:30, c'est là où l'ambiance commence. C'est-à-dire, on commence avec les trucs un peu comme les merengues. Vers les 23 heures là, quand le bikutsi commence, c'est jusqu'à la gare".

12 Original French: "Parce que vendredi était le grand jour, c'était le vendredi des banquiers. Le vendredi, c'était grave".

13 Original French: "C'était divisé en deux. Une partie pour tout le commun, les mortels, et derrière c'était réservé à ceux qui avaient les moyens. Les grands moyens".

14 Original French: "Les vendredi, tout le monde est allé à la messe".

15 Original French: "tous ceux qui passent pour 'in' doivent être vus de ce côté-là", "C'était presque un déshonneur d'entendre qu'un tel n'était pas venu à Escalier".

16 Original French: "Si on parle des Vétérans, c'est le bikutsi".

17 Original French: "Je leur ai dit que, si on met sur un disque exactement ce qu'on joue au bar, il ne rond que le publique du bar, et le reste ne va pas suivre cette chose-là".

18 Original French: "De temps en temps, certains instruments dont la prise de son est complètement ratée sont effacés tout simplement et re-exécutés par d'autres musiciens en France, exemple de la basse du dernier album de Vétérans exécutée je crois par Michel Alibo. Pourtant tous ceux qui ont déjà mis pied à Escalier-bar connaissent la maîtrise de la basse typique de cluei qui tient cet

instrument de ledit bar, mais voilà, il est trahi par la prise de son du multipiste de Yaoundé. Ceci s'applique aussi aux suires car le travail de deux garçons comme Essono et Mebenga (trompette et saxo) a été systématiquement éliminé parce que, malgré la bonne exécution des instruments, la prise de son n'était pas à la hauteur du son général donné à l'album 'traditions'".

19 One song in Les Vétérans' output is an exception: 'Osun' on the LP *Traditions* is labelled as "koué", referring to a specific dance (also written "koé"). It is possible that this dance had not yet been included in what was commonly labelled "bikutsi", or the group wanted to highlight the specificity of the dance that was rather rare in modern music, probably due to its 18-pulse-structure and the fact that it is usually played not on xylophones but on slit drums.

20 Original French: "Mais, finalement, c'est Kulu qui a pris la tête. Et bon. C'est pour ca que c'est parti".

21 Original French: "On attendait Kulu dans la salle toujours avec impatience. On attendait toujours Kulu, comme ça venait vers les deux heures du matin. C'est tout le monde qui était impatient. Mais qu'on intonait Kulu, c'est tout la salle qui étais rempli. Personne ne restait assis, quand ils lançaient Kulu".

22 Original French: "On mettait d'abord un tempo au début, pour que les gens suivent d'abord les paroles, qui soient interessé. Et après, on faisait un break pour envoyer l'ambiance, là, où les gens, dès qu'on met la 'bem' ... c'est début á la fin la meme chose. C'est-à-dire, tu te leves, tu te decoules, tout est en haut, jusqu'à la fin !"

23 Owona Nguini said that it means something similar to "so that it moves" ("que ça bouge", Owona Nguini 1995: 272). It seems to be a word created for the purpose of animating dancing in the cabaret, possibly in reference to a specific dance step or movement.

24 In Congolese music, the part "seben" involves a specific person, the "atalaku", who is responsible for "shouts" during the *animation* and emerged as a central figure throughout the 1980s (White 2009: 59–64), a development not mirrored in bikutsi.

25 Original French: "Nous, on s'est vraiment battu, chez nous, c'était du folklore".

26 Original French: "pas franchement comme les femmes chantent, comme les grand- parents ont chanté. Mais en plus, en dehors de ça, c'est une composition, c'est comme une rédaction".

27 Such issues of cultural property in connection to community and traditional music are well known and much debated in ethnomusicology, especially in the 1990s with the emergence of the marketing term "World Music", or, for example, around Paul Simon's collaboration with the South African music group Ladysmith Black Mambazo (Meintjes 1990; Connell and Gibson 2004) or the use of samples of ethnomusicological recordings in popular music (e.g., Feld 2000; see also Binas-Preisendörfer 2010). John Collins identified various problems with applying European copyright conceptions to African music realities (Collins 1993).

28 Original French: "C'est tous les musiciens qui s'inspirent de quelqu'un ou de quelque chose. Mais pour l'essentiel, nos morceaux viennent de nous-mêmes, …"

29 Original French: "C'est un commerce, c'est un marché, ça les intéressait, on était oblige de le faire".

30 Original French: "Quand ils enregistraient, ils limitaient vraiment le message, parce que le message devrait être approprié au public".

31 Original French: "Quand c'est en boite, là, c'était le direct. C'est-à-dire là, on allait directement droit au but. On prononçait directement ce qu'il fallait prononcer. Mais, quand il fallait enregistrer, il fallait jouer cache-cache. Non, en boite, c'était grave, je vous le dis, c'était direct, brute".

32 Original French: "Oui, c'était là. Mais, c'était un peu caché sur le disque. Mais dans Escalier, c'était ouvert".

33 This was due to two complementary reasons. First, my mainly male interlocutors did not feel comfortable talking openly on matters like these, especially to a (foreign) woman; and second, people are attentive towards the image of bikutsi music that they present to foreigners, including European researchers, and avoid talking about issues that they object to morally themselves, out of fear that they could cast a negative light on their cultural background.

34 Original French: "Au lieu de parler de sex, nous avons des petits expressions d'appeler les choses, il y a des expressions, mais il n'y avait que nous, les Beti qui comprenions ce qu'on voulait dire".

Chapter 7

1 For details see, e.g., DeLancey 1989; DeLancey, Neh Mbuh, and DeLancey 2010; Bayart 1986.

2 Allowing private media next to state-owned media has not ended political oppression completely, as for example could be seen with the forced temporary closure of the private radio station *Magic FM* (which was very popular in and around Yaoundé) in 2008 because of critical commentaries about Biya's government (cf. http://globaledge.msu.edu/countries/cameroon/government/, accessed April 18, 2011; personal communication with Donald Tsala, radio presenter at *Magic FM*).

3 On the record it is in fact entitled 'A Nti Kaa', but this is probably a spelling mistake (cf. LP Sita Mengue, AOLP 013, J.-M. Ahanda 1982a).

4 Original French: "Quand on partait jouer dans les manifestations, soit du mariage, les gens ne nous permettaient pas de jouer du bikutsi, ils disaient, ah, c'est trop village".

5 Original French: "Zanzibar accède donc au firmament des géants du Bikutsi".

6 Original French: "Donc, c'est Foty, qui nous propose, vous laissez la modernité, vous dechirrez vos trikots, et vos pantalons. Moi, je vais proposer qu'on rase

nos têtes, comme les Indiens, parce que le groupe s'appelait Les Têtes Brulées, l'inspiration est venu; j'ai dit il faudrait que chacun trouve un look pour sa tête. Ca a donné. Et Jean Marie Ahanda, il nous a invité chez lui, dès que nous avons fini à raser les têtes, il se levait, tout doucement, et allait dans sa chambre, il a pris de la peinture et le pinceau, et il l'a mis sur ma tête, et vraiment, c'était beau. Tout le monde à applaudi, c'est ainsi qu'on a commeneé à mettre la peinture".

7   Original French: "Arrivé à la television, j'ai caché les Têtes Brulées, mais quand on les a annoncé, 'et voici Les Têtes Brulées', le presentateur les a pas vu encore. Donc, lui-meme a eu une surprise terrible".

8   Original French: "Pour nous, c'était une façon de representer la pauvreté, les habilles dechiré, même volontairement, le manque, avec – comment je peux le dire – paradoxalement des pantalons des clowns, avec des sneakers qui font un peut militaire, et des sac-a-dos".

9   It should be mentioned that in the 1980s, another group also used body painting in their look: the Golden Sounds, the music group of the Republican Guards (see Chapter 2). In 1986 they released the LP *Zangalewa*, produced by Ebobolo Fia. In a video accompanying the popular song 'Zangalewa Zaminamina', the group made fun of the military, especially military officers. The three protagonists had white painted faces, wore military shirts stuffed with material to make them fat, short trousers, and colonial pith helmets. In their dancing they mimicked military parades and the military as a whole – which they themselves were a part of as members of the Republican Guards. In contrast to Les Têtes Brulées, however, the look was part of the joke of the song and not a look created for the group, although they kept it for some time.

10 I thank Joachim Oelsner for providing this information about the group's early releases.

11 The recording I mainly used for this analysis was a live version released in 2000 on the *Best Of* CD, which I frequently compared to a recording released in the 1990s, the only copy of which I had available was of very bad sound quality.

12 I thank Mvondo Ateba Albert for providing me with a digital version of the song, which is probably from the LP *Révélation Télé-Podium*; however, it might be from a later LP recording. Unfortunately, we could not clarify the respective LP release.

13 Original French: "Les Camerounais accusaient *Les Têtes Brulées* d'avoir tué Zanzibar".

14 Original French: "Notre succès restait en Europe".

15 For a description and report on this event see Rathnaw 2009: 61–80.

16 https://musique.rfi.fr/musique/20090305-le-nouveau-visage-tetes-brulees (accessed March 30, 2021).

17 In a 1981 report in *Cameroon Tribune*, the prices for LPs were cited as being 3400 to 3500 CFA, 7-inch singles as 1000 CFA. In 1984 LPs could cost up to 5000 CFA. To record a cassette from an LP cost around 1000 to 1200 CFA. Even

including the cost of 800 to 1000 CFA for the blank cassette, copying of music from LPs to cassette was clearly cheaper (Ibrahima 1984).

18   I witnessed this dance style performed in 2008 in a cabaret in Yaoundé and in 2012 at the festival *Festi Bikutsi*. Both times, Mbarga Soukous was invited and performed, among others, his hit 'Essamba Essamba'. The people screamed and did not hesitate to get in line and dance accordingly (see, e.g., recording done at the *Festi Bikutsi* 2012, archived at the Phonogrammarchiv, the Austrian Audiovisual Research Archive of the Austrian Academy of Sciences in Vienna).

19   Original French: "Chansons camerounaises: quel message?"

20   For more on the singer K-Tino and a possible interpretation of her performance, see Brunner 2015 and Rathnaw 2009.

21   For more on these conflicts see Konings 2002; Nyamnjoh 2005; Monga 2000.

Bibliography

Abega, Séverin Cécile. 1987. *L'Esana chez les Beti*. Yaoundé: Éditions Clé.

Abui Mama. 1985. "L'Oncle Medjo me Nsom en cassette". *Cameroon Tribune*, December 31, 1985.

Agawu, Kofi. 2003. *Representing African Music: Postcolonial Notes, Queries, Positions*. New York: Routledge.

Ahanda, Antoine. 1982. "C'était la vogue du merengue". *Cameroon Tribune*, April 20, 1982.

Ahanda, Jean-Marie. 1982a. "Celui qui vient à point". *Cameroon Tribune*, December 29, 1982.

Ahanda, Jean-Marie. 1982b. "La mort des orchestres". *Cameroon Tribune*, March 6, 1982.

Ahanda, Jean-Marie. 1982c. "Le dernier refuge". *Cameroon Tribune*, March 6, 1982.

Ahanda, Jean-Marie. 1982d. "Le retour de Cheramy de la Capitale". *Cameroon Tribune*, April 13, 1982.

Ahanda, Jean-Marie. 1982e. "Mbida Douglas: 'le disque coûte trop cher'". *Cameroon Tribune*, January 9, 1982.

Ahanda, Jean-Marie. 1986a. "'Jazz sous les manguiers' à l'Université". *Cameroon Tribune*, May 3, 1986.

Ahanda, Jean-Marie. 1986b. "Les 'Têtes Brulées' à Nkol-Afeme". *Cameroon Tribune*, September 20, 1986.

Ahanda, Jean-Marie. 1986c. "Musique en Liberté avec Les Têtes Brulées". *Cameroon Tribune*, April 19, 1986.

Ahanda, Jean-Marie. 1987. "Epeme Théodore dit Zanzibar. Du bikutsi surprise". *Cameroon Tribune*, January 7, 1987.

Ahanda, Jean-Marie. 1988a. "Le 'village' se transporte chez 'Tailleur Bar'". *Cameroon Tribune*, October 21, 1988.

Ahanda, Jean-Marie. 1988b. "Les Têtes Brûlées perdent un magicien de la guitare". *Cameroon Tribune*, October 23, 1988.

Ahanda, René. 1986. "'Je fais attention à ce que je dis'". *Cameroon Tribune*, October 2, 1986.

Alexandre, Pierre, and Jacques Binet. 1958. *Le groupe dit Pahoun (Fang-Bulu-Beti)*. Paris: Presses Universitaires de France.

Alobwede, Charles Esambe. 2006. *Cameroon: Research Findings and Conclusions*. Tech. report. African Media Development Initiative.

Amoah-Ramey, Nana Abena. 2018. *Female Highlife Performers in Ghana: Expression, Resistance, and Advocacy*. Lanham, MD: Lexington.

Anderson, Benedict. 1983. *Imagined Communities: Reflections on the Origin and Spread of Nationalism*. London: Verso.

Askew, Kelly M. 2002. *Performing the Nation: Swahili Music and Cultural Politics in Tanzania*. Chicago: University of Chicago Press.

Ateba Ndoumou, Alphonse. 1986. "Nous voulons changer les habitudes en matière de danse". *Cameroon Tribune*, August 14, 1986.

Austerlitz, Paul. 1997. *Merengue: Dominican Music and Dominican Identity*. Philadelphia: Temple University Press.

Averill, Gage. 1997. *A Day for the Hunter: A Day for the Prey. Popular Music and Power in Haiti*. Chicago: University of Chicago Press. https://doi.org/10.7208/chicago/9780226032931.001.0001

Awona, Stanislaus. n.d. [1967?]. "Bikud-Si et Mvet". In *Danses du Cameroon. Cameroonian Dances*, edited by Ministère de l'Éducation, de la Jeunesse et de la Culture, 87–104. Yaoundé: Centres d'édition et de production de manuels et d'auxiliaires de l'enseignement.

Ayissi-Essomba, André. 1984. "Les Vétérans: un cercle au village". *Bingo* 377: 50–51.

Bahoken, J. C., and Engelbert Atangana. 1976. *Cultural Policy in the United Republic of Cameroon*. Paris: Unesco Press.

Bayart, Jean-François. 1979. *L'État au Cameroun*. Paris: Presses de la Fondation Nationale des Sciences Politiques.

Bayart, Jean-François. 1986. "La société politique camerounaise (1982–1986)". *Politique Africaine* 22: 5–35.

Beling-Nkoumba, Dominique. 1985. *Contes du Cameroun II*. Yaoundé: Éditions Clé.

Bender, Wolfgang. 2000. *Sweet Mother: Moderne afrikanische Musik*. Wuppertal: Peter Hammer Verlag.

Betene, Pierre. 1973. "Le Beti vu à travers ses Chants Traditionnels". *Abbia. Revue Culturelle Camerounaise / Cameroon Cultural Revues* 26: 43–93.

Binas-Preisendörfer, Susanne. 2010. *Klänge im Zeitalter ihrer medialen Verfügbarkeit. Popmusik auf globalen Märkten und in lokalen Kontexten*. Bielefeld: transcript. https://doi.org/10.14361/transcript.9783839414590

Binyam, Junior. 2005. "Escalier bar: Le temple du bikutsi est une église". *Mutations*, November 15, 2005.

Bissi, Mouelle. 1983. "'Les mauvais patrons sont à l'origine de la mort des orchestres'". *Cameroon Tribune*, June 15, 1983.

B.M. 1979. "Le retour de 'Richard Band' de Zoétélé". *Cameroon Tribune*, September 12, 1979.

Bolap, Henri-Paul. 1974. "Le Richard Band de Zoétélé... une valeur sûre de la musique authentiquement camerounaise". *Cameroon Tribune*, July 19, 1974.

Bourdieu, Pierre. 1984. *Distinction: A Social Critique of the Judgement of Taste.* Cambridge, MA: Harvard University Press.

Bourdieu, Pierre. 1993. *The Field of Cultural Production: Essays on Art and Literature.* New York: Columbia University Press.

Bourdieu, Pierre. 2001. *Die Regeln der Kunst. Genese und Struktur des literarischen Feldes.* Frankfurt am Main: Suhrkamp taschenbuch wissenschaft.

Boyomo Assala, Laurent-Charles. 1975a. "De nouveaux 'tubes'". *Cameroon Tribune*, August 7, 1975.

Boyomo Assala, Laurent-Charles. 1975b. "'L'affaire' Los Camaroes ou la dislocation d'une amitié". *Cameroon Tribune*, July 24, 1975.

Boyomo Assala, Laurent-Charles. 1975c. "Mama Ohandja dit Rossignol. Faire la musique qui se vend". *Cameroon Tribune*, September 24, 1975.

Boyomo Assala, Laurent-Charles. 1975d. "Une sensibilité exaspérée par l'amour conventionnel". *Cameroon Tribune*, July 17, 1975.

Boyomo Assala, Laurent-Charles. 1976a. "Yongoua Ngoubissam: Quelle musique?" *Cameroon Tribune*, January 12, 1976.

Boyomo Assala, Laurent-Charles. 1976b. "Beaucoup de candidats mais peu de musiciens". *Cameroon Tribune*, July 21, 1976.

Boyomo Assala, Laurent-Charles. 1978. "La musique camerounaise en quête d'une expression – 5. Au royaume de la muse, la chaîne règne". *Cameroon Tribune*, September 23, 1978.

Brunner, Anja. 2010. *Die Anfänge des Mbalax. Zur Entstehung einer senegalesischen Popularmusik.* Wien: Department of Musicology, University of Vienna.

Brunner, Anja. 2012. "Local Cosmopolitan Bikutsi". *Norient Academic Online Journal.* https://norient.com/academic/local-cosmopolitan-bikutsi/ (accessed March 30, 2021).

Brunner, Anja. 2013. "The Singer Anne-Marie Nzié and the Song 'Liberté': On Popular Music and the Postcolonial State in Cameroon". *African Music* 9(3): 40–58. https://doi.org/10.21504/amj.v9i3.1910

Brunner, Anja. 2015. "Bikutsi von Frauen. Weibliche Strategien im Kameruner pop-musikalischen Feld". In *Transgressions of a Musical Kind. Festschrift on the occasion of Regine Allgayer-Kaufmann's 65th birthday*, edited by Anja Brunner, Cornelia Gruber and August Schmidhofer, 249–65. Aachen: Shaker.

Brunner, Anja. 2017. "Popular Music and the Young Postcolonial State of Cameroon, 1960–1980". *Popular Music and Society* 40(1): 37–48. https://doi.org/10.1080/03007766.2016.1230380

Butler, Judith. 1990. *Gender Trouble.* New York: Routledge.

Collins, John. 1993. "The Problem of Oral Copyright: The Case of Ghana". In *Music and Copyright*, edited by Simon Frith, 146–58. Edinburgh: Edinburgh University Press.

Connell, John, and Chris Gibson. 2004. "World Music: Deterritorializing Place and Identity". *Progress in Human Geography* 28(3): 342–61. https://doi.org/10.1191/0309132504ph493oa

Coplan, David. 1982. "The Urbanisation of African Music: Some Theoretical Observations". *Popular Music* 2: 113–29. https://doi.org/10.1017/S0261143000001252

Dave, Nomi. 2019. *The Revolution's Echoes: Music, Politics, and Pleasure in Guinea*. Chicago and London: University of Chicago Press. https://doi.org/10.7208/chicago/9780226654775.001.0001

"Decouvrons les Tetes Brulees". 1987. *Cameroon Tribune*, July 11, 1987.

DeLancey, Mark W. 1989. *Cameroon: Dependence and Independence*. Boulder, CO: Westview Press.

DeLancey, Mark W., and H. Mokeba Mbella. 1990. *Historical Dictionary of the Republic of Cameroon*. Metuchen, NJ: Scarecrow Press.

DeLancey, Mark Dike, Rebecca Neh Mbuh, and Mark W. DeLancey. 2010. *Historical Dictionary of the Republic of Cameroon*. 4th ed. Metuchen, NJ: Scarecrow Press.

Dibango, Manu. 1994. *Three Kilos of Coffee: An Autobiography by Manu Dibango*. Chicago: University of Chicago Press.

Drewett, Michael, and Martin Cloonan, eds. 2006. *Popular Music Censorship in Africa*. Aldershot: Ashgate.

Emielu, Austin. 2018. "Tradition, Innovations, and Modernity in a Music of the Edo of Nigeria: Toward a Theory of Progressive Traditionalism". *Ethnomusicology* 62(2): 206–229. https://doi.org/10.5406/ethnomusicology.62.2.0206

Emvana Emiro, Michel Roger. 1986. "La mort du balafon". *Cameroon Tribune*, October 16, 1986.

E.N.B. 1977. "Une artiste camerounais récompensé par la C.C.C. Finoline". *Cameroon Tribune*, October 9, 1977.

Engama, Stella. 2001. "La thématique du Bikut-si de Sally Nyolo (1ère Partie)". *Patrimoine*, January 10, 2001.

Englert, Birgit. 2008. "Popular Music and Politics in Africa – Some Introductory Reflections". In *Popular Music and Politics in Africa*, edited by Birgit Englert, 1–15. Wien: ECCO.

Eonè, Tjadè. 1986. *Radios, Publics et Pouvoirs au Cameroun. Utilisations officielles et besoins sociaux*. Paris: L'Harmattan.

Erlmann, Veit, ed. 1991. *Populäre Musik in Afrika*. Berlin: Staatliche Museen Preußischer Kulturbesitz.

Erlmann, Veit. 1996. *Nightsong: Performance, Power, and Practice in South Africa*. Chicago: University of Chicago Press.

Essame, Biyiti bi. 1974. "Après l'éclatement des 'Titans' de Sangmélima, les Vétérans préparent la suite savoureuse de 'Minsounga'". *Cameroon Tribune*, December 7, 1974.

Essola, Donatien. 1975. "Consécration de jeunes talents". *Cameroon Tribune*, May 22, 1975.

Ewens, Graeme. 1991. *Africa O-Ye! A Celebration of African Music*. London: Guinness Publishing.

Fabbri, Franco. 1981. "A Theory of Musical Genres: Two Applications". In *Popular Music Perspectives: Papers from the First International Conference on Popular Music Research, Amsterdam, June 1981*, edited by David Horn and Phillip Tagg, 52–81. Göteborg and Exeter: International Association for the Study of Popular Music.

Feld, Steven. 2000. "A Sweet Lullaby for World Music". *Public Culture* 12(1): 145–71. https://doi.org/10.1215/08992363-12-1-145

Feld, Steven. 2012. *Jazz Cosmopolitanism in Accra: Five Musical Years in Ghana*. Durham, NC and London: Duke University Press.

Frow, John. 2006. *Genre*. London: Routledge.

Fumtim, Joseph, and Anne Cillon Perri. 2013. *Zanzibar Epémé Théodore et les Têtes brûlées du Cameroun: la passion bikutsi*. Yaoundé: Éditions Ifrikiya.

Gebesmair, Andreas. 2008. *Die Fabrikation globaler Vielfalt. Struktur und Logik der transnationalen Popmusikindustrie*. Bielefeld: transcript. https://doi.org/10.14361/9783839408506

Gildo, Adala. 1978. "Titi, un musicien égal à lui-même depuis 20 ans". *Cameroon Tribune*, August 13, 1978.

Gildo, Adala. 1979. "Musiques 'made in Yaoundé'. La percée pour bientôt. I – Messi, le prohète". *Cameroon Tribune*, April 16, 1979.

Graham, Ronnie. 1989. *Stern's Guide to Contemporary African Music*. London: Pluto Press.

Graham, Ronnie. 1992. *The World of African Music: Stern's Guide to Contemporary African Music. Volume 2*. London: Pluto Press.

Grupe, Gerd. 2005. "Notating African Music: Issues and Concepts". *The World of Music* 47(2): 87–103.

Guthrie, Malcom. 1970. *Comparative Bantu: An Introduction to the Comparative Linguistics and Prehistory of the Bantu Languages*. Vol. 3. Farnborough: Gregg International Publishers.

Haynes, Jo. 2005. "World Music and the Search for Difference". *Ethnicities* 5(3): 365–85. https://doi.org/10.1177/1468796805054961

Hennion, Antoine. 1989. "An Intermediary between Production and Consumption: The Producer of Popular Music". *Science, Technology, and Human Values* 14(4): 400–424. https://doi.org/10.1177/016224398901400405

Hesmondhalgh, David. 2006. "Bourdieu, the Media and Cultural Production". *Media, Culture & Society* 28(2): 211–31. https://doi.org/10.1177/0163443706061682

"Hit Parade de C.T.". 1985. *Cameroon Tribune*, 6/7 January: 27.

Holt, Fabian. 2007. *Genre in Popular Music*. Chicago: University of Chicago Press. https://doi.org/10.7208/chicago/9780226350400.001.0001

Holt, Fabian. 2008. "A View from Popular Music Studies: Genre Issues". In *The New (Ethno)Musicologies*, edited by Henry Stobart, 40–47. Lanham, MD: Scarecrow Press.

Hornbostel, Erich M. von. 1913. "Musik (Abschnitt XX.)". In *Die Pangwe*, edited by Günter Tessmann, 320–57. Berlin: Ernst Wasmuth.

Ibrahima, Daniel. 1984. "Discotheques: la guerre des decibels". *Cameroon Tribune*, August 3, 1984.

Kaye, Andrew L. 1998. "The Guitar in Africa". In *Africa: The Garland Encyclopedia of World Music*, Vol. 1, edited by Ruth M. Stone, 350–69. New York: Garland Publishing.

Kazadi, Pierre Cary. 1973. "Trends of Nineteenth and Twentieth Century Music in the Congo-Zaïre". In *Musikkulturen Asiens, Afrikas und Ozeaniens im 19. Jahrhundert*, edited by Robert Günther, 267–83. Regensburg: Gustav Bosse Verlag.

Keye, Ndogo Alleluia. 1978. "Conquerir le public de la capitale". *Cameroon Tribune*, August 25, 1978.

Konings, Piet. 2002. "University Students' Revolt, Ethnic Militia, and Violence during Political Liberalization in Cameroon". *African Studies Review* 45(2): 179–204. https://doi.org/10.1017/S0002020600031486

Kubik, Gerhard. 1969. "Afrikanische Elemente im Jazz – Jazzelemente in der populären Musik Afrikas". *Jazzforschung/Jazz Research* 1: 84–98.

Kubik, Gerhard. 1971–72. "Die Verarbeitung von Kwela, Jazz und Pop in der modernen Musik von Malawi". *Jazzforschung/Jazz Research* 3/4: 51–115.

Kubik, Gerhard. 1985. "African Tone-Systems: A Reassessment". *Yearbook for Traditional Music* 17: 31–63. https://doi.org/10.2307/768436

Kubik, Gerhard. 2001. "Cameroon". In *The New Grove Dictionary of Music and Musicians*, Vol. 4, edited by Stanley Sadie, 872–78. London: Macmillan.

Kubik, Gerhard. 2004. *Zum Verstehen afrikanischer Musik*. 2nd ed. Wien: LIT-Verlag.

Kubik, Gerhard. 2009. *Central African Guitar Song Composers: The Second and Third Generation. Field Recordings 1962–2009 by Gerhard Kubik and associates*. Wien: Department of Musicology, University of Vienna.

Kubik, Gerhard. 2010. *Theory of African Music. Volume II*. Chicago: University of Chicago Press.

Laburthe-Tolra, Philippe. 1977. *Mînlaaba. Histoire et Société traditionnelle chez les Béti du Sud Cameroun*. Lille: Reproduction des Theses Université de Lille III.

Laburthe-Tolra, Philippe. 1981a. "'Essai de synthèse sur les populations dites beti' de la région de Minlaba (sud du Nyong)". In *Contribution de la recherche Éthnologique à l'histoire des civilisations du Cameroun*, edited by Claude Tardits, 533–46. Paris: Éditions du Centre National de la Recherche Scientifique.

Laburthe-Tolra, Philippe. 1981b. *Les seigneurs de la forêt*. Paris: Publications de la Sorbonne.

Lemana, Louis-Marie. 1980. "Festival de musique scolaire". *Cameroon Tribune*, February 2, 1980.

Lena, Jennifer C., and Richard A. Peterson. 2006. *Resources and Phases in Music Genre Development*. Proposed presentation for the American Sociological Association Meetings.

Lena, Jennifer C., and Richard A. Peterson. 2008. "Classification as Culture: Types and Trajectories of Music Genres". *American Sociological Review* 73: 697–718. https://doi.org/10.1177/000312240807300501

"Les orchestres scolaires commencent à se manifester". 1976. *Cameroon Tribune*, November 11, 1976.

Madiba, Hilda. 1990. "De l'attente à la casse". *Cameroon Tribune*, December 27, 1990.

Manuel, Peter. 1988. *Popular Musics of the Non-Western World: An Introductory Survey*. New York: Oxford University Press.

Manuel, Peter. 1993. *Cassette Culture: Popular Music and Technology in North India*. Chicago: University of Chicago Press.

Manuel, Peter. 1995. *Caribbean Currents: Caribbean Music from Rumba to Reggae*. Philadelphia: Temple University Press.

Martin, Denis-Constant. 2004. "Les musique face aux pouvoirs". *Géopolitique africaine* 13: 1–13.

Mba, Wenzeslaus. 1981. "L'influence de la musique religieuse européene sur la musique religieuse des Beti ainsi que ses rapports avec la musique traditionelle du peuple Beti du Cameroun". Dissertation. Saarbrücken: Universität des Saarlandes.

Mbala, Agnès Marie épouse Nkili. 1985. "Bikutsi: chants des femmes chez les Mvele". PhD thesis. Lille: Université de Lille.

Mbembe, Achille. 2001. *On the Postcolony*. Berkeley: University of California Press. https://doi.org/10.1525/9780520917538

Mboua, Venant. 2004. "L'Ensemble national: msière et oisiveté". *Africultures* 60: 80–83. https://doi.org/10.3917/afcul.060.0080

Mefe, Tony. 2004. "Des vedettes d'une musique qui dérange". *Africultures* 60: 100–103. https://doi.org/10.3917/afcul.060.0100

Mehler, Andreas. 1993. *Kamerun in der Ära Biya. Bedingungen, erste Schritte und Blockaden einer demokratischen Transition*. Hamburg: Institut für Afrikakunde.

Meintjes, Louise. 1990. "Paul Simon's Graceland, South Africa, and the Mediation of Musical Meaning". *Ethnomusicology* 34(1): 37–73. https://doi.org/10.2307/852356

Modo, Asse. 1995. "La Chanson dans la Communication Politique au Cameroun". *Frequence Sud* 13: 121–31.

Monga, Yvette. 2000. "'Au village!': Space, Culture, and Politics in Cameroon". *Cahiers d'Études africaines* 160: 723–49. https://doi.org/10.4000/etudesafricaines.46

Mono Ndjana, Hubert. 1999. *Les Chansons de Sodome et Gomorrhe. Analyses pour l'éthique*. Yaoundé: Éditions du Carrefour.

Mpessa Mouangue. 1988. "Les autres 'Têtes' témoignent". *Cameroon Tribune*, October 23, 1988.

Mukuna, Kazadi wa. 2001. "Congo, Democratic Republic of the". In *The New Grove Dictionary of Music and Musicians*, Vol. 6, edited by Stanley Sadie, 291–93. London: Macmillan.

"Musique scolaire dimanche au Capitole. Quatre orchestres au programme". 1978. *Cameroon Tribune*, July 27, 1978.

Mviena, P. 1970. *Univers culturel et religieux du peuple beti*. Yaoundé: Saint-Paul.

N.A. 1976. "Le second 33 T de musique religieuse camerounaise vient précitpiter la mort du cantique latin". *Cameroon Tribune*, March 11, 1976.

NAP. 1975. "Un festival de nouveautés camerounaises". *Cameroon Tribune*, May 15, 1975.

Nbouwza, Français Émile. 1974. "Festival de la musique camerounaise. Rencontre avec l'organisateur et ses vedettes". *Bingo* 252: 80–82.

Ndachi Tagne, David. 1985. "Quels problèmes pose la production de disques au Cameroun?" *Cameroon Tribune*, January 5, 1985.

Ndachi Tagne, David. 1988. "Là où Albert Broeuk's cuisine les musiques d'aujourd'hui". *Cameroon Tribune*, November 6, 1988.

Ndachi Tagne, David. 1990. *Anne Marie Nzié: Secrets d'or*. Yaoundé: SOPECAM.

Ndjo, Basile. 2005. "*Carrefour de la Joie*: Popular Deconstruction of the African Postcolonial Public Sphere". *Africa* 75(3): 265–94. https://doi.org/10.3366/afr.2005.75.3.265

Negus, Keith. 1999. *Music Genres and Corporate Cultures*. London: Routledge.

Negus, Keith. 2002. "The Work of Cultural Intermediaries and the Enduring Distance between Production and Consumption". *Cultural Studies* 16(4): 501–515. https://doi.org/10.1080/09502380210139089

Nekes, Hermann. 1911. *Lehrbuch der Jaunde-Sprache*. Berlin: Georg Reimer. Reprint. https://doi.org/10.1515/9783111346731

Nettl, Bruno. 1978. *Eight Urban Musical Cultures: Tradition and Change*. Urbana: University of Illinois Press.

Nettl, Bruno. 2005. *The Study of Ethnomusicology: Thirty-One Issues and Concepts*. Champaign, IL: University of Illinois Press.

Ngumu, Pie-Claude. 1971. *Maitrise des Chanteurs à la Croix d'Ébène de Yaoundé*. Victoria: Presbook.

Ngumu, Pie-Claude. 1976a. "Beitrag zur Religion der Ewondo-sprechenden Beti (Kamerun) auf Grund schriftlicher und mündlicher Quellen". Dissertation. Wien: Universität Wien.

Ngumu, Pie-Claude. 1976b. *Les Mendzang des Chanteurs de Yaoundé*. Wien: Elisabeth Stiglmayr.

Ngumu, Pie-Claude. 1989. "Poésie chantée beti". *Notre librairie. Littérature Camerounaise* 99: 59–64.

Nixon, Sean, and Paul du Gay. 2002. "Who Needs Cultural Intermediaries?" *Cultural Studies* 16(4): 495–500. https://doi.org/10.1080/09502380210139070

Nken, Badjang ba. 1990. "La vogue des chansons obscènes". *Cameroon Tribune*, October 18, 1990.

Nkolo, Jean-Victor, and Graeme Ewens. 1999. "Cameroon: Music of a Small Continent". In *World Music: The Rough Guide. Volume 1: Africa, Europe and the*

Middle East, edited by Simon Broughton, Mark Ellingham, and Richard Trillo, 440–47. London: Rough Guides.

Nkwi, Paul Nchoji, and Antoine Socpa. 1997. "Ethnicity and Party Politics in Cameroon: The Politics of Divide and Rule". In *Regional Balance and National Integration in Cameroon: Lessons Learnt and the Uncertain Future*, edited by Paul Nchoji Nkwi and Francis B. Nyamnjoh, 138–49. Leiden and Yaoundé: ASC/ICASSRT.

Nnana, Marie-Claire. 1989. "Ensemble national: l'heure du bilan". *Cameroon Tribune*, October 18, 1989.

Noah, Jean Maurice. 2004. *Le Bikutsi du Cameroon. Ethnomusicologie des Seigneurs de la forêt*. Yaoundé: Carrefour/Erika.

Noah, Jean Maurice. 2010. *Le Makossa. Une musique africaine moderne*. Paris: L'Harmattan.

Noah Messomo, Albert. 1980. "Mendzan. Etude ethno-littéraire du xylophone des Beti". MA thesis. Yaoundé: Ecole Normale Supérieure.

Noah Messomo, Albert. 1995. *The Crisis of Cameroonian Culture: Problems and Expectations*. Bayreuth: Iwalewa-Haus.

Nyamnjoh, Francis B. 2005. *Africa's Media: Democracy and the Politics of Belonging*. London: Zed Books.

Nyamnjoh, Francis B., and Jude Fokwang. 2005. "Entertaining Repression: Music and Politics in Postcolonial Cameroon". *African Affairs* 104(415): 251–74. https://doi.org/10.1093/afraf/adi007

Nyano, Patrice. 1975. "La chorale Saint Kisito de Mvog-Mby fête ses dix ans". *Cameroon Tribune*, September 6, 1975.

Ondigui, Dieudonné. 1986. "Pourquoi René Ahanda veut-il berner les gens?" *Cameroon Tribune*, September 24, 1986.

Onguene Essono, Louis-Martin. 1996. "La démocratie en chanson: les Bikut-si du Cameroun". *Politique Africaine* 64: 52–61.

Onguene Essono, Louis-Martin. 2012. *Grammaire de l'ewondo. Essai de grammaire méthodique*. Yaoundé: Cerdotola.

Owona, Roger. 1988. "Jean-Marie Ahanda à C.T.: On ne remplace pas un Zanzibar". *Cameroon Tribune*, November 23, 1988.

Owona, Roger. 1989. "Première fête annuelle de RDPC. La musique, super star". *Cameroon Tribune*, April 2, 1989.

Owona, Roger. 1990a. "Bonjour, morceaux choisis!" *Cameroon Tribune*, September 23, 1990.

Owona, Roger. 1990b. "La crise de fonds et de la qualité". *Cameroon Tribune*, June 20, 1990.

Owona, Roger. 1990c. "Mon problème, c'est faire danser les gens". *Cameroon Tribune*, October 18, 1990.

Owona, Roger. 1990d. "Polémique autour d'une paternité". *Cameroon Tribune*, October 14, 1990.

Owono-Kouma, Auguste. 2004. "Langage de la sexualité et tendances de la pratique sexuelle chez les Beti aujourd'hui. Essai d'analyse lexico-sémantique des textes de quelques chanteurs de bìkùd sí des années 1990". *Cahier de l'UCAC* 7: 37–67.

Owona Nguini, Mathias Eric. 1995. "La controverse bikutsi-makossa: musique, politique et affinités régionales au Cameroun (1990–1994)". *L'Afrique politique*: 267–76.

Perret, Thierry. 2005. *Le temps des journalistes. L'invention de la presse en Afrique francophone*. Paris: Karthala.

Quinn, Frederick. 1980. "Charles Atangana of Yaoundé". *Journal of African History* 21(4): 485–95. https://doi.org/10.1017/S0021853700018703

Quinn, Frederick. 2006. *In Search of Salt: Changes in Beti (Cameroon) Society, 1880–1960*. New York: Berghahn Books.

Rathnaw, Dennis Michael. 2005. "Strategic Minstrelsy: Les Têtes Brulées and the Claim for Black Modernism". In *Urbanization and African Cultures*, edited by Toyin Falola and Steven J. Salm, 185–99. Durham, NC: Carolina Academic Press.

Rathnaw, Dennis Michael. 2009. "Waiting for Gumbo: Cargo Cults, Media and the Bikutsi of Cameroon". PhD thesis. Austin: University of Texas.

Rathnaw, Dennis Michael. 2010. "The Eroticization of Bikutsi: Reclaiming Female Space through Popular Music and Media". *African Music* 8(4): 48–67. https://doi.org/10.21504/amj.v8i4.1866

Regev, Motti. 2007a. "Cultural Uniqueness and Aesthetic Cosmopolitanism". *European Journal of Social Theory* 10(1): 123–38. https://doi.org/10.1177/1368431006068765

Regev, Motti. 2007b. "Ethno-National Pop-Rock Music: Aesthetic Cosmopolitanism Made from Within". *Cultural Sociology* 1(3): 317–41. https://doi.org/10.1177/1749975507082051

Regev, Motti. 2013. *Pop-Rock Music: Aesthetic Cosmopolitanism in Late Modernity*. Cambridge: Polity.

Sango, Jackson P. 1976. "La Fête de la Jeunesse à l'Université de Yaoundé". *Cameroon Tribune*, February 18, 1976.

Sango, Jackson P. 1977. "Les orchestres du Lycée Leclerc et du Collège Vogt tiennent en émoi un public de jeunes". *Cameroon Tribune*, March 13, 1977.

Scheibelhofer, Elisabeth. 2005. "A Reflection upon Interpretive Research Techniques: The Problem-Centered Interview as a Method for Biographic Research". In *Narrative, Memory and Everyday Life*, edited by Nancy Kelly, Christine Horrocks, Kate Milnes, Brian Roberts, and David Robinson, 19–32. Huddersfield: University of Huddersfield.

Scheibelhofer, Elisabeth. 2008. "Combining Narration-Based Interviews with Topical Interviews: Methodological Reflections on Research Practices". *International Journal of Social Research Methodology* 11(5): 403–416. https://doi.org/10.1080/13645570701401370

Schicho, Walter. 2001. *Handbuch Afrika. Band 2: Westafrika und die Inseln im Atlantik*. Frankfurt am Main: Brandes und Apsel.

Shuker, Roy. 2016. *Understanding Popular Music Culture*. Milton Park, NY: Routledge. https://doi.org/10.4324/9781315694870

Simgba, Jean Bosco, and Badjang ba Nken. 1987. "Une soirée à 'Chacal Bar'". *Cameroon Tribune*, July 11, 1987.

Simon, Artur. 1987. "Afrikanische und indonesische Musik zwischen Tradition und Pop". In *Zur Tradition, Rezeption und Produktion von populärer Musik*, edited by Helmut Rösing, 5–14. Hamburg: ASPM.

Simon, Artur. 1992. "Traditionelle Wurzeln und moderne Entwicklungen in populärer Musik Afrikas". In *Aspekte zur Geschichte populärer Musik*, edited by Helmut Rösing, 31–41. Baden-Baden: ASPM.

Simon, Artur, and Albert Noah Messomo. 2005. *Mvet ai Mendzang. Die Musik der Beti in Kamerun / Music of the Beti in Cameroon. Booklet to CD "Mvet ai Mendzang. Beti – Cameroon"*. Mainz: Wergo.

Sindjoun, L. 1996. "Le champ social camerounais : désordre inventif, mythes simplificateurs et stabilité hégémonique de l'État". *Politique Africaine* 62: 57–667.

Slobin, Mark. 1993. *Subcultural Sounds: Micromusics of the West*. Hanover: Wesleyan University Press.

Smith Maguire, Jennifer, and Julian Matthews. 2012. "Are We All Cultural Intermediaries Now? An Introduction to Cultural Intermediaries in Context". *European Journal of Cultural Studies* 15(5): 551–62. https://doi.org/10.1177/1367549412445762

Soupa, Casimir Datchoua. 1978. "L'ensemble national se distingue au Centre Culturel Français". *Cameroon Tribune*, September 4, 1978.

Stapleton, Chris, and Chris May. 1987. *African All-Stars: The Pop Music of a Continent*. London: Quartet Books.

Stapleton, Chris, and Chris May. 1990. *African Rock: The Pop Music of a Continent*. Dutton: Obelisk.

Steingo, Gavin. 2016. *Kwaito's Promise: Music and the Aesthetics of Freedom in South Africa*. Chicago: University of Chicago Press. https://doi.org/10.7208/chicago/9780226362687.001.0001

Stewart, Gary. 2000. *Rumba on the River: A History of Popular Music of the Two Congos*. London: Verso.

Tadadjeu, Maurice, and Etienne Sadembouo. 1979. *General Alphabet of Cameroon Languages*. Yaoundé: Université de Yaoundé.

Tchoungui, Gisele. 2000. "Unilingual Past, Multilingual Present, Uncertain Future: The Case of Yaoundé". *Journal of Multilingual and Multicultural Development* 21(2): 113–28. https://doi.org/10.1080/01434630008666397

Tessmann, Günter. 1913. *Die Pangwe*. Berlin: Ernst Wasmuth.

Touré, Aladji. 2005. *Les Secrets de la Basse Africaine*. Paris: HLMusic.

Tsala, Théodore. 1985. *Mille et un proverbes Beti. La société Beti à travers ses proverbes. Recueillis par Théodore Tsala*, edited by Jeanne-Françoise Vincent and Luc Bouquiaux. Paris: SELAF.

Tsala, Théodore. n.d. [1950s]. *Dictionnaire Ewondo-Français*. Lyon: Emmanuel Vitte.

Turino, Thomas. 2000. *Nationalists, Cosmopolitans, and Popular Music in Zimbabwe*. Chicago: University of Chicago Press.
https://doi.org/10.7208/chicago/9780226816968.001.0001

Turino, Thomas. 2003. "Are We Global Yet? Globalist Discourse, Cultural Formations and the Study of Zimbabwean Popular Music". *British Journal of Ethnomusicology* 12(2): 52–79.

Vamoulké, A. Madéouma. 1978. "La fin du 'pifomètre'". *Cameroon Tribune*, February 18, 1978.

Waterman, Christopher A. 1990. *Jùjú: A Social History and Ethnography of an African Popular Music*. Chicago: University of Chicago Press.

White, Bob W. 2009. *Rumba Rules: The Politics of Dance Music in Mobutu's Zaire*. Durham, NC and London: Duke University Press.
https://doi.org/10.1215/9780822389262

Winter, Martin. 2013. "'So, What Kind of Music Do You Like?' An Intersectional Theory of Genres as Boundary-Work in the Social Field of Music". In *Umfang, Methoden und Ziele der Musikwissenschaften. Ausgewählte Beiträge vom 25. internationalen Symposium des Dachverbands der Studierenden der Musikwissenschaft, Graz 2012*, edited by Malik Sharif, Christina Lessiak, Susanne Sackl, and Tobias Neuhold, 190–208. Wien: LIT.

Witzel, Andreas. 2000. "Das problemzentrierte Interview". *Forum: Qualitative Sozialforschung / Forum: Qualitative Research* 1(1), Art. 22.
https://www.qualitative-research.net/index.php/fqs/article/view/1132/2519 (accessed March 30, 2021).

Wright, David. 2005. "Mediating Production and Consumption: Cultural Capital and 'Cultural Workers'". *British Journal of Sociology* 56(1): 105–121.
https://doi.org/10.1111/j.1468-4446.2005.00049.x

XIX Article 19. 1997. *Cameroon: A Transition in Crisis. Tech. rep. Article 19 – Global Campaign for Free Expression*.
https://www.article19.org/data/files/pdfs/publications/cameroon-a-transition-in-crisis.pdf (accessed October 9, 2017).

Index

www.ingramcontent.com/pod-product-compliance
Lightning Source LLC
Chambersburg PA
CBHW062026270326
41929CB00014B/2330